Windows 3™ Made Easy

Windows 3™ Made Easy

Tom Sheldon

Osborne **McGraw-Hill**
Berkeley New York St. Louis San Francisco
Auckland Bogotá Hamburg London Madrid
Mexico City Milan Montreal New Delhi Panama City
Paris São Paulo Singapore Sydney
Tokyo Toronto

Osborne **McGraw-Hill**
2600 Tenth Street
Berkeley, California 94710
U.S.A.

For information on translations and book distributors outside of the U.S.A., please write to Osborne **McGraw-Hill** at the above address.

A complete list of trademarks appears on page 449.

Windows 3™ Made Easy

Copyright © 1990 by McGraw-Hill. All rights reserved. Printed in the United States of America. Except as permitted under the Copyright Act of 1976, no part of this publication may be reproduced or distributed in any form or by any means, or stored in a database or retrieval system, without the prior written permission of the publisher, with the exception that the program listings may be entered, stored, and executed in a computer system, but they may not be reproduced for publication.

34567890 DOC 99876543210

ISBN 0-07-881537-1

Acquisitions Editor: Jeff Pepper
Technical Reviewers: William Murray and Chris Pappas
Copy Editor: Barbara Conway
Word Processor: Bonnie Bozorg
Composition: Bonnie Bozorg
Proofreaders: Julie Anjos, Jeff Green
Cover Design: Bay Graphics Design, Inc.
Production Supervisor: Kevin Shafer

Information has been obtained by Osborne McGraw-Hill from sources believed to be reliable. However, because of the possibility of human or mechanical error by our sources, Osborne McGraw-Hill, or others, Osborne McGraw-Hill does not guarantee the accuracy, adequacy, or completeness of any information and is not responsible for any errors or omissions or the results obtained from the use of such information.

CONTENTS AT A GLANCE

PART I   Windows Concepts

1	Introducing Windows	5
2	Installing Windows	27
3	Ways to Start Windows	47
4	Learning the Windows Interface	59
5	Windows Applications and Their Shared Features	87
6	DOS Concepts for Windows	117
7	Working with the File Manager	131
8	Working with Printers	169
9	Customizing Windows with the Control Panel	187
10	Getting Organized with the Program Manager	207

PART II   Running Applications

11	Running Applications Under Windows	227
12	Windows Desktop Accessories	241

13	**Windows Write**...	**277**
14	**Windows Paintbrush**.....................................	**307**
15	**Windows Terminal**...	**337**
16	**Playing Games**..	**353**
17	**A Typical Day with Windows**.......................	**357**

PART III Advanced Topics

18	**Modifying Windows Startup**........................	**377**
19	**Operating in Real Mode**..............................	**391**
20	**Operating in Standard Mode**.......................	**397**
21	**Operating in 386 Enhanced Mode**..............	**407**

PART IV Appendixes

A	**Using Windows Setup**...................................	**427**
B	**Optimizing Techniques**...............................	**431**
C	**Using Windows with a Network**..................	**437**
D	**Advanced Scientific Calculator Functions**...	**443**

TABLE OF CONTENTS

Introduction xxi
Why This Book Is for You 1

PART I Windows Concepts

1 Introducing Windows 5

What Windows Can Do 6
Features and Benefits of Windows 9
    Foundation for Program Development 10
    Consistent User Interface 10
    Multitasking Capabilities 10
    Data Transfer Capabilities 11
    Desktop Accessories 12
    Windows Control Panel 13
    Dynamic Data Exchange 15
    DOS Compatibility 15
    Increased Productivity 15
    OS/2 Look and Feel 16
New Features for Windows 3 16
    Program Manager: The Group Organizer 16
    File Manager 17
    Task List 18
    Network Support 19
    Additional New Features 19
Windows Operating Modes 20
Hardware Requirements for Windows 3 21

  Other Considerations 22

2 **Installing Windows ....** **27**

 Installation Considerations 28
  Expanded and Extended Memory 28
  Disk Space 29
  Optimizing Your Hard Drive 29
 Installation Procedure 30
  Starting the Installation 31
  SETUP Configuration Phase 34
  Modifying the System Files 36
  Installing Your Printers 37
  Setting Up Applications 41
  Reading the Release Notes 42
  SETUP Completion 43
 Configuration Options 43
  Options for 8088/8086 Systems 43
  Options for 80286 Systems 44
  Options for 80386/80486 Systems 45

3 **Ways to Start Windows ....** **47**

 Starting Windows 48
  Basic Startup Command 48
  Starting an Application and Windows
   Simultaneously 49
  Starting with a Specific Operating Mode 49
  Starting Windows with a Batch File 50
  Starting Windows Automatically 51
  Quitting Windows 51
 Startup Considerations 53
  Minimizing Memory Usage 53
  Memory-Resident Software 55
  Running Older Windows Applications 56
  Running Non-Windows Applications 56

4 Learning the Windows Interface 59

    Elements of the Windows Screen 60
        The Desktop Metaphor 60
        Types of Windows 62
        Elements of a Window 66
    The Features and Use of Dialog Boxes 70
        Elements of Dialog Boxes 70
        Warning and Message Boxes 74
    Mouse Techniques 74
        Mouse Terminology 74
        Moving and Sizing Windows with the Mouse 75
        Scrolling with the Mouse 78
        Selecting with the Mouse 78
    Keyboard Techniques 79
        Menu Selection with the Keyboard 79
        Moving and Sizing Windows
          with the Keyboard 81
        Using Dialog Boxes with the Keyboard 83
    Changing the Active Window 84
        Switching Windows with the Keyboard 84
        Using the Mouse to Switch Applications 85
        Switching Windows with the Task List Utility 86
        Arranging Windows 86

**5 Windows Applications and Their
Shared Features 87**

    The Program Manager 88
    The Main Group 90
        File Manager 90
        Control Panel 91
        Print Manager 92
        Clipboard 92
        DOS Prompt 93
        Windows Setup 93

   The Accessories Group 94
     Calculator 94
     Calendar 95
     Cardfile 95
     Clock 96
     Notepad 96
     Paintbrush 96
     PIF Editor 97
     Recorder 98
     Terminal 99
     Write 99
   Shared Menu Commands 101
     The File Pull-Down Menu 101
     The Edit Pull-Down Menu and the Clipboard 107
     Using Windows Help 110
   Shared Keyboard Techniques 111
     Correcting Typing Mistakes 111
     Moving the Insertion Point 112
     Selecting Text 112
     Cut and Paste Shortcut Keys 113

6 Dos Concepts for Windows 117

   File Concepts 118
     File Types 119
     Naming Files 120
   Directory Concepts 125
     Organizing with Directories 128

7 Working with the File Manager 131

   A Quick Introduction to the File Manager 132
     The File Manager Menu Bar 133
   Working with Directory Trees 135
     Changing Drives 136
     Viewing the Directory Tree 136
     Working with Directory Windows 137

Changing the Way Files Are Listed   142
Using Other File Manager Options   148
    Changing Display Options   148
    Arranging and Updating Directory Windows   148
Manipulating Files   149
    Selecting Multiple Files for an Operation   149
    Creating Directories and Files   152
    Viewing Files   153
    Moving and Copying Files Using Menus   154
    Moving and Copying Files Using the Mouse   157
    Renaming Files   159
    Printing Files   160
    Setting File Attributes and Protecting Files   160
    Associating a File with a Program   162
    Deleting Files and Directories   163
Other Program Manager Techniques   165
    Searching for Files   165
    Running DOS Commands   166
    Formatting Diskettes   166
    Labeling Diskettes   167
    Copying Diskettes   167

8 Working with Printers 169

Printer Setup and Configuration   170
    Copying a New Printer Driver from Diskette   171
    Setting the Printer Port   172
    Configuring New Printer Drivers   174
    Selecting the Active and Default Printers   176
Fonts   177
    Why Add New Fonts?   177
    How Fonts Are Used in Documents   178
    How Fonts Are Displayed and Printed   179
    Adding Fonts   181
The Print Manager   181
    The Print Manager Menu Options   182

Print Manager Activities   184
Handling Printer Problems   185

9 Customizing Windows with the Control Panel 187

Color   188
    Selecting Existing Color Schemes   189
    Changing Existing Color Schemes   190
    Creating Custom Colors   191
Date/time   194
Desktop   194
    Altering Desktop Patterns   196
    Selecting a Wallpaper   197
    Changing the Cursor Blink Rate   198
    Changing Granularity   198
    Changing the Border Width   199
Fonts   199
International   199
Keyboard   201
Mouse   202
Network   203
Ports   203
Printers   205
Sound   205
386 Enhanced   206

10 Getting Organized with the Program Manager 207

Working with the Program Manager   208
    Another Look at the Program Manager   209
    Opening and Minimizing Group Windows   212
Arranging Windows and Icons   212
    Moving and Sizing Windows   213
    Arranging Windows and Icons   213
    Saving Your Changes   214

Creating Groups   215
    Creating a Group Window   215
    Adding Items to a Group   217

PART II   Running Applications

11   Running Applications Under Windows 227

Ways to Start an Application   228
    Using the Program Manager   228
    Using the DOS Prompt   228
    Using the File Manager Direct Execution
       Method   229
    Using the File Manager Run Option   230
Types of Applications   231
    Windows 3 Applications   232
    Pre-Windows 3 Applications   233
    Non-Windows Applications   235
    Memory-Resident Software   237
Using Program Information Files   239

12   Windows Desktop Accessories 241

Notepad   242
    Startup and Overview   242
    Writing and Editing in Notepad   243
    Printing and Saving Your Document   246
    The Notepad Time-Log Feature   247
Calculator   247
    Startup and Overview   248
    Calculator Function Buttons   250
    Standard and Scientific Calculator
      Shared Keys   250
    Converting Numbers with the Scientific
      Calculator   253

    Statistical Functions with the Scientific
        Calculator   253
Calendar   254
    Startup and Overview   254
    Calendar Setup   257
    Entering Appointments   258
    Setting Calendar Alarms   260
    Marking Dates   261
    Saving and Printing Appointments   260
Cardfile   262
    Startup and Overview   263
    Cardfile Setup and Editing   265
    Viewing and Searching for Cards   266
    Manipulating Cards and Card Information   268
    Printing and Saving Card Files   269
Recorder   270
    Startup and Overview   270
    Recording a Macro   272
    More About Recorder   275

13   Windows Write..**277**

Startup and Overview   278
    Elements of the Write Window   280
Write Concepts   280
    Character and Paragraph Elements   281
    The Invisible Paragraph Marker   282
    Layout   282
    The Ruler   282
    Selecting Text and Paragraphs   283
    How Write Saves Files   285
Typing and Editing in Write   285
    Reviewing Your Document   285
    Moving to a Specific Page   286
    Finding and Changing Text   287
    Selecting Text to Edit or Format   289

Other Editing Features   290
    Inserting Hyphens   291
    Paginating and Breaking Pages   291
    Adding and Editing Graphics   293
Formatting in Write   294
    Character Formatting   294
    Paragraph Formatting   297
    Altering the Page Layout   299
    Headers and Footers   301
    Setting Margins and the Starting Page Number   302
Saving and Printing Your Document   303
    Saving Your Documents   303
    Printing Your Documents   304

14 Windows Paintbrush 307

Startup and Overview   308
    The Color Palette   309
    The Toolbox   309
    The Line Size Box   311
    The Paintbrush Menus   312
Paintbrush Concepts   314
    The Cursor   314
    The Drawing Area   315
    Securing an Object   318
    Line Width and Color Effects   319
    Foreground and Background Colors   320
Drawing Techniques   320
    Detailed Drawing   320
    Using the Painting Tools   321
    Using the Text Tool   324
    Using the Line and Curve Tools   325
    Using the Box, Circle and Polygon Tools   326
Text and Graphic Editing Techniques   327
    Using the Cutout Tools   327
    Using the Eraser Tools   328

  Special Techniques 330
    Sweeping a Cutout 330
    Shrinking and Enlarging a Cutout 331
    Flipping, Inverting, and Tilting Techniques 332
    Creating Custom Colors 332
  Retrieving, Saving, And Printing 334
    Saving Your Work 334
    Printing a Drawing 335

15 Windows Terminal 337

  Establishing a Communications Session 338
    Saving and Retrieving
     Communications Settings 339
    Basic Settings 339
  Dialing and Connection 345
    When You Have Connection Problems 345
  On-line Activities 347
    Types of Files and Transfer Methods 347
    Transmitting Text Files 348
    Transmitting Binary Files 350
    Working in the Terminal Window 351
    Ending a Communications Session 352

16 Playing Games 353

  Reversi 353
  Solitaire 355
    The Solitaire Options Menu 356

17 A Typical Day with Windows 357

  Opening the Calendar 358
    Keeping a Personal Calendar 358
  Writing Notes 359
  Organizing the Desktop 359
    Moving the Files to Their Own Directory 361

Creating Startup Icons for the Daily Files   362
Tips and Techniques for Writing   363
    Writing and Consolidating Notes   364
    Comparing and Copying Between Files   364
Writing A Letter   365
    Boilerplates   365
    Retrieving an Address   367
    Adding a Letterhead   367
File Manager Techniques   368
    Switching to the File Manager   368
    Sending Disk Files   369
    Copying Files to Disk   370
Playing a Game   370
Creating Scrapbooks   371
    Graphics Scrapbooks   371
    Text Scrapbooks   371
    Creating a File Catalog   372
Archiving Files   373

PART III   Advanced Topics

18   Modifying Windows Startup 377

Altering the Windows Startup Files   378
    Loading Programs   379
    Running Programs   380
    Specifying How Programs Are Listed   380
    Specifying How Documents Are Listed   381
    Associating Filename Extensions   381
    Saving and Rebooting   382
Working With Your System's Startup Files   382
    Editing the Startup Files   383
    The CONFIG.SYS File   384
    The AUTOEXEC.BAT File   389

19 Operating In Real Mode 391

Starting in Real Mode   392
    Starting with Expanded Memory Switches   393
Running Applications in Real Mode   394
    When Applications Require
      Expanded Memory   394
Running Non-Windows Applications
  in Real Mode   395

20 Operating in Standard Mode 397

When Applications Require
  Expanded Memory   398
Running Non-Windows Applications   398
    Using the PIF Editor   400
    Changing the Default PIF Settings   405

21 Operating in 386 Enhanced Mode 407

Control Panel Settings for 386 Enhanced
  Mode   408
    Device Contention Options   408
    Scheduling Options   409
Running Non-Windows Applications in
  386 Enhanced Mode   410
    Using the PIF Editor   412
    Advanced PIF Options for 386
      Enhanced Mode   416
Control Menu Settings for Non-Windows
  Applications   422

PART IV   Appendixes

A   Using Windows SETUP 427

Starting SETUP   427
Making Changes with Setup   428

Running SETUP from DOS 429

B Optimizing Techniques 431

Increase the Disk Cache 432
Use a Disk Optimizing Utility 432
Backup-and-Restore Method 433
Advanced Backup-and-Restore Method 434

C Using Windows with a Network 437

Adding Network Support with SETUP 438
    Network Features and Guidelines 438
    Setting the Network Option in the
        Control Panel 439
Using Network Drives 439
Printing on a Network 440
    Connecting to a Network Printer 440
    Network Printing with Print Manager 441

**D Advanced Scientific Calculator
Functions 443**

Operators 444
Number Base Functions 444
Statistical Functions 445
Other Functions 445

Index 451

INTRODUCTION

Windows is a success. After many years of competing with other graphic shells for the PC DOS environment, Windows has come out on top. Many users and PC managers are still debating the need for advanced operating systems like OS/2 and UNIX. While these operating systems can give you the power to work more efficiently, a lack of applications or understanding of products often prohibits their use. Windows 3 has arrived just in time to fill the gap for DOS users who need more functions from their DOS machine or those users in transition to OS/2.

Windows has been around for a number of years, but version 3, about which this book is written, offers a radical advancement in the way Windows looks and operates. Many of the problems DOS users have experienced with memory, graphics compatibility, and the need to run multiple applications are resolved with the new Windows. Version 3 provides enhanced support for 80386 computer systems and emerging 80486 systems. And with Windows 3, new and better applications are being introduced by almost every DOS software vendor. Windows has become the new standard. It has come of age.

For those still debating the move to OS/2, Windows offers a good interim solution that extends the life of current applications and hardware until the world of OS/2 becomes more stable and more applications become available. At the same time, the Windows graphic interface is similar in look and feel to the OS/2 Presentation Manager; users who learn Windows today will be ready for the transition to OS/2 tomorrow.

ABOUT THIS BOOK

This book is written for those who need instruction in the use of Windows and its applications. The chapters are meant to be read in order but are easy to access for later reference. Chapter 1 starts by introducing you to the concepts of Windows and its many features. You will learn about the various Windows operating modes and how it will run on your particular system. Chapter 2 describes the installation process, with special attention given to those users unfamiliar with previous versions of Windows. Chapter 3 then explains various ways you can start Windows.

Chapter 4 introduces you to the Windows interface. You will learn how to work with the windows, menus, and dialog boxes of Windows using both mouse and keyboard techniques. Chapter 5 discusses the features of Windows that are the same in just about every application you run under Windows. For example, loading, saving, and printing documents and files are similar for all Windows applications, so you need only learn the techniques once.

Chapter 6 introduces various DOS concepts you must be familiar with to use the Windows file-management utilities. Those already familiar with DOS file-naming conventions, directory structures, and other DOS concepts may want to skim through this chapter. Chapter 7 then introduces the Windows File Manager, which is a new feature of Windows for version 3. This powerful program makes it easy to organize and manage your computer filing system. This feature alone makes it worthwhile to start Windows every time you turn on your computer.

Chapter 8 covers working with printers, and Chapter 9 discusses the features of the Windows Control Panel, which you use to set the operating characteristics of Windows. Chapter 10 wraps up the first section of this book by discussing the Program Manager, which is a Windows tool you can use to organize your Windows desktop and programs you run on a regular basis.

Part II of this book discusses the applications that come with Windows, such as Notepad, Calendar, Cardfile, Write, Paintbrush, and Terminal, as well as some games. Part III discusses technical topics, such as how to change the startup procedure for Windows and how to run Windows in its various operating modes. If you need to run Windows on a network, refer to Appendix C.

CONVENTIONS USED IN THIS BOOK

This book is meant to be read while you are working at your computer. Become more familiar with Windows by working out the many examples that are given. Many screen illustrations let you easily follow the discussion. You will also find them helpful if you are reading away from your computer.

Text that you are to type will be typed in boldface. To avoid confusion, the keys you are to press when executing commands are shown as they appear on the keyboard. A few examples are shown here:

- ENTER
- ESC
- BACKSPACE
- DEL

Some key strokes must be typed together. This is done by holding down the first key listed while pressing the second key listed. A few examples are shown here:

- ALT-ESC
- CTRL-HOME
- SHIFT-F1

ADDITIONAL HELP FROM OSBORNE/McGRAW-HILL

Osborne/McGraw-Hill provides top-quality books for computer users at every level of computing experience. To help you build your skills, we suggest that you look for the books in the following Osborne/McGraw-Hill series that best address your needs.

The "Teach Yourself" Series is perfect for beginners who have never used a computer before or who want to gain confidence in using program basics. These books provide a simple, slow-paced introduction to the fundamental usage of popular software packages and programming languages. The "Mastery Learning" format ensures that concepts are learned thoroughly before progressing to new material. Plenty of exercises and examples are used throughout the text, and answers are at the back of the book.

The "Made Easy" Series is also for beginners or users who may need a refresher on the new features of an upgraded product. These in-depth introductions guide users step-by-step from the program basics to intermediate-level usage. Plenty of hands-on exercises and examples are used in every chapter.

The "Using" Series presents fast-paced guides that quickly cover beginning concepts and move on to intermediate-level techniques, and even some advanced topics. These books are written for users who already are familiar with computers and software, and who want to get up to speed quickly with a certain product.

The "Advanced" Series assumes that the reader is already an experienced user who has reached at least an intermediate skill level and is ready to learn more sophisticated techniques and refinements.

The "Complete Reference" Series of handy desktop references list every command, feature, and function of popular software and programming languages, along with brief, detailed descriptions of how they are used. Books are fully indexed and often include tear-out command cards. This series is ideal for all users—beginners and pros.

The "Pocket Reference" is a pocket-sized, shorter version of the "Complete Reference" series and provides only the essential commands, features, and functions of software and programming languages for users who need a quick reminder of the most important commands. This series also is written for all users and every level of computing ability.

The "Secrets, Solutions, Shortcuts" Series is written for beginning users who are already somewhat familiar with the software and for experienced users at intermediate and advanced levels. This series gives clever tips and points out shortcuts for using the software to greater advantage. Traps to avoid are also mentioned.

Osborne/McGraw-Hill also publishes many fine books that are not included in the series described here. If you have questions about which Osborne book is right for you, ask the salesperson at your local book or computer store.

OTHER OSBORNE/MCGRAW-HILL BOOKS OF INTEREST TO YOU

We hope that *Windows 3 Made Easy* will assist you in mastering this graphic interface, and will also peak your interest in learning more about other ways to better use your computer.

If you're interested in expanding your skills so you can be even more "computer efficient," be sure to take advantage of Osborne/McGraw-Hill's large selection of top-quality computer books that cover all varieties of popular hardware, software, programming languages, and operating systems. While we cannot list every title here that may relate to OS/2 and to your special computing needs, here are just a few related books that complement *Windows 3 Made Easy*.

OS/2 Presentation Manager Programming Primer, by Asael Dror and Robert Lafore, helps users quickly learn the Presentation Manager, OS/2's graphic user interface. Short, clear programming examples and detailed explanations of features are provided.

If you're already programming with OS/2, see *OS/2 Presentation Manager Graphics: An Introduction*, by Chris H. Pappas and William H. Murray, for a guide to unlocking the power of Presentation Manager graphics. The book starts with basic concepts and a discussion of individual Presentation Manager commands, and then builds to increasingly complex programs for line, bar, and pie charts.

OS/2 Programmer's Guide, Second Edition, Volume 1, by Ed Iacobucci, leader of the IBM OS/2 design team, is the first book in a two-book set and provides a complete overview of OS/2 versions 1.1 and 1.2, and the Presentation Manager.

To learn more advanced OS/2 programming skills with Ed Iacobucci, see *OS/2 Programmer's Guide, Second Edition, Volume 2*. The second volume of this two-book set emphasizes coverage of OS/2 version 1.2's API structure.

OS/2 Programming: An Introduction, by Herbert Schildt, is a fast-paced guide that quickly gets you up to speed on OS/2 version 1.1 intermediate-level programming techniques. A background in assembly langauage programming is not a prerequisite, but many samples of C programs are used in the text. Applications are emphasized.

Using OS/2, by Kris Jamsa, quickly moves from fundamental to advanced techniques and covers major OS/2 version 1.0 strengths in detail, including multitasking.

Assembly Language Programming Under OS/2, by William H. Murray and Chris H. Pappas, is a practical hands-on guide that serves as an excellent introduction to OS/2 version 1.1 assembly language programming. Over 75 complete Real and Protected mode programs are provided to give you a resource from which to draw when developing your own programs. After discussing beginning concepts, the authors quickly move on to develop more sophisticated programming methods.

WHY THIS BOOK IS FOR YOU

This book has been written to help you quickly learn Microsoft Windows and use applications that run with the Windows graphic interface. You'll become familiar with the terminology and concepts of Windows and how to use it in your everyday activities. The book takes a step-by-step approach for new computer users or those using Windows for the first time. Those who have used previous versions of Windows will be able to learn quickly the features of the new version.

This book is of particular interest to the following:

- *New PC users.* New computer users will find Windows an excellent system to learn as the basis for their computer training. Windows will familiarize you with the features and commands of DOS.

- *New Windows users.* This book provides an excellent tutorial for readers who may be familiar with computers but not Windows. You'll learn the Windows interface in a step-by-step approach that can be integrated into your daily activities.

- *Experienced Windows users.* If you have upgraded to Windows 3 from a previous version, this book will introduce you to its new features. You'll find the material easy reading and will be able to quickly locate areas of interest.

- *Network managers.* Network managers will find this an excellent tutorial or reference manual to give to users on their networks who use the network versions of Windows.

- *Windows applications users.* Those who use software applications that run under the Windows graphic interface will find this book useful for exploring the Windows interface and for using its features and commands outside their normal application.

LEARN MORE ABOUT WINDOWS

Here is another excellent Osborne/McGraw-Hill book on Windows that will help you build your skills and maximize the power of this graphic interface with multitasking capabilities. For a concise introduction to Windows programming that focuses on intermediate-level techniques and some advanced concepts, see *Windows Programming: An Introduction*, by William Murray and Chris Pappas. This book also discusses migrating programming concepts from Windows to the OS/2 Presentation Manager.

WINDOWS CONCEPTS

1

INTRODUCING WINDOWS

What Windows Can Do
Features and Benefits of Windows
New Features for Windows 3
Windows Operating Modes
Hardware Requirements for Windows 3

Microsoft Windows is a windowing and multitasking environment for personal computers that run PC-DOS and MS-DOS. A *window* is a rectangular box that holds a running application. You can have several windows open at once. These windows can overlap one another, and the topmost window usually holds the currently running application. Since multiple applications can be open at once, you need not exit one to use another. Instead, you simply switch windows. *Multitasking* is an additional feature of Windows that gives it the ability to run more than one application at the same time. This means you can actively sort a database in one window while writing a letter in another. Multitasking is only possible on 80386 or more advanced machines.

Windowing and multitasking are probably the most important characteristics of Windows, but the *data transfer* feature also enhances the value of the package. It gives you the ability to grab a block of text, a table of numbers, or a picture from a document in one window and "paste" it into another window. This means you can easily insert a graphics image in a letter, or insert spreadsheet information in a report. Transferring information between programs is possible because all applications written for Windows support the same data transfer capabilities. You can even cut and paste between some applications not specifically written for Windows.

Windows is similar in look and feel to its OS/2 cousin—the Presentation Manager. In fact, if you plan to use OS/2 and the Presentation Manager in the future, Windows is an excellent environment in which to work in preparation for your transition.

Although Windows has been around since 1985, version 3 is a radical departure from previous versions in its power, flexibility, ease of use, and graphics interface. Many new features have been added, including the ability to handle memory beyond the 640K barrier normally associated with DOS. In addition, an enhanced appearance along with new ways of organizing your programs and working with files make Windows a program you will want to have running at all times, not just when you need to run multiple applications or transfer data between documents. Essentially, the DOS command prompt is a thing of the past.

WHAT WINDOWS CAN DO

At its most basic level, Windows offers a way to organize your programs on top of an *electronic desktop,* as shown in Figure 1-1. Each window holds its own set of *program icons,* and each icon represents a program or utility that starts when you double-click on the icon with the mouse.

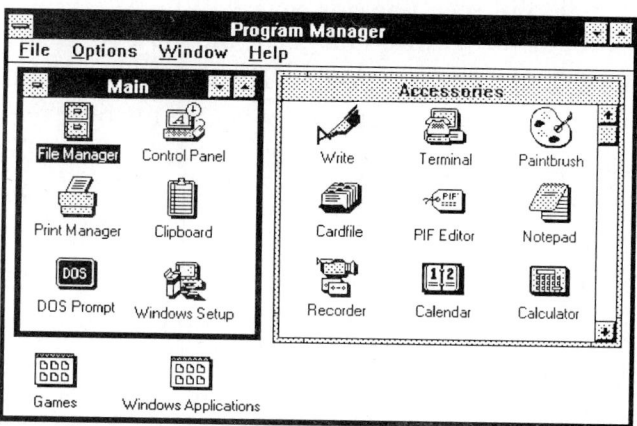

FIGURE 1-1. The Windows Program Manager with its Main and Accessories windows open

Figure 1-1 shows three stackable, overlapping windows that can be opened or closed as you see fit. Note that the Main window is

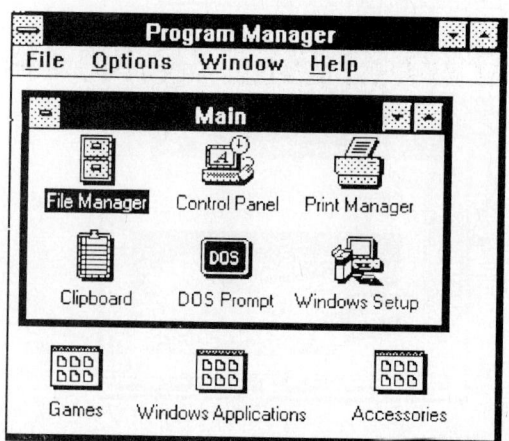

FIGURE 1-2. The Program Manager window resized, with the Accessories window reduced to an icon

overlapping the Accessories window. These are both contained within the Program Manager, which is a window used to manage all of your icons in groups. The Program Manager window and most other windows can be expanded to cover the entire screen or reduced to an icon while working in other windows.

In Figure 1-2, the Program Manager window has been reduced to a smaller size and the Accessories window has been reduced to an icon at the bottom right of the screen. Windows reduced to icons are available for immediate use. Simply double-click on the icon to reopen the window.

Figure 1-3 shows two programs loaded in separate windows. The Windows Paintbrush drawing program is the active top window, and the Windows Cardfile accessory is the inactive window beneath it. Notice that the Program Manager has been reduced to an icon since it is not being used. The Paintbrush and Cardfile windows are both open at the same time so the art in the Paintbrush window can easily be copied and pasted to the Cardfile window. Cardfile can store both graphics images and text for later use. In

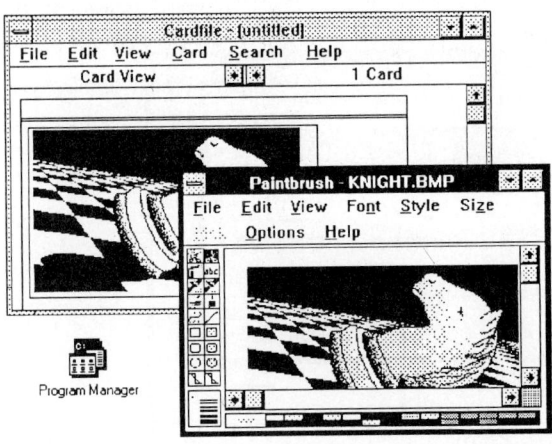

FIGURE 1-3. Pictures or text in one window can be cut and pasted into another window

Introducing Windows   9

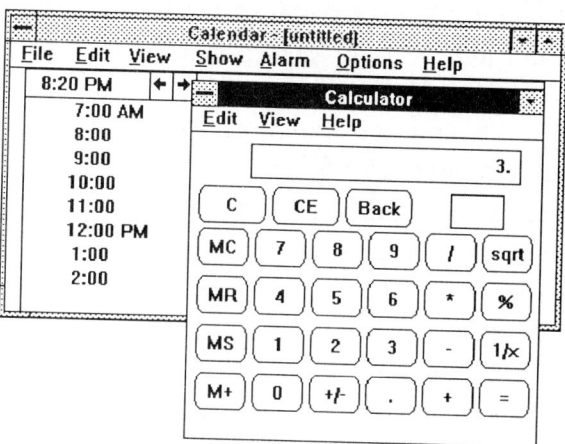

FIGURE 1-4.   The Windows Calculator can be opened on the desktop for quick calculations while working in other applications

this way it acts as a glossary, but as you will see later, it has many other uses.

As another example, Figure 1-4 shows the Windows Calculator open at the same time as the Calendar accessory. You can have the calculator resting on your desktop to perform calculations as you go through the previous days' activities and expenses.

You can see there are many ways to use multiple windows and multiple applications at the same time. The more you use Windows, the more you'll find that you can't do without it.

FEATURES AND BENEFITS OF WINDOWS

Windows offers many features that benefit both new and experienced PC users. Several of the operating features were discussed and illustrated in the previous section. This section describes other features that may not be so apparent.

Foundation for Program Development

A wide range of software applications have been written to the Windows environment, including Aldus PageMaker, Microsoft Excel, and Micrografx Designer. The Windows user interface is already in place, so programmers simply design their programs to work with that interface. This lets them concentrate on the real guts of the program itself and thus create programs with advanced features that are relatively free of problems and easy to use.

Windows contains a complete programmers toolbox that speeds the development of software. You can be assured that just about any type of application will be available in the Windows environment now that Windows (together with the Presentation Manager) has become a standardized graphics user interface.

Consistent User Interface

Since programmers design their applications to fit within the Windows user interface, you will already know how to start using most of the applications you buy for Windows. You will spend less time learning how to use your applications and more time getting productive work done.

Multitasking Capabilities

Multitasking gives you the ability not only to load multiple applications in multiple windows, but also to actually run those applications simultaneously. This is not to be confused with *multiloading,* a term used to describe multiple loaded applications that do not run simultaneously. A loaded application resides in memory but sits idle while another application runs. When you switch to another application, it begins to run and the other becomes idle. True Windows multitasking occurs when two or more applications in different windows actually run or process information simultaneously. Technically, even this is an illusion since each application is simply given a small piece of the microprocessor's time, a process known as *time slicing*. But with advanced processors like the 80386 and 80486, this happens so quickly that you can take advantage of multitasking to do several things at once, like write a letter while your mailing list is being sorted or printed.

Multiloading simply saves you the trouble of exiting one application and loading another as you go from one to the other. Each sits idle in its own window until you make the window active. Obviously, true multitasking would seem to be more desirable, but your system must have at least an 80386 microprocessor to take advantage of it. As you run additional applications, you will see some slowdown as the microprocessor time is sliced up among each running application. But consider the advantages. For example, a chess playing computer may take some time to calculate its next move against you, the opponent. This time often increases with the skill level you have chosen. Multitasking lets you switch to another window and write a letter while the computer "thinks."

Data Transfer Capabilities

The Windows Clipboard utility is used to exchange graphics, scanned images, spreadsheet data, or text between applications. The Clipboard makes all of your Windows applications (and some non-Windows applications) act as if they are part of a single integrated software package. You can think of it as a translator, because in most cases it will convert images in one format to another during the transfer between applications. Imagine the Clipboard as you would a real clipboard—a place where you clip pieces of art or text while moving to another location. In Windows, the Clipboard holds this information as you switch between win-

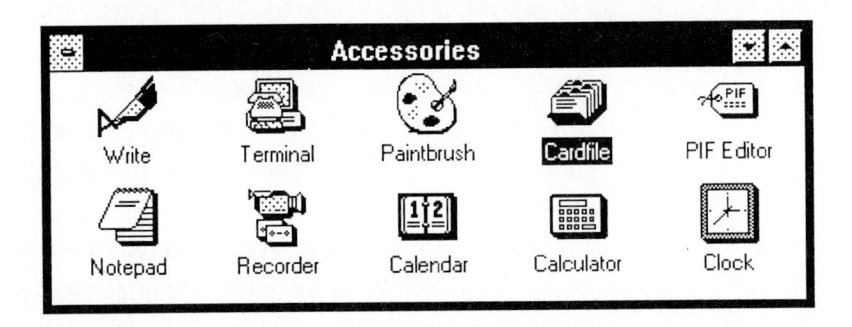

FIGURE 1-5. The Accessories window

dows, allowing you to mimic the common routines of cutting and pasting.

Desktop Accessories

Windows offers several accessories and utilities you will want to use every day. These are located in the Accessories Group window, shown in Figure 1-5.

A description of each item follows. During your normal Windows sessions, you may want to keep one or more of these accessories loaded on the desktop for easy access.

Write	Used to write, edit, format, and print documents. Although not a full-featured word processor like Microsoft Word, it is useful for memos, letters, reports, and other everyday documents.
Paintbrush	A convenient, easy-to-use drawing program. Used to create simple to complex drawings for your Write documents or any document created with any Windows application.

Terminal	A communications program used with a modem to connect with other computer systems or on-line data services over the phone lines.
Notepad	Allows you to create, store, and quickly retrieve notes and memos during your Windows sessions.
Recorder	Allows you to save keystrokes and mouse movements so you can repeat them at any time. Useful for establishing procedures for novice users or for replaying keystrokes and mouse sequences you perform on a regular basis.
Cardfile	An electronic card filing system with many of the sorting and searching features of advanced database systems.
Calendar	An appointment scheduling utility with day and month views, appointment scheduling, alarms, and other features.
Calculator	A desktop calculator with two modes, standard and scientific.
Clock	Produces an analog or digital time display you can place on the screen during idle computer time.
PIF Editor	Program Information File (PIF) editor creates and alters files used by Windows to run non-Windows applications.

Windows Control Panel

The Windows Control Panel offers a complete set of utilities for controlling the operation of your computer and Windows. The Control Panel window with the utility icons it contains is shown in Figure 1-6.

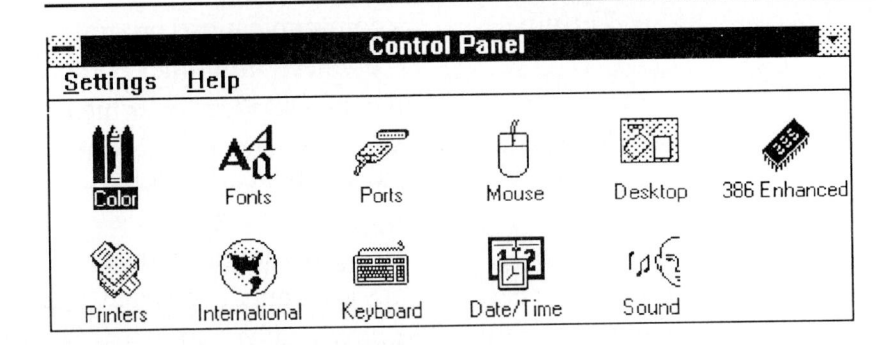

FIGURE 1-6. The Control Panel

Here is a description of each utility in the Control Panel:

Color	Used to alter the foreground, background, border, and other color schemes of Windows.
Fonts	Used to add, alter, and remove screen fonts.
Ports	Controls parallel and serial ports for printers, modems, and other devices that connect to your computer.
Mouse	Controls the operating characteristics of the mouse.
Desktop	Used to alter the features of the desktop.
386 Enhanced	Only appears on 80386 and 80486 systems and is used to control multitasking features.
Printers	Used to add and remove printers or alter their settings.
International	Sets keyboard, date, time, currency, and number features and formats to US or international standards.
Keyboard	Sets the keyboard repeat rate.
Date/Time	Sets the date and time.
Sound	Sets the warning beep on or off.

Dynamic Data Exchange

Another feature used to exchange data is Dynamic Data Exchange (DDE), which is more automatic than the Clipboard and relies on features programmed into the application being used. For example, a data analysis package in one window could supply data points to a graphics program running in another window. As the analysis package processes in the background, you can watch the bar charts change in real time. The plotting of election results comes to mind. Taking this a step further, election results could be entered in a database by an operator or input device as they arrive. The new data is fed to the analysis package as required, which then updates the graphics display.

DOS Compatibility

Since Windows is a shell over the DOS environment, you can still run most DOS applications by simply opening a window to the DOS command prompt. In addition, many DOS commands can be executed from the File Manager using the familiar Windows interface. These include the DOS commands for copying, deleting, renaming, and changing file attributes, as well as commands for creating and removing directories. You can also format and label floppy disks.

Increased Productivity

While increasing productivity may sound like computer jargon from the '80s, the concept is valid when it comes to Windows 3. In the past, some people probably wondered whether a computer really made them more productive, since the process of learning and using the computer took more time than it was worth. But, as hardware and software become more sophisticated, we can begin to see what increased productivity is all about, and Windows is no doubt one of its realizations. It brings you a working computer environment that offers software integration, speed, and ease of use. At the same time, your learning time decreases because Windows applications have the same consistent user interface that you need not relearn with every new application you buy.

OS/2 Look and Feel

If you are interested in making a transition to the OS/2 Presentation Manager environment at some time in the future, or if you often move to other systems that run OS/2, you will find Windows an excellent environment to use and grow with.

NEW FEATURES FOR WINDOWS 3

If you have been using previous versions of Windows, you will be interested in learning about the new features in Windows version 3. The most significant additions are the Program Manager, File Manager, and Task List.

Program Manager: The Group Organizer

The Program Manager is the first window displayed when you start Windows 3 and is used to organize your applications, utilities, and files into meaningful groups, making access to them easier. The following illustration shows how a typical Program Manager screen appears with all windows reduced to icons.

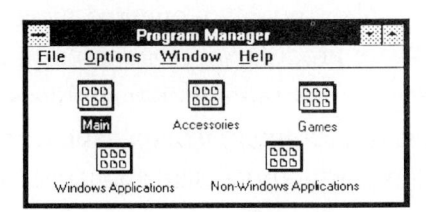

The icons are created during the installation process by Windows to hold the various programs and utilities that come with Windows, or that may already exist on the system. A powerful feature of Windows 3 is its ability to completely search a system for existing applications and create startup icons for those it recognizes.

Not all group windows necessarily hold programs and utilities. In the following illustration, a group window called Department Budgets has been opened to reveal *document icons,* in this case, Excel spreadsheet documents.

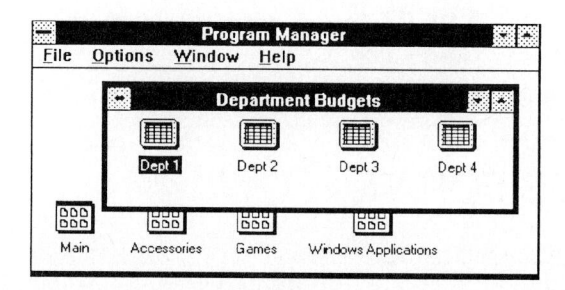

By double-clicking on any of the document icons, Excel is started and the spreadsheet for the associated department is loaded. This example reveals how the Program Manager can be used to organize your system according to the tasks you perform on a regular basis. It also points out Windows' ability to start an application and load a document by clicking on the document icon.

File Manager

The File Manager is one of the most practical additions to Windows. It allows you to use the mouse to work with files and directories in a whole new way. The File Manager is illustrated in Figure 1-7. Inside its window is the Directory Tree window on the left, which shows a graphic representation of your hard drive filing system. On the right is a *directory window,* which shows the files in a directory called WIN3. Notice that files have icons associated

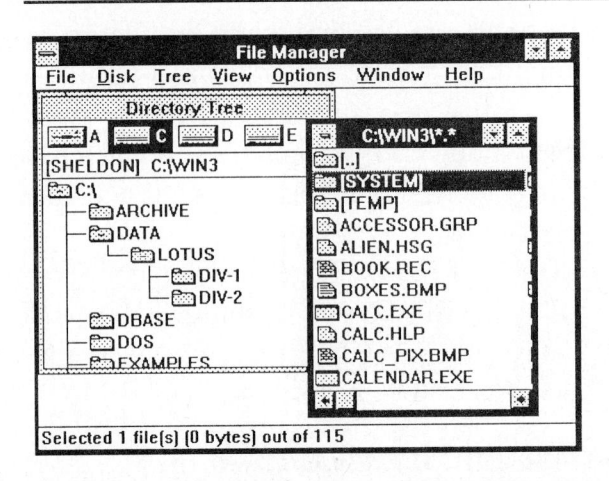

FIGURE 1-7. The File Manager

with them to help you differentiate between programs, directories, and normal files. Copying a file is easy: simply drag a file icon from a directory window to one of the directory icons on the Directory Tree.

Floppy disk and hard-disk drives are represented as icons to which you can switch by clicking with the mouse. Directories are also easy to get to by clicking the mouse. Subdirectories branch from their parent directories, making it easy to move to any directory quickly and easily. Files can be viewed and managed by double-clicking on any directory or subdirectory icon.

Task List

The Task List is a useful tool for moving from one window to another, especially when a lot of windows are on the desktop. The Task List can be opened at any time by double-clicking on the desktop. In the following illustration, a number of applications are listed in the Task List, each representing an application in an open window or icon.

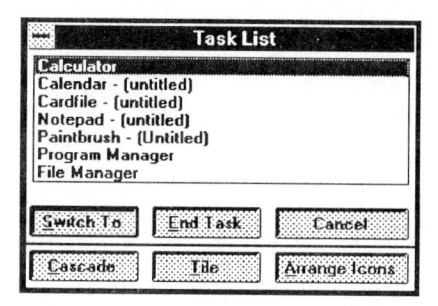

```
┌─────────────────────────────────┐
│ ▬           Task List           │
│ ┌─────────────────────────────┐ │
│ │ Calculator                  │ │
│ │ Calendar - (untitled)       │ │
│ │ Cardfile - (untitled)       │ │
│ │ Notepad - (untitled)        │ │
│ │ Paintbrush - (Untitled)     │ │
│ │ Program Manager             │ │
│ │ File Manager                │ │
│ └─────────────────────────────┘ │
│  [Switch To] [End Task] [Cancel]│
│  [Cascade]  [Tile]  [Arrange Icons] │
└─────────────────────────────────┘
```

To quickly switch to any application, simply click on its name. The Task List is also used to rearrange the windows and icons on the desktop.

Network Support

Windows 3 recognizes network connections and allows you to display and work with files on network drives and to use network printers. Popular networks such as Novell NetWare, Microsoft LAN Manager, and Banyan VINES are supported.

Additional New Features

Windows 3 presents a whole new appearance that is the result of enhanced colors, proportionally spaced fonts, and interesting graphics icons. Along with this new interface are these features:

- Easy installation. Windows determines how it should be installed and searches your hard drive for applications that can be run under Windows. It then creates startup icons for the applications.

- Full, on-line help facilities.

- Enhanced Print Manager now supports network printing.

- The Recorder accessory allows you to save keystrokes and mouse movements so they can be repeated at any time.

- Enhanced terminal communications program.

- Expanded printer support.

- New, expanded symbol font.

- An enhanced 386 mode provides even more compatibility with non-Windows applications.

- Solitaire, a new game.

WINDOWS OPERATING MODES

Windows operates in one of three modes, depending on the type of hardware you have. When Windows is first started, it automatically determines which mode to use, but you can choose to run Windows in a particular mode if the software you are attempting to run will not operate in the mode Windows selects. This may be the case with older Windows applications or non-Windows applications.

The three operating modes are discussed here.

REAL MODE Windows automatically runs in Real mode if your system has less than 1 megabyte of memory or if it uses an Intel 8086 or 8088 microprocessor. Real mode is the slowest and least desirable running mode for Windows. In addition, it does not take advantage of extended memory, which means that Windows has less memory available to run multiple applications and may not be able to do so at all. In some cases, you may want to run Windows in Real mode, even if you have a more advanced system, because applications written for previous versions of Windows may only be able to run in Real mode. If you have such applications, Real mode can be activated by starting Windows with the /R option, as discussed in Chapter 3, "Ways to Start Windows."

STANDARD MODE   Windows automatically runs in Standard mode if your system has 1MB or more of memory and if it has an Intel 80286 microprocessor. In Standard mode, Windows can access extended memory, and you can switch among non-Windows applications.

386 ENHANCED MODE   Windows loads in 386 Enhanced mode if your system has an Intel 80386/80486 microprocessor and 2MBs or more of memory. True multitasking of Windows and non-Windows applications is possible in this mode. When Windows runs in 386 Enhanced mode, it uses a special operating mode of the 80386/80486 microprocessor known as the virtual 86 mode. In this mode, the 80386/80486 acts like separate 8086 microprocessors for each open window with a running application. Each virtual 8086 machine runs in its own protected environment—if a program crashes in another virtual 8086 window, the entire computer system is not brought down.

Each operating mode is discussed in a separate chapter in Part III of this book. You should read the chapter that pertains to the mode you will be using since it will present topics you must consider when running programs, transferring data, or handling problems.

HARDWARE REQUIREMENTS FOR WINDOWS 3

Windows operates on most DOS-based computers, including personal computers with Intel 8088 and 8086 processors, although the performance on these systems is not spectacular. Windows runs best on AT-type systems with Intel 80286 microprocessors or advanced systems with Intel 80386 or 80486 microprocessors.

In general, the hardware you use should be 100 percent compatible with the tested hardware list you received with Windows. If you have problems running Windows, you may need to obtain special software from the hardware manufacturer to make your system compatible with Windows.

The minimum software and hardware requirements are outlined here:

- PC-DOS or MS-DOS 3.1 or higher.

- A personal computer based on the Intel family of 8088/8086 microprocessors. This family also includes the Intel 80286, 80386, and 80486.

- Memory requirements as listed in the next section.

- A hard-disk drive and at least 8MBs of free space.

- Graphics monitor.

- Although a mouse is not required, operating Windows without a mouse is difficult. This book is written with the assumption that you have a mouse.

- If you intend to use the Windows Enhanced Terminal communications software, you need a Hayes-compatible modem.

Other Considerations

There are a few things you must consider before you install Windows. These have to do mainly with the type of system you intend to use and the mode it will be operating in.

MEMORY Windows may use expanded or extended memory, depending on the run mode. Expanded memory is only used in the Real mode, so if you have an application that requires expanded memory, you may need to run your system in this mode. Standard and 386 Enhanced modes use extended memory because it is much faster and efficient than expanded memory. If you have an 80386 system and you need to run an application that requires expanded memory, you can install a special expanded memory simulator, as discussed in Chapter 21, "Operating in 386 Enhanced Mode."

The expanded memory used in Real mode must conform to version 4.0 of the Lotus-Intel-Microsoft Expanded Memory Specification (LIM EMS 4.0). Because extended memory is preferable to expanded memory, you should use whatever method possible to take advantage of it. While this is not possible on systems based on the 8088 and 8086 microprocessor, 80286 systems with installed memory boards like the AST RAMpage! or Intel Above Board/AT should be installed with those boards set for extended memory. You should then run in the Standard mode whenever possible.

The following is an outline of the memory requirements for the three different types of systems:

8088/8086	Systems in this class can only run in Real mode and can only use expanded memory. Set your memory expansion boards for expanded memory. You will need 640K of conventional memory and as much expanded memory as possible to conform to the LIM EMS 4.0 specification.
80286	Systems in this class can run in the Standard mode. One megabyte of memory is required but 2 megabytes or more are recommended.

80386/80486   Systems in this class will run 386 Enhanced mode. Two megabytes of memory are required but more are recommended.

OLDER WINDOWS APPLICATIONS   If you have applications that were written for older versions of Windows, you may not be able to run them in the Standard or 386 Enhanced mode. You will need to start Windows in the Real mode to use these programs until you can get an update from the software manufacturer.

MEMORY-RESIDENT SOFTWARE   Memory-resident software remains in memory after you start it, even if you start another application. This type of software may pose problems for Windows. Most applications that are simply loaded and have no further interaction with the user can be loaded in the normal way before starting Windows. So called *pop-up programs* that interact with users at any time may need to be loaded after Windows is started. Chapter 3, "Ways to Start Windows," discusses different ways of starting and using memory-resident software with Windows.

DISK-CACHING PROGRAMS   Windows uses its own disk-caching program called SMARTDrive to improve access to your hard drive. In most cases, you should replace your existing disk caching program with SMARTDrive. SMARTDrive increases the efficiency of your system by keeping previously read hard-disk information in memory just in case you need it again. Most computer systems typically read the same blocks of information from a disk system on a regular basis, so programs like SMART-Drive offer a dramatic improvement in overall speed. This is especially true if you are running several applications at once.

SMARTDrive requires at least 512K of extended memory or 256K of expanded memory. The utility is installed automatically by the SETUP program covered in Chapter 2, "Installing Windows," but you can alter its operating characteristics as will be outlined in Chapter 18, "Modifying Windows Startup."

During installation various files are copied to your system to match your hardware and peripherals. Some of these files, called *software drivers,* contain code that helps Windows use the hardware and peripherals of your particular system. The Windows disks come with a large assortment of these software drivers to match the most popular equipment. If you find during installation that a driver is not available for your particular equipment, you may need to contact the hardware manufacturer or Microsoft. Alternatively, you often can select a driver for a comparable piece of equipment. This usually means setting internal switches on the hardware. For example, many printers can be set to emulate IBM and Epson printers. You can run your hardware in an emulation mode until you obtain a suitable driver.

The Windows SETUP program copies drivers only for the equipment you specify during the initial installation. If you upgrade your system at a later date, you may need to copy new drivers from the Windows disk set to your system. This can be done by running the internal version of SETUP that is invoked from within Windows. It installs new drivers only, not the entire system.

Before you begin installation, make sure that your system meets the hardware and software requirements outlined at the end of Chapter 1.

INSTALLATION CONSIDERATIONS

This section points out a few things you should be aware of before proceeding with installation. Although Windows does a good job of determining the best way to configure itself for your system, you may want to consider these points before starting.

Expanded and Extended Memory

If you plan to install additional memory in your system, do so before running the SETUP program. SETUP will set various parameters based on the amount of memory it finds. If you have an 80286 system with a memory expansion board, you should install the board as extended memory, not expanded memory. If you have applications that require expanded memory, such as Lotus 1-2-3, but you want to take advantage of extended memory, you should configure the board with enough expanded memory for the application and configure the rest as extended memory, assuming your board allows this. Place the appropriate expanded or extended memory configuration commands in the CONFIG.SYS file before running the SETUP program.

> **Note:** If you are not familiar with expanded and extended memory, refer to your memory board's manual or to Part III of this book.

Disk Space

Not only is adequate disk space required to install Windows properly, but you must have enough left over to save your documents and work with applications. In addition, some applications, including Windows, use a unique swapping method to compensate for low memory. When memory starts to become scarce, part of the program or part of a document may be temporarily transferred to disk to free additional memory. The information is placed in a temporary *swap file,* which is usually removed once you quit the application. If your system is based on the 80386, SETUP establishes a permanent swap file on your drive, the size of which is determined by available free space. If your drive has enough space, you should verify creation of this file during the SETUP program.

Optimizing Your Hard Drive

You can use various techniques to make your system operate more efficiently. Most of these techniques are covered in Appendix B, "Optimizing Techniques." Of interest here, however, are methods for optimizing your hard drive before you install Windows and any other new applications. Through a process known as *file fragmen-*

tation, hard drives can slowly lose their efficiency. A hole left by a deleted file may be filled inefficiently by a new file if the new file is bigger than the space left by the deleted file. The new file is then split and stored in separate areas of the disk drive, causing slower access. You can "unfragment" your drive by using special software like the Norton utilities, or you can back up the drive completely, format it, and then restore the software. Before unfragmenting a drive, it is best to delete all unnecessary files. These and other methods are covered in Appendix B, but they are necessary only if you have an older system and feel your system's performance has been degraded.

INSTALLING OTHER SOFTWARE One of the best features of the SETUP program is its ability to search your hard drive for applications and create startup icons for those it finds. You can take advantage of this feature by installing your applications before installing Windows. SETUP will then find the program files and configure Windows accordingly, saving you the trouble of doing it yourself.

INSTALLATION PROCEDURE

The Windows SETUP program is simple to operate, and you need little instruction to run it. Along the way, however, you must make several decisions. This section guides you through the installation process. Part of the process is run using Windows itself, so if you are new to Windows, you can use this section to guide you through the mouse and keystroke movements you must make.

You will need to know the following during the installation:

- *Directory where Windows will be stored.* SETUP recommends WINDOWS. If you have an old version of Windows in a directory called WINDOWS that you want to keep, specify another directory, such as WIN3.

- *Monitor, keyboard, and mouse type.* Windows automatically determines the type of computer you have (80286, 80386, etc.). You should know the type of monitor (EGA, VGA, etc.), keyboard (101-key, US, or foreign), and mouse (Microsoft, IBM, etc.). This sets features such as US or Foreign Language type, date and number format.

- *Network type.* If your system is connected to a network, you must specify which type (Novell, Microsoft, Banyan, etc.).

- *Printer type and computer connection port.* A wide range of printers will appear in the list. If your printer does not appear, determine if it is compatible with one in the list and choose that printer. You must know the port it is connected to on the back of your computer. For parallel printers, this is usually LPT1 for the first printer, LPT2 for the second, and so on. For serial printers, COM1 is the first port, although modems are usually connected to COM ports on DOS-based personal computers.

Starting the Installation

To begin installation, place the number 1 installation disk in the floppy drive and switch to that drive. In the following example, drive A is used. Press (ENTER) after typing each of these commands.

A:

SETUP

The first screen to appear offers you a choice of either going ahead with the installation, reviewing SETUP help information, or stopping the installation process. You can use the (F1) key to review help information at any time. Other keys used during installation are listed here:

(F1)   Display help information

(ESC)	Return to SETUP after reviewing help information
Arrow keys	Move the cursor to items in a list
(ENTER)	Choose a recommended option or continue
(F3)	Exit SETUP at any time

> **Note** If you exit SETUP with (F3), you must rerun SETUP from the beginning for a proper installation.

SETUP determines the type of system and associated hardware you are using and configures Windows for that hardware as best it can. In most cases, you can simply press (ENTER) to accept the recommended options and settings.

The next screen to appear, if you continue with installation, asks for the name of the directory where Windows will be stored. SETUP recommends a directory called WINDOWS and creates that directory if you press (ENTER.) To create and use another directory, backspace and type in the new name.

A screen with the information similar to Figure 2-1 appears next. The settings on your system will differ, depending on the type of hardware you have. You can change these if you wish. Scan through the list to make sure SETUP has determined your hardware configuration properly. If you need to make changes, press the (UP ARROW) key to locate the appropriate selection, and press (ENTER) to see alternate choices.

WHEN WINDOWS MAKES INCORRECT RECOMMENDATIONS SETUP may not correctly determine your hardware configuration. For example, it may select an IBM 8514/a VGA monitor when you have a VGA monitor from another company. In this case, you would select VGA from the monitor list instead of 8514/a. If you have a VGA system with a monochrome monitor, be sure that you choose the selection for VGA with monochrome monitor.

<u>Windows SETUP</u>

SETUP has determined that the following components make up your computer system. Please review the list below to confirm that your system includes these hardware and software components.

Computer:	MS or PC DOS System
Display:	8514/a
Mouse:	Microsoft or IBM PS/2
Keyboard:	Enhanced 101 or 102 key US and Non US keyboards
Keyboard Layout:	Standard (US)
Language:	English (American)
Network:	Microsoft Network (or 100% compatible)
No Changes:	The above list matches my computer

If all the items in the list are correct, press `ENTER` to indicate "No Changes." If you want to change any item in the list, press the `UP` or `DOWN ARROW` key to move the highlight to the item you want to change. Then press `ENTER` to see alternative choices for that item.

FIGURE 2-1. Windows SETUP displays its determination of your system components

SETUP may select the wrong type of network for your system or select a network even if you are not connected to one. Press the `UP ARROW` key to the network field, and press `ENTER` to see the list of alternatives. Select No Network Installed from the list, or select an alternate network. If your network is not listed, choose a network that most closely matches yours.

Windows SETUP may lock up if the incorrect hardware is selected. Simply reboot and start again using a different selection. In most cases, you can make choices that will not inhibit the installation, even if you are not sure the choice you have made is correct for your system. Don't worry too much about making incorrect selections, since you can alter them later by running SETUP from inside Windows.

SETUP Configuration Phase

After you verify the hardware list and press (ENTER), SETUP begins copying the Windows program files to the directory you specified. You are prompted for each disk as needed. From this point on, SETUP runs under Windows. Because Windows is running, you can make selections from dialog boxes and pull-down menus with the mouse, if you have one. If you do not have a mouse, this section will help you determine which keys on your keyboard to use for making selections.

In a moment, the Windows SETUP screen, as shown in Figure 2-2, appears. You can set up your printers, set up any applications currently installed on the hard drive, or read on-line documentation. You can opt to install these later using the internal version of SETUP by removing the checkmark from any item.

The screen options are explained here:

- *Set Up Printers.* Windows needs special instructions in order to use your particular printer. These instructions are contained in the driver files discussed earlier in this chapter. The Set Up Printers option is used to specify which driver file should be copied to your system. If you have more than one printer, you can install each printer individually.

- *Set Up Applications Already on Hard Disk.* Applications are software packages you have already installed on the hard disk. Windows searches your hard drive, finds applications, and creates special Program Information Files (PIFs) to help it load and run the applications. Windows creates desktop icons for the applications it recognizes.

- *Read On-Line Documents.* Several documents may have come with your version of Windows that contain information not available at the release date. You can select this option to review or print the files.

```
┌─────────────────────────────────────────────────────────┐
│ ─                    Windows Setup                       │
│  ┌──┐                                    ┌────────────┐ │
│  │💻│  Installing Windows 3.0            │  Continue  │ │
│  └──┘                                    └────────────┘ │
│                                                          │
│       In addition to installing Windows 3.0, you can:   │
│                                                          │
│              ☒ Set up Printers                           │
│              ☒ Set up Applications Already on Hard Disk  │
│              ☒ Read On-line Documents                    │
│                                                          │
└─────────────────────────────────────────────────────────┘
```

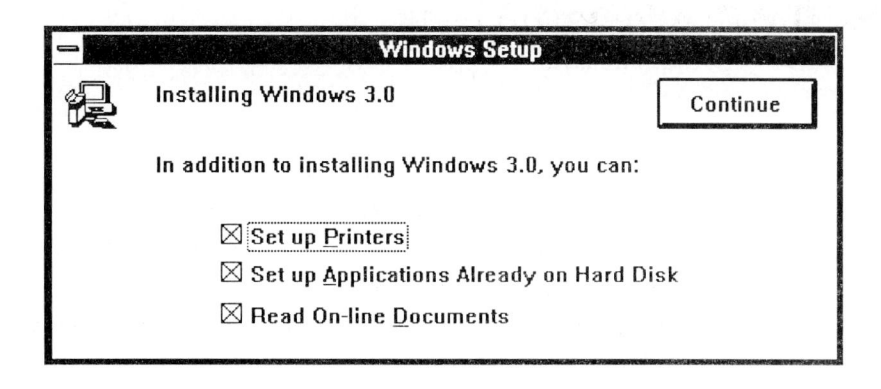

FIGURE 2-2. The Windows (SETUP) screen

SELECTING SETUP OPTIONS Each of the options on the (SETUP) screen should have an "X" in its checkbox, indicating that the selection will be performed when you click on the Continue button or press (ENTER). You can deselect any item by clicking its selection box. If you are using the keyboard, use the arrow keys to move to the appropriate selection and press the (SPACEBAR) to select or deselect it.

The remainder of this chapter assumes each item has been selected. Click on the Continue button, or press (ENTER) to continue SETUP. You are prompted for additional disks as installation continues. Keep in mind that whenever you see an OK button, you can click it with the mouse or press (ENTER) to continue. As SETUP asks for each disk, it extracts only the files it needs from the disks, based on the hardware configuration specified earlier. If you decide to change the installation at a later time, SETUP may once again ask for the disks to extract files it has not yet copied to the hard drive.

Modifying the System Files

The SETUP program can make changes to the DOS startup files that configure memory and set options required by Windows. You can choose one of the options shown on the menu in Figure 2-3.

The options are explained here:

- *Make all modifications for you.* The SETUP program modifies your current AUTOEXEC.BAT and CONFIG.SYS programs. The old files are renamed AUTOEXEC.OLD and CONFIG.OLD.

- *Let you review and edit changes before modifications are made.* SETUP makes the necessary changes and then displays the files so you can make further changes.

- *Let you make the modifications later.* SETUP saves modified versions of your startup files so you can review them at a later time and make changes to your existing files as you see fit. This option is only recommended for experienced DOS users.

```
┌─────────────────────── Windows Setup ───────────────────────┐
│ In order for Windows to be installed optimally, Setup       │
│ needs to modify your CONFIG.SYS file.          [ Continue ] │
│                                                             │
│ Setup can:                                                  │
│   ◉ make all modifications for you                          │
│   ○ let you review and edit changes, before modifications are made │
│   ○ let you make the modifications later                    │
└─────────────────────────────────────────────────────────────┘
```

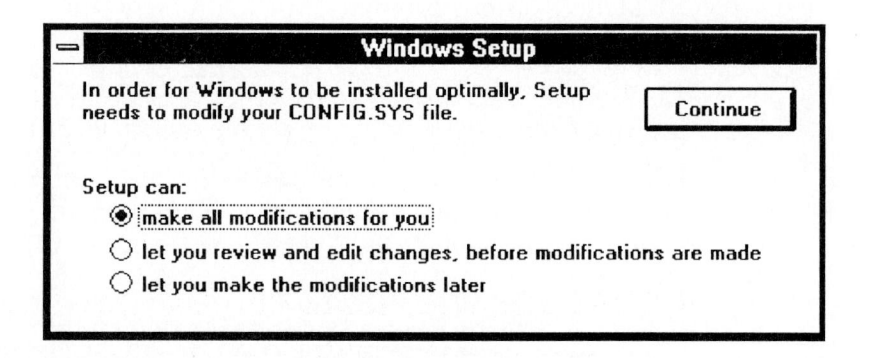

FIGURE 2-3. Changing the startup files with SETUP

The following changes are made to the AUTOEXEC.BAT file:

- The new WINDOWS directory is added to the PATH command.
- Any existing Windows path statements are removed from the PATH command.

The following lines are added to the CONFIG.SYS file:

```
FILES=30
DEVICE=HYMEM.SYS
DEVICE=SMARTDRIVE.SYS
```

In addition, any incompatible memory drivers are removed, such as 386MAX.SYS or CEMM.SYS.

It is recommended that you select the first option from the Windows Setup menu, since you can always change the files later at the DOS level.

Installing Your Printers

The Printers screen, shown in Figure 2-4, appears next. You can use the arrow keys to scroll through the list of printers at the bottom of the screen. You can also press the first letter of your printer name to select your printer.

When you locate the printer to install, press (ENTER). SETUP asks for the disk containing the printer driver file. It then copies the driver files for the disk to your hard drive and makes the printer active. You can repeat these steps for each printer you want to install.

CONFIGURE THE PRINTERS After the printers have been copied and their names appear in the Installed Printers field of the Printers menu, you must select each printer one after the other and configure them. Highlight a printer using the arrow keys, and click

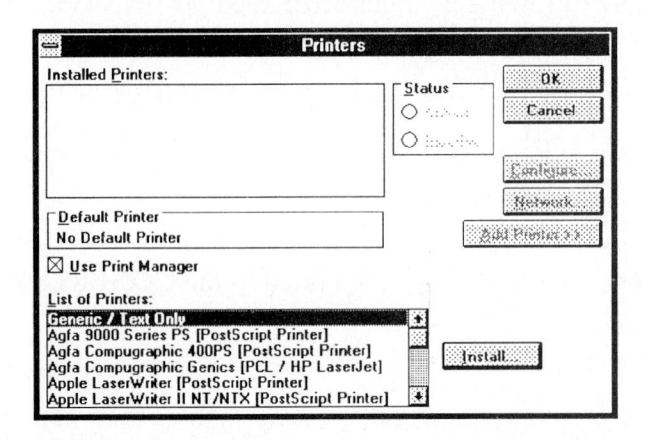

FIGURE 2-4. The Printers Installation menu

on the Configure button with the mouse or press **ALT-C**. A Printers-Configure window appears, similar to this one:

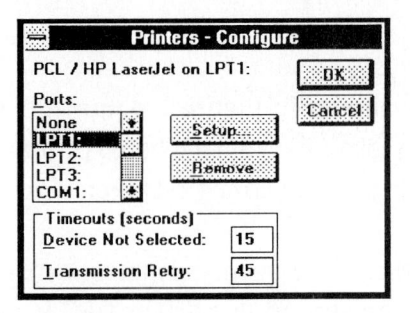

Select a printer port by choosing a parallel (LPT) port or a serial (COM) port. If you are not sure which port to use, refer to Chapter 8. You can now use the **TAB** key or mouse to move to the other selections in the window. You can leave the Timeouts field as it is for now and make adjustments later by referring to Chapter 8, "Working With Printers."

Installing Windows 39

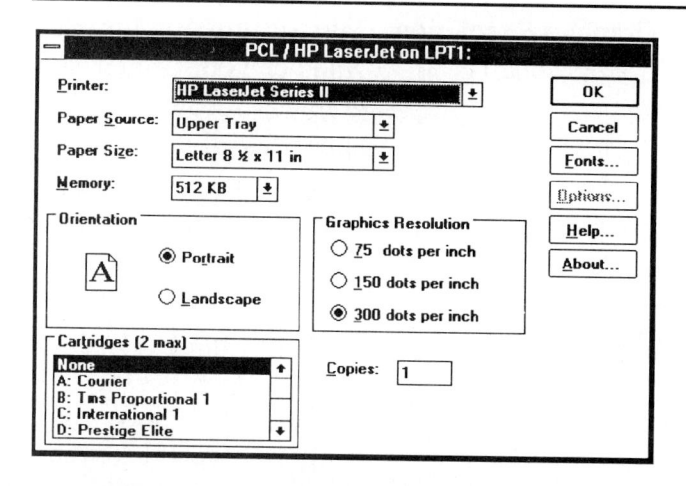

```
┌─────────────────────────────────────────────────────────┐
│ —           PCL / HP LaserJet on LPT1:                  │
│  Printer:    [HP LaserJet Series II      ][±]  [  OK  ] │
│  Paper Source: [Upper Tray              ][±]  [Cancel ] │
│  Paper Size:   [Letter 8 ½ x 11 in      ][±]  [Fonts...]│
│  Memory:       [512 KB][±]                    [Options..]│
│  ┌─Orientation──────┐ ┌─Graphics Resolution─┐ [ Help... ]│
│  │       ⦿ Portrait │ │  ○ 75 dots per inch │ [ About...]│
│  │ [A]              │ │  ○ 150 dots per inch│           │
│  │       ○ Landscape│ │  ⦿ 300 dots per inch│           │
│  └──────────────────┘ └─────────────────────┘           │
│  ┌─Cartridges (2 max)─┐                                 │
│  │ None            ↑ │  Copies: [1]                     │
│  │ A: Courier        │                                  │
│  │ B: Tms Proportional 1                                │
│  │ C: International 1                                   │
│  │ D: Prestige Elite ↓│                                 │
│  └───────────────────┘                                  │
└─────────────────────────────────────────────────────────┘
```

FIGURE 2-5. The Printer Setup menu

Select Setup from the Printers-Configure window using the (TAB) key or mouse or by pressing (ALT-S). A screen similar to Figure 2-5 appears, which shows options for the Hewlett-Packard LaserJet Series II printer.

Using the (TAB) key or mouse, move to each field and make adjustments. Descriptions of the fields and buttons follow. Use the arrow keys in each field to make further selections.

Paper Source	The paper source differs depending on the type of printer you install. It may have upper and lower paper trays, paper bins, or envelope feeders.
Paper Size	The size of the paper you intend to use.
Memory	Enter the amount of memory installed in the printer.
Orientation	Select Portrait (normal) or Landscape (sideways) mode.

Graphics Resolution	The setting in this field depends on whether your printer supports different graphics resolutions. The options may appear as High, Medium, or Low, or as dots per inch. Most laser printers will print at 300 dots per inch. High resolution causes slow printing but produces high-quality output.
Copies	Enter the number of copies you want to print.
Cartridges	Many printers have slots for font cartridges. Select the font cartridge you plan to use from the list.
Fonts button	On some dialog boxes, the Fonts button will appear. Press the Fonts button if you wish to set up fonts not included with Windows. These are supplied from other sources on disk or as cartridges.
Options button	On some dialog boxes the Options button will appear. Press this button to select unique options for the printer.

Note: You may find that no one selection is appropriate for the way you want to print. Chapter 8, "Working With Printers," discusses how to create several different configurations for one printer.

After making your selections on the Printers window, press (ENTER) or click on OK. The Printers-Configure window reappears. Make any other changes as necessary and press (ENTER). You can return to the main Printers menu where you can configure another printer if necessary. To save the configurations and continue with SETUP, press (ENTER) or click on the OK button.

Setting Up Applications

The next phase of the SETUP program sets up the applications you currently have on the hard drive. The following Set Up Applications screen appears:

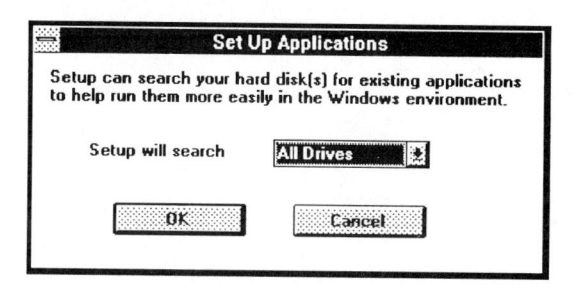

[Set Up Applications dialog box: "Setup can search your hard disk(s) for existing applications to help run them more easily in the Windows environment. Setup will search [All Drives]" with OK and Cancel buttons]

This setup procedure provides a convenient way of making your current applications work with Windows. It searches through your system, locates executable applications, and creates the appropriate files to make those aplications work with Windows. You can sit back and let Windows do all the work. These options can be selected when you click on the Set Up Applications list box:

All Drives	All current hard drives are searched. Use caution with this command if you have network drives installed.
Path Only	Only the directories specified in the current path are searched.
Drive x	Only the drive specified by x is searched.

Use the arrow keys to select an option from the search field, and press (ENTER) or click on OK to start the procedure.

In a moment the screen shown in Figure 2-6 appears. It displays a list of found applications on the left and allows you to actually install them as Windows applications by clicking on the Add

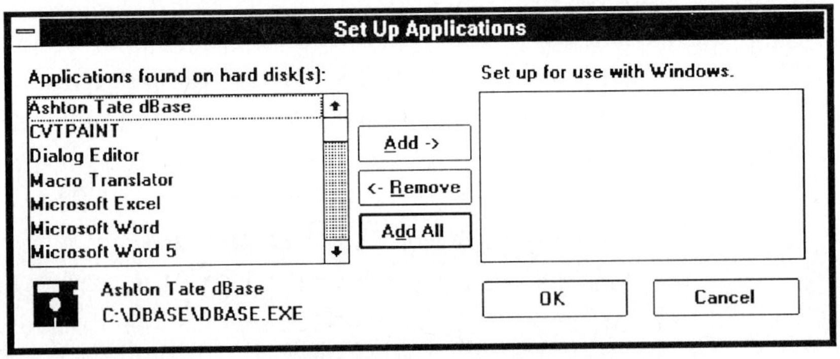

FIGURE 2-6. The Applications Setup menu

button or by pressing (ALT-A). Use the arrow keys to select the application on the left you want to add, and then click the Add button. To add all the applications, click the Add All button or press (ALT-D). Use the Remove button to remove applications on the right if necessary.

When all the applications you want to install are in the right window, click on OK or press (ENTER) to continue. The SETUP program will then add the programs to appropriate windows and give each a special name and icon you can select to start the program.

Reading the Release Notes

SETUP starts the Notepad editor and displays the current release notes for your version of Windows as the last step in the installation process. You can print the notes by choosing Print on the File menu. If you don't have a mouse, press (ALT-F), and then select Print from the menu by typing **P**.

After the notes have been printed, exit Notepad by selecting Exit on the File menu. Click on the File menu and then click on Exit. If you don't have a mouse, press (ALT-F) and type **X** to exit.

SETUP Completion

When Windows installation is complete, the final window to appear gives you the option of rebooting the system or returning to DOS. You must reboot your system in order to activate the options or changes made in the CONFIG.SYS file. You can choose to return to DOS if you need to make further alterations to the AUTOEXEC.BAT or CONFIG.SYS files before rebooting. To do so, choose the Return to DOS option; otherwise select the Reboot option.

Chapter 3 discusses how to start Windows.

CONFIGURATION OPTIONS

After SETUP installs Windows, you may want to check the CONFIG.SYS and AUTOEXEC.BAT startup files and make alterations to their settings if you are familiar with DOS and know how to make such adjustments. This section discusses the settings made by SETUP. You will find additional information on the contents and alteration of the startup files in Part III of this book.

Options for 8088/8086 Systems

Intel 8088- and 8086-based systems operate in Real mode only. They must have 640K of conventional memory and as much expanded memory as possible. The CONFIG.SYS file should have a command to configure the memory on the expanded memory board. Refer to the board's documentation for more details.

Windows also includes the SMARTDrive command for disk caching if your system has enough expanded memory. The SMARTDrive command has the /A option to indicate expanded memory usage. Chapter 18, "Modifying Windows Startup," covers the SMARTDrive command in more detail.

The CONFIG.SYS file should also contain the following:

FILES = 30

BUFFERS = 20

You may need to increase these settings for some software or you may need to reduce them to save memory. If SMARTDrive is used, BUFFERS equals 10 rather than 20.

If you will be running non-Windows applications and have an EGA monitor, the following command should be included.

DEVICE = C:\WINDOWS\EGA.SYS

Options for 80286 Systems

Systems based on the Intel 80286 run Windows in Standard mode if more than 1MB of memory is present; otherwise Windows runs in Real mode. It is recommended that memory expansion boards be configured as extended memory and that appropriate commands be placed in the CONFIG.SYS file for this purpose. This should have been done before installing Windows and the command should be included in the new CONFIG.SYS file created by SETUP.

The Windows HIMEM.SYS and SMARTDrive commands should be included in the CONFIG.SYS file to take advantage of extended memory. HIMEM.SYS is a memory management utility; SMARTDrive is a disk-caching program. Both are covered in Chapter 18, "Modifying How Windows Starts."

The CONFIG.SYS file should also contain the following:

FILES = 30

BUFFERS = 20

You may need to increase these settings for some software. You may need to reduce them to save memory usage, or if SMART-Drive is used, set BUFFERS equal to 5.

Those running non-Windows applications on an EGA monitor should include the following command:

DEVICE = C:\WINDOWS\EGA.SYS

Options for 80386/80486 Systems

The CONFIG.SYS file for 80386 and higher systems should include commands to configure add-in memory boards as extended memory, not expanded memory. You may need to add the EMM386.SYS command to install expanded memory emulation for programs that run only on expanded memory. Refer to Chapter 21, "Operating In 386 Enhanced Mode," for more details.

The Windows HIMEM.SYS command should be included in the CONFIG.SYS file to take advantage of extended memory. HIMEM.SYS is a memory management utility that is installed in the file by SETUP. The SMARTDrive configuration command should also be included to set up disk caching, as covered in Chapter 18, "Modifying Windows Startup."

The CONFIG.SYS file should also contain the following:

FILES = 30

BUFFERS = 20

You may need to increase these for some software or you may need to reduce them to save memory. If SMARTDrive is used, set BUFFERS to 5.

- If you will be running non-Windows applications and have an EGA monitor, the following command should be included.

DEVICE = C:\WINDOWS\EGA.SYS

3

WAYS TO START WINDOWS

Starting Windows
Startup Considerations

This chapter explains how to start Windows. In most cases, you can type a simple command such as **WIN** to start Windows. There may be times, however, when you need to alter the startup method to access a different Windows operating mode. These modes and the startup commands for them are covered here.

Before starting Windows you may want to refer to the "Startup Considerations" section of this chapter. It explains the procedures you may need to follow to get memory-resident software or non-Windows applications running. In addition, you'll find tips on maximizing the amount of memory in your system and on running older Windows applications.

STARTING WINDOWS

Starting Windows can be as simple as typing a three-letter command. However, depending on the Windows run mode you want to use and the type of software you have, you may need to specify additional parameters on the command line. This section covers various startup procedures.

Basic Startup Command

The basic startup procedure is to type **WIN** at the DOS prompt after your system starts.

A screen similar to Figure 3-1 appears. The Program Manager is always the first screen to appear when Windows starts, unless you have made changes to the startup procedure.

You can include the WIN command in the AUTOEXEC.BAT file so Windows starts every time you boot your system (see "Starting Windows Automatically" later in this chapter).

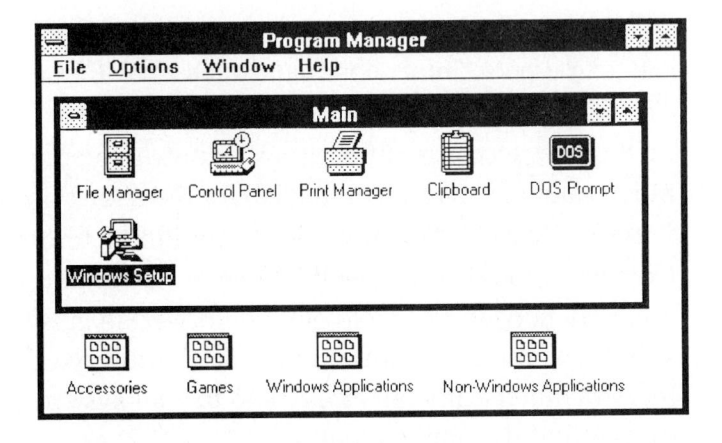

FIGURE 3-1. The opening Windows screen

Starting an Application And Windows Simultaneously

You can start an application at the same time you start Windows by specifying the name of the application and its directory path, if necessary, on the command line. For example, the following command starts Word for Windows, which is located in the WINWORD directory of drive C:

WIN C:\WINWORD\WORD.EXE

The second portion of the command is known as the *run command* and must come after any switches, as discussed in the next section.

Starting with a Specific Operating Mode

When started by the methods just described, Windows determines its startup method, depending on the type of equipment you have. You may want to start Windows in another mode, even if you have an advanced system. To do this, invoke the WIN command using the special switch described in the following sections.

> **Note** If you use switches and run commands (discussed in the previous section), the switches must come before the run commands.

REAL MODE Start Windows in Real mode if you cannot get an older Windows application to run in one of the other modes. This is the mode automatically selected if your system has less than 1MB of memory or is based on an Intel 8088 or 8086 microprocessor.

To start in Real mode, type **WIN /R** on the DOS command line.

Real mode has additional command-line switches that control how expanded memory is used, although the default used by

Windows is usually adequate. Refer to Chapter 19, "Operating in Real Mode," for additional information.

STANDARD MODE   Standard mode is the normal mode for systems based on the Intel 80286 processor. You may want to run in this mode if you have an 80386-based system and are not running non-Windows applications. Windows on an 80386 system actually runs faster in Standard mode than in 386 Enhanced mode because it does not have to manage the overhead required to run non-Windows applications. Note that 2MB or more of memory must be available. Standard mode should also be used if your 80386 computer system is not compatible with the 386 Enhanced mode.

To start in Standard mode, type **WIN /S** on the DOS command line.

386 ENHANCED MODE   If you have an 80386-based system but less than 2MB of memory, Windows will start in Standard mode due to a lack of memory. You can type **WIN /3** to force 386 Enhanced mode on a low memory 80386 system, although the system will run slower than normal.

Starting Windows with a Batch File

The Windows startup commands can become lengthy if you use switches and run commands. To make Windows easier to start, you can create a batch file that includes all the parameters you need. A batch file saves you the trouble of typing the entire startup commands. The startup command WIN C:\WORD5\WORD could be placed in a batch file called WORD.BAT for example. To start Windows and Word, you would then type **WORD** on the command line.

With batch files you also can start Windows in different modes or with different programs. You simply create a separate batch file for each application or mode you want to start.

To create a batch file, move to the ROOT directory or a directory that is on your search path, and use the COPY CON command at the DOS level or the Windows Notepad accessory (see Chapter 12, "Windows Desktop Accessories"). The following example creates the WINWORD.BAT file discussed earlier:

```
COPY CON WINWORD.BAT
WIN C:\WINWORD\WORD
```

Press (F6) and then (ENTER) to write the file.

Starting Windows Automatically

You can place the Windows startup command in your AUTOEXEC.BAT file to start Windows every time you turn your system on. Since most applications run from Windows and it offers superior file- and directory-handling facilities, you have every reason to work in the Windows environment on a regular basis. Simply make the Windows startup command the last line of the AUTOEXEC.BAT file.

Quitting Windows

You should always quit Windows using one of the methods described here and never by simply turning the system off. Windows may be opened with unsaved documents, which would be lost unless you quit properly. You can use one of several methods to quit Windows. The first method is the simplest but requires a mouse. Double-click on the Control menu selector in the top left corner of the Program Manager window, as shown here:

52 Windows 3 Made Easy

── Control menu selector

```
 ▓  Program Manager
File  Options  Window  Help
```

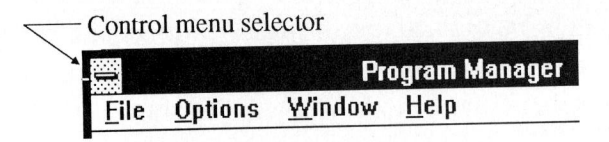

The next two methods can be done with the keyboard. You can also click with the mouse to open the menus and select the options shown. Press the key combination (ALT-SPACEBAR) to display the Control menu shown here:

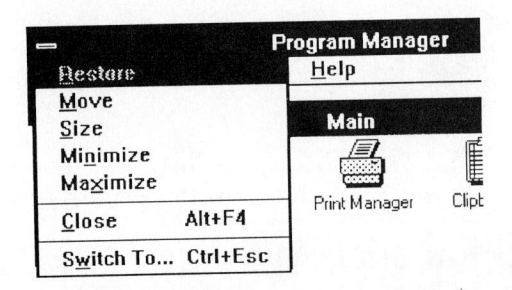

```
─           Program Manager
 Restore     Help
 Move
 Size           Main
 Minimize
 Maximize
               Print Manager  Clipb
 Close   Alt+F4
 Switch To... Ctrl+Esc
```

Type C to select Close or press (ALT-F4).

The last method is to type (ALT-F) to open the File menu and type X to choose the Exit Windows option, as shown here:

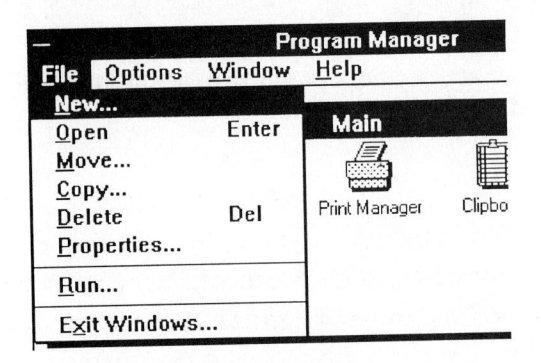

```
─              Program Manager
File  Options  Window  Help
 New...
 Open        Enter    Main
 Move...
 Copy...
 Delete      Del     Print Manager  Clipbo
 Properties...

 Run...

 Exit Windows...
```

Windows never lets you end a session using any of these methods without displaying the following warning screen.

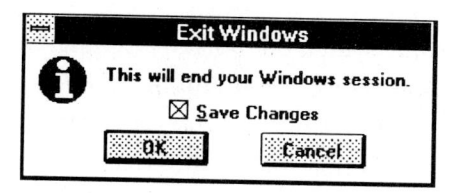

Click on the OK button or press (ENTER) to confirm that you want to quit. If you moved or resized the windows of the Program Manager in a way that you want to save, be sure an "X" appears in the Save Changes box. If you do not have a mouse, press the (TAB) key until the box is outlined, press the (SPACEBAR), and then tab back to the OK button and press (ENTER) to exit.

> **Note** If applications are still open, Windows displays a warning screen and does not allow you to exit until the Windows are closed.

STARTUP CONSIDERATIONS

You may need to alter your Windows startup procedure with the techniques discussed here if Windows does not start or if applications do not start from Windows.

Minimizing Memory Usage

You are less likely to have problems starting Windows or running applications in Windows if you reduce the amount of memory in use before you start it. This is especially true if you are attempting to run non-Windows applications that require a set amount of memory.

Memory-resident programs that are loaded when your system starts are the most likely memory hogs. Commands to start these programs are usually located in the CONFIG.SYS and AUTOEXEC.BAT files, which reside in the ROOT directory of your system. You may want to review the contents of these files and remove any commands that load nonessential programs.

The main idea is to avoid loading programs that use too much memory at boot time. You should experiment with the programs to see if they can be loaded after Windows has been started. This involves a process of temporarily disabling commands in either CONFIG.SYS or AUTOEXEC.BAT until you find a combination that works. You then should determine whether you really need the program or whether it can be loaded from Windows.

Note You can place a REM statement before a command in a startup file to temporarily disable it. Ignore the error message produced by the REM statement at boot time until you have solved your memory problem.

The commands normally associated with CONFIG.SYS and AUTOEXEC.BAT are discussed in the next two sections.

THE CONFIG.SYS STARTUP FILE The CONFIG.SYS file normally contains DEVICE commands used to load device drivers. Two commands that should not be disabled are

```
DEVICE = HIMEM.SYS
DEVICE = SMARTDRV.SYS
```

These start the memory-management and cache programs used by Windows. Other DEVICE commands might load drivers for peripherals you have attached to your system, such as optical drives and tape drives. You may want to temporarily disable these commands until you can locate the source of the memory problem.

The most common memory hog is a RAM drive or "phantom" drive, which is a pseudo-drive established in memory. It appears to DOS and Windows as a super-fast drive that can be used to speed access to programs or data that are stored in it rather than on a physical disk. RAM drives should be disabled.

There are other commands normally associated with CONFIG.SYS such as FILES, BUFFERS, LASTDRIVE, and STACKS. A small amount of memory can be saved by lowering the setting for these commands or removing them if possible. Complete information can be found in Chapter 18, "Modifying How Windows Starts," or your DOS manual.

THE AUTOEXEC.BAT STARTUP FILE The AUTOEXEC.BAT file is a batch file that automatically runs when your system starts. You can place the Windows startup command in the file to start Windows every time you turn your system on. Other commands in the file normally include those that set the system search path and change the system prompt.

The commands in AUTOEXEC.BAT most likely to cause memory problems are those that start pop-up-type memory-resident software, like Borland's Sidekick. The commands used to start these programs should be removed from AUTOEXEC.BAT. Instead, you should execute them from Windows once it has been loaded. See the next section for more information. Alteration of the AUTOEXEC.BAT file is covered in Chapter 18, "Modifying How Windows Starts."

Memory-Resident Software

Memory-resident software is loaded into memory and stays there, even as you run other applications. Some memory-resident software is interactive, which means that you can press a key combination to pop it up on the screen. As discussed in the previous section, memory-resident software is normally loaded when the system is first turned on through commands in the CONFIG.SYS and AUTOEXEC.BAT startup files.

Typically, noninteractive memory-resident software pose only memory problems to Windows. Interactive pop-up software, on the other hand, may pose more serious problems. Windows or programs running in Windows could crash when you interact with the software. For this reason, you may want to disable the commands that start the software from the startup files and try loading them from inside Windows instead. These measures are only required if you are having memory or program conflicts.

See Chapter 11, "Running Applications Under Windows," for more information on using memory-resident pop-up software.

Running Older Windows Applications

You may need to alter your Windows startup procedure if you cannot start applications written for previous versions of Windows. The best thing to do is get an updated version of the software from the manufacturer.

To run an older application, start Windows in Real mode by typing **WIN /R**. Keep in mind that Real mode does not use extended memory. Some applications may require expanded memory, which you may have disabled in preference to extended memory. Because of differences between Windows 3 and older versions, your old Windows application might not run the same as it did with the older version: Fonts may appear incorrectly in dialog boxes and colors may be displayed wrong. At worst, the application may suddenly terminate. You should experiment with its use before doing any serious work.

Running Non-Windows Applications

Non-Windows applications are those not designed to work with any version of Windows. If a non-Windows application can be started under Windows, it will require the entire screen in Real and Standard modes and will not have any of the typical Windows features such as pull-down menus and scroll bars. Its operation will be exactly the same as if started from the DOS command line. If you are running 386 Enhanced mode, most non-Windows applications will run inside a window of their own. This is possible because 80386-based machines allow each program to run in its own protected partition.

The benefit of running non-Windows applications under Windows rather than by themselves as normal is that you can easily switch to Windows and other applications and even cut and paste information between other applications.

Since non-Windows applications were not written with Windows in mind, they are not capable of cooperatively sharing memory with other applications you may attempt to run. Non-Windows applications tend to dominate memory. You will probably need to free up memory elsewhere to supply the non-Windows application with more memory. This is covered in the previous section, "Minimizing Memory Usage," and is covered in more detail in Chapter 11, "Running Applications Under Windows."

4

LEARNING THE WINDOWS INTERFACE

Elements of the Windows Screen
The Features and Use of Dialog Boxes
Mouse Techniques
Keyboard Techniques
Changing the Active Window

This chapter explains the features of windows and how to control them. What you learn here will be the foundation of your future interaction with Windows, because the techniques given here are applicable to most programs that run under Windows.

You will notice immediately that Windows can be used with the keyboard or with the mouse. Neither device is preferred exclusively over the other because both have their advantages in certain situations. The mouse is the quickest method for accessing menus and making selections, but when you do not want to remove your hands from the keyboard, the keyboard method is the best. Both methods are explained when necessary, but this book is written with the assumption that you are using a mouse.

ELEMENTS OF THE WINDOWS SCREEN

This section defines all areas of the Windows screen and some of their features. This should help you to follow along with the topics of this book.

Note: Keep in mind that your screen may not appear exactly as shown in the illustrations of this chapter due to differences in setup.

The Desktop Metaphor

A major concept in the development of Windows and your use of the product is the desktop. Windows attempts to imitate a typical desktop as closely as possible, not only in the way it looks, but also in the way you work with it.

You probably work on several projects at one time, with papers scattered about or stacked neatly on your desk. You undoubtedly use "tools of the trade," like your phone, appointment book, and notepad, as you meet with people, make calls, or catch up on work. Windows is designed to mimic these activities with electronic tools. In the process, the resulting notes, documents, spreadsheets, appointments, and other information you produce are centralized into your computer's filing system, as shown in Figure 4-1. Because information is stored in one place and is accessed using the same Windows graphics interface, you can easily cut and paste between applications. The multiple window and multitasking features of Windows make the desktop metaphor possible.

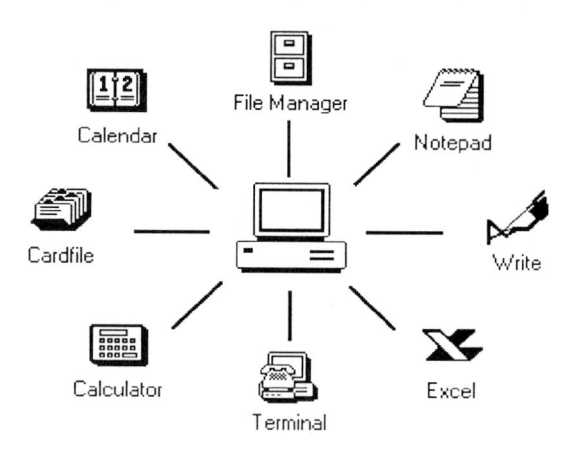

FIGURE 4-1. The Windows desktop centralizes the output of your activities into the computer filing system

When Windows is running the whole screen becomes the desktop. You can then open windows to different applications on the desktop, as shown in Figure 4-2.

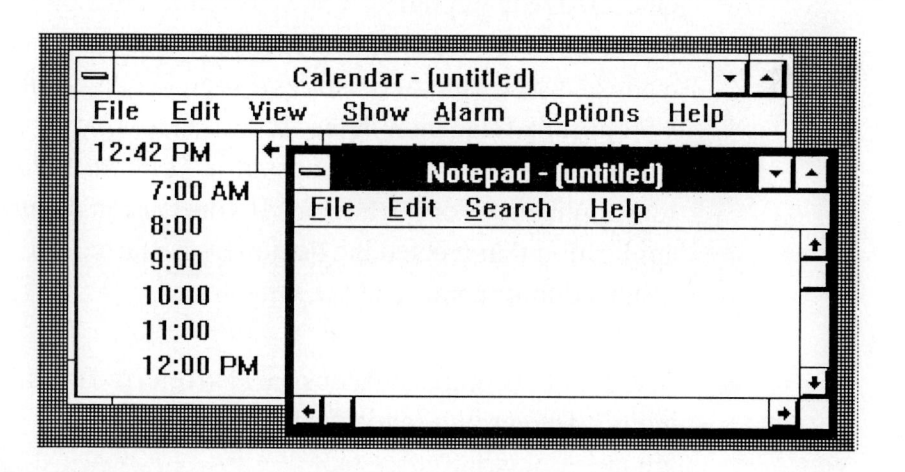

FIGURE 4-2. Open applications rest on the Windows desktop

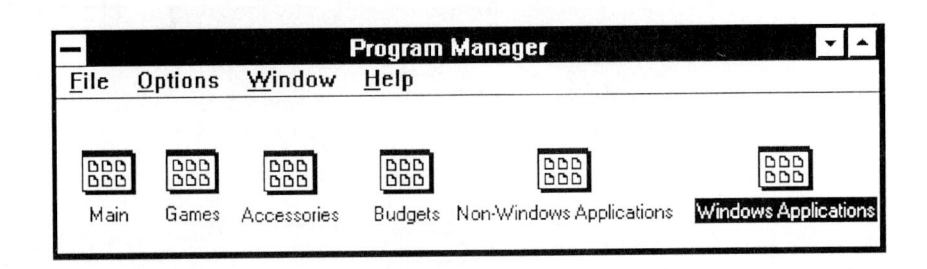

FIGURE 4-3. All icons are initially located in one of the Program Manager group icons

Types of Windows

An application can exist in several states on the Windows desktop. To see these different states, follow the Notepad accessory as it goes from one state to another. Recall from Chapter 1 that all application icons are located on the Program Manager work area in *group icons*. These group icons can be seen in Figure 4-3.

UNLOADED ICONS You can double-click on the Accessories icon to open its window, or type (ALT-W) to pull down the Window menu and select the Accessories option. A screen similar to Figure 4-4 appears. Each icon in the Accessories window is an unloaded application waiting for you to start it. *Unloaded icons* may represent applications or documents. If you select a document icon, the application that created the document is started and the document is loaded into memory at the same time.

Note In Chapter 10, unloaded icons are also referred to as "program item icons." The term *unloaded icons* describes exactly what state they are in.

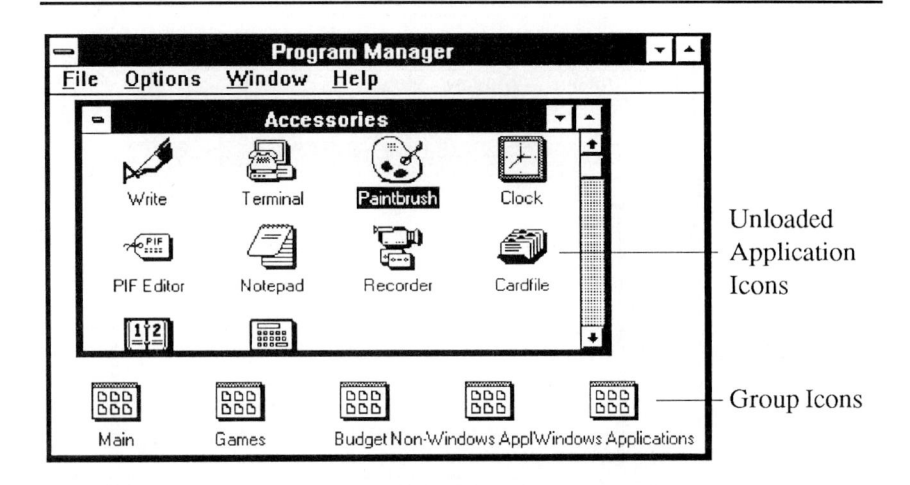

FIGURE 4-4. Unloaded icons in the Accessories window

ACTIVE WINDOW When you double-click on the Notepad icon, it is started and placed in an *active window* on the desktop, as shown in Figure 4-5. If you have a keyboard, you can use the arrow keys to highlight Notepad in the Accessories window, and then press (ENTER). Active windows have a dark band in the window title area. If you have a color screen, this title bar is a different color than the rest of the windows on the screen.

The active window is always brought to the top. If you click on another underlying window, it is brought to the top. The application in the active window is allowed to run. Those in inactive windows are put on hold, unless you are running in 386 Enhanced mode.

INACTIVE WINDOW In Figure 4-5 the Program Manager window has moved beneath the active Notepad window, indicating that it is currently inactive. Its title bar is dimmed. Applications in

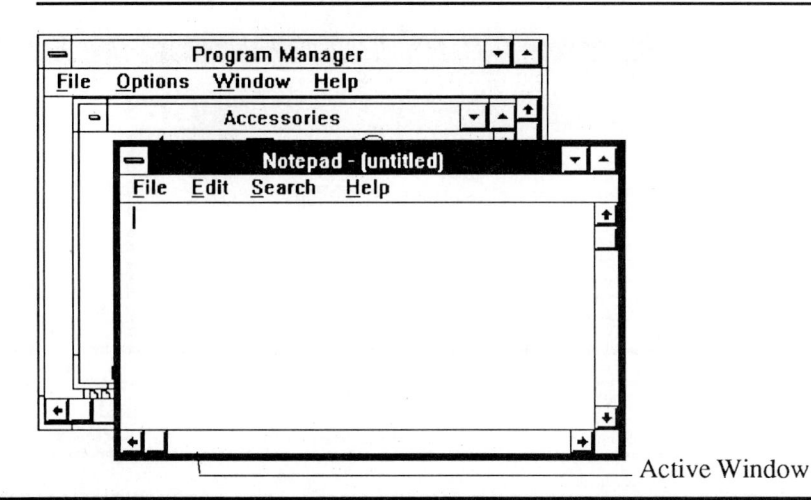

FIGURE 4-5. The active window is characterized by a dark or colored title bar

inactive windows are kept open but are not actually running. In other words, any processing that was taking place is temporarily halted unless you are running in 386 Enhanced mode, which allows multitasking.

LOADED ICON Inactive windows can begin to clutter the screen if you open too many applications. To remove the screen clutter, you can click on a window's minimize button. The window is reduced to an icon, as shown in Figure 4-6. The icon is placed on the desktop outside its group window. In Figure 4-6, the Program Manager and Notepad have been reduced to icons, while Cardfile is open as an active window. If a named file is open in a reduced window, the name of the file appears with the icon. This is a distinguishing feature if you have two or more versions of the same application open simultaneously.

It is important to realize that loaded icons are inactive windows whose applications are still loaded in memory. They are not the

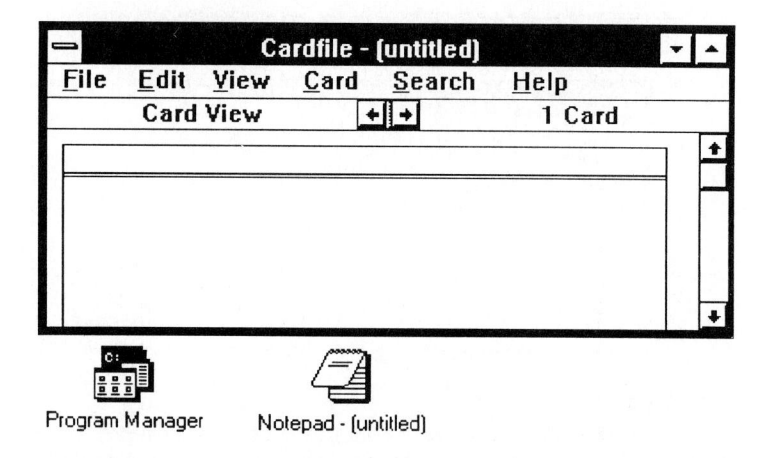

FIGURE 4-6. Minimized windows become icons on the desktop

same as unloaded icons, which are not yet loaded in memory. Loaded icons are available for immediate use and retain the contents of the window while it is reduced.

SUBORDINATE WINDOWS   Some applications may let you open two or more document windows simultaneously. A word processing program, for example, might let you view two separate documents side-by-side. The Windows Program Manager shown in Figure 4-7 shows examples of *subordinate windows*. The Main and Accessories windows are subordinate to the Program Manager window; you cannot move them out of the Program Manager window. An important feature of this arrangement is that the commands in the menu bar of the Program Manager window affect only the active subordinate window.

Note: In the Windows documentation and Chapter 10 of this book, subordinate windows are also referred to as *document windows*.

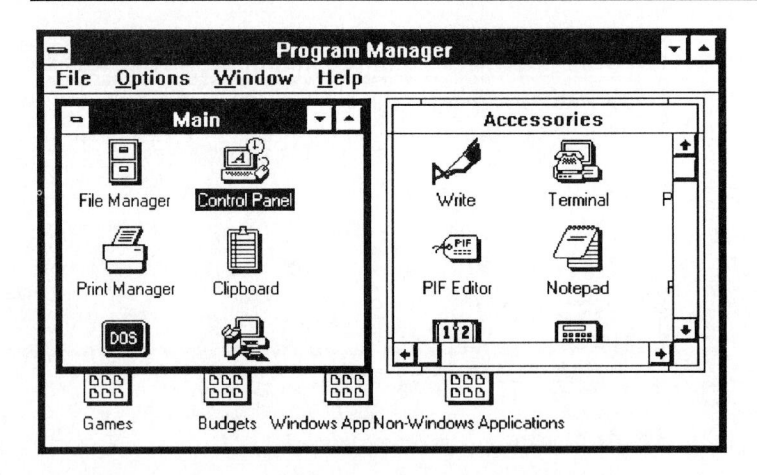

FIGURE 4-7. The Main window and Accessories window are subordinate to the Program Manager window

DIALOG BOXES A dialog box appears only after making a selection from a menu or performing some other tasks. Dialog boxes have buttons, checkboxes, and list boxes of various types that when set provide information Windows needs to complete a command. Dialog boxes also appear to verify the execution of some commands. A discussion of dialog boxes is reserved for a separate section.

Elements of a Window

Each window has the same basic features and operating characteristics, which means you can move from one Windows application to another without learning new techniques. This section describes the various elements of a window, which are shown in Figure 4-8.

HIGHLIGHTING/SELECTING Highlighting and selecting are synonymous in Windows. To *highlight* an item is to select it for an operation. Highlights are applied by clicking on an item with a

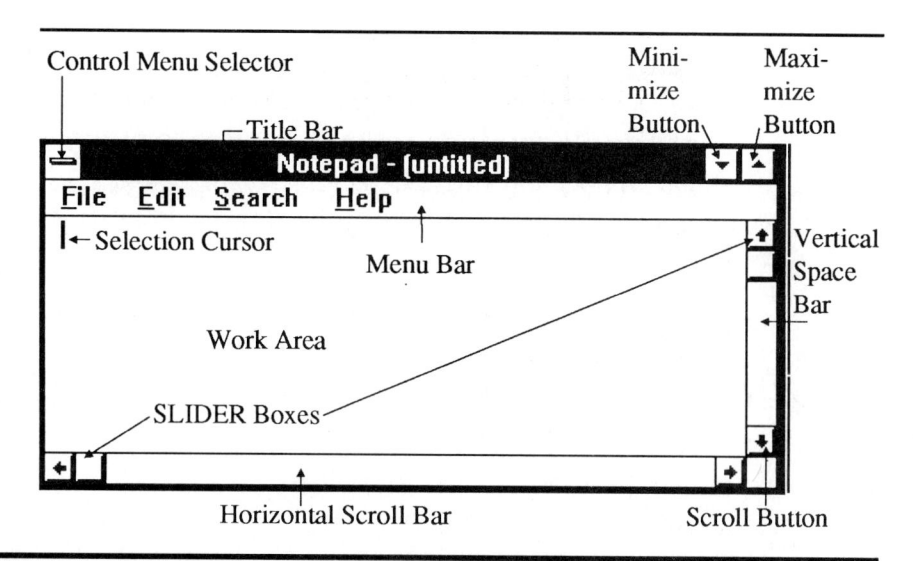

FIGURE 4-8. The elements of a window

mouse or using the arrow keys on the keyboard. You can extend a highlight by dragging the mouse over several items. Items are usually file names in a list or even icons on the screen.

You can also highlight blocks of text. For example, if you are writing a letter in Windows Write, you can highlight a block of text and then apply formats to the block such as underlining or boldface. Highlights can be applied with the mouse or the keyboard.

WORK AREA The *work area* is the open space where text, graphics, or other information is normally typed or drawn. Some applications may allow you to have more than one work area open at once.

TITLE BAR The *title bar* contains the name of the application running in a window. If the contents of its work area have been saved as a file, the name of the file also appears in the title bar.

MENU BAR The *menu bar* consists of headings for pull-down menus. You gain access to the menu bar by clicking on one of the headings or pressing the (ALT) key and then using an arrow key. Menu bars may differ depending on the application running in the window.

PULL-DOWN MENUS When you open a pull-down menu, you can select options on it by clicking with the mouse or typing the underlined letter in each option. You can also move the highlight with an arrow key.

Pull-down menus may have unavailable options, as well as options that are active or inactive. In the example in Figure 4-9, the black menu options are available for selection and the grayed options are unavailable. The checkmarked items are currently active. Think of the checkmark as a toggle switch for the option.

Grayed options may be unavailable because the current window does not support them, or because another option must be selected

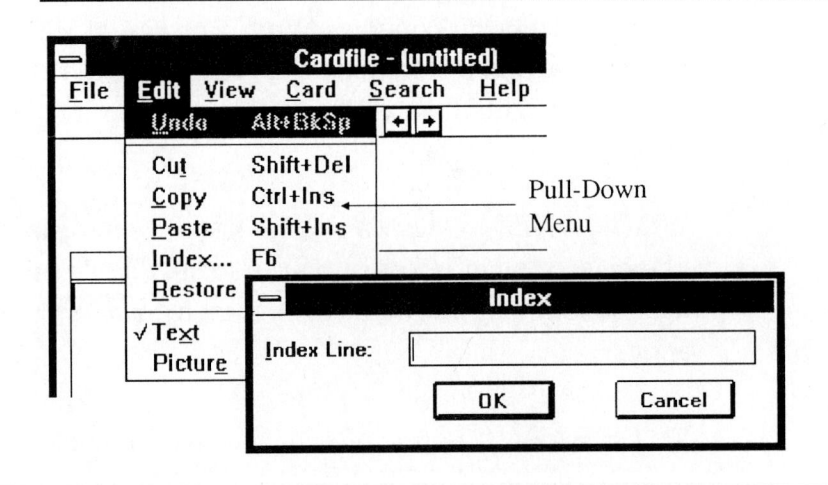

FIGURE 4-9. Available options in menus are black and unavailable options are grayed

before they can be used. If an option name is followed by an ellipsis, as in Index..., a submenu appears when it is selected.

> **Note:** If you open a menu and do not want to use it, press (ESC) or click outside of the menu.

CONTROL MENU SELECTOR The Control menu, shown here, is a pull-down menu that displays commands used to alter or close the current window.

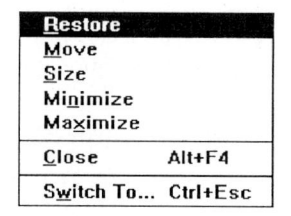

```
Restore
Move
Size
Minimize
Maximize
Close         Alt+F4
Switch To...  Ctrl+Esc
```

It is accessed by clicking on the Control menu selector. Using a keyboard, it can be accessed by pressing (ALT) and then (SPACEBAR).

The Control menu is basically the same for all windows. It is useful to those using a keyboard instead of a mouse. If you have a mouse, it is unlikely you will be using the Control menu because it is easier to make selections with the mouse.

MAXIMIZE AND MINIMIZE BUTTONS The maximize button is the up-arrow button. It expands the window to fit the entire screen. The minimize button is the down-arrow button, which shrinks the screen to an icon. If a window is maximized, the maximize button converts to a double arrow that can be used to restore the menu to its previous state.

SCROLL BARS The scroll bars are used with the mouse to move up and down or left and right in a window. Generally, you only need to move up and down in most documents, but some lists and spreadsheet programs require left and right movement of the window contents. You can use the scroll bar in three ways: to press in the arrow box to actively scroll, to click and drag the slider box, and to click above or below the slider box to move up or down one window.

BORDERS AND CORNERS The borders and corners of a window are active if you have a mouse. Point to a border or corner until the mouse pointer turns into a double-headed arrow, then click and drag to resize the window to any shape. If you are using a keyboard, you must choose Size from the Control menu and use the arrow keys to resize a window. Press (ENTER) when the preferred size is arranged.

THE FEATURES AND USE OF DIALOG BOXES

Dialog boxes are used to get information and set various operating parameters. They usually appear after selecting a menu item when additional information is required. A dialog box appears on a pull-down menu item that has an ellipsis (...) in its name. Figure 4-10 illustrates the elements of a typical dialog box.

Elements of Dialog Boxes

No two dialog boxes within the same application look exactly the same, because they request specific information for the menu command you have selected. On the other hand, you will notice a similarity in these dialog boxes as you move to different applications. For example, the printer dialog box shown in Figure 4-10 looks the same in most Windows applications, so once you become familiar with its features, you won't need to relearn them.

[Figure 4-10 shows a dialog box with labeled elements: Drop-down List Box, Command Buttons, Option Button, Text Box, List Box]

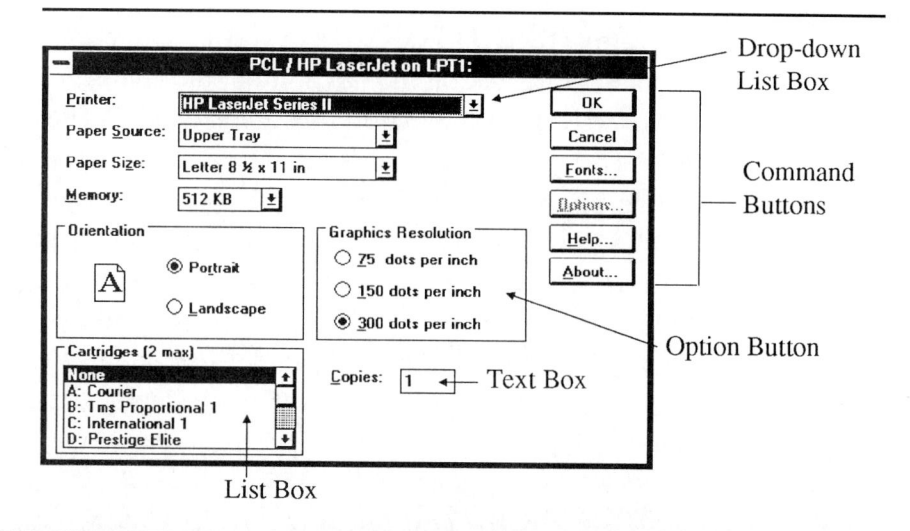

FIGURE 4-10. The elements of a dialog box

Each area of a dialog box is used to collect different kinds of information. You need not make changes to all areas, only those with options you want to change. Each area of a dialog box is discussed in the following sections.

MOUSE AND KEYBOARD TECHNIQUES FOR DIALOG BOXES The mouse or the keyboard is used to make one area active at a time so you can make selections within it. If you have a mouse, simply click on the appropriate button or area to work in.

Using the keyboard, press the (TAB) key to move through the areas of the dialog box. A dotted rectangle or highlight appears in the currently selected area. You then can follow the instructions for selecting options given later in the next sections.

Note: Changes to dialog boxes are confirmed and executed when you press the (ENTER) key or click on the OK button with the mouse. Be sure you have set the proper options before doing so.

COMMAND BUTTONS The *command buttons* initiate actions. If you click on the OK button, the changes you have made in other parts of the dialog box are executed. The Cancel button closes the dialog box without making any changes. When the title of the button ends with an ellipsis (...) or greater-than symbols (>>), additional options appear. Dimmed buttons are unavailable.

If you are using a keyboard, press **TAB** to move the dotted rectangle to the appropriate button, and then press **ENTER** to execute it. Some buttons have underlined letters. You can choose and execute one of these buttons in one step by pressing **ALT** and then the letter.

TEXT BOXES *Text boxes* are areas where you type information. The flashing insertion bar appears in the selected text box. You can type information and use editing keys to alter the information you have typed. For example, you can backspace over previously typed information, or use the **LEFT ARROW** key to move back to a particular letter. You can also press the **DEL** key to remove letters.

> **Note** You may need to highlight part of the text in a text box. Click and hold down the mouse button as you drag over the text you want to select. With the keyboard, you can hold down the **SHIFT** key while using an arrow key.

LIST BOXES Many dialog boxes contain *list boxes,* where files or other information may be listed. Click the item you want with the mouse, or double-click an item to choose it and complete the command. You can use the arrow keys to move up and down through the list. When the target item is highlighted, press the spacebar to select it. You can use the **HOME** and **END** keys to jump to either the top or bottom of the list and the **PG UP** or **PG DOWN** keys to move the list itself up or down.

> **Note:** Type the first letter of the item you are trying to find in order to quickly jump to it.

You can select multiple items in some list boxes. With the mouse, click on each item to highlight it. With the keyboard, press the spacebar to select each item, and use the arrow keys to move to other items you want to select.

DROP-DOWN LIST BOXES   A *drop-down list box* is initially a single rectangle that opens when selected to reveal additional items. Drop-down list boxes are characterized by the arrow on the right side of the box. To open a drop-down box, click on the arrow with the mouse. If you have a keyboard, press `ALT` and the `DOWN ARROW` key to open the box.

OPTION BUTTONS   *Option buttons* come in groups, and only one can be on at one time. To change a selection, a different button in the group is turned on. In Figure 4-10, only one graphics resolution can be selected in the Graphics Resolution area. To select an option, click on it with the mouse. Using the keyboard, you can tab to the selection area, then use the arrow keys to move the dotted rectangle to the appropriate selection.

CHECKBOXES   *Checkboxes* are used to turn a selection on or off. Unlike option buttons, checkbox items are not related to the on or off state of other checkboxes or buttons, unless the option is currently unavailable. Here is an example of a checkbox.

Checkbox

The Confirm Page Breaks option is selected because an "X" appears in its checkbox. Click a checkbox with the mouse, or press the `TAB` and the `SPACEBAR` to move and select a box with the keyboard.

Warning and Message Boxes

Some dialog boxes appear to confirm your response or warn you of problems. Other boxes appear to display system messages. Warning boxes usually have an OK or Cancel button, which allows you to verify or cancel the command about to be executed. Message boxes usually have an OK button, which you press after reading the message.

MOUSE TECHNIQUES

You can use various mouse techniques to control a window, to select pull-down menus, to make selections in dialog boxes, and to work with documents, including letters you are typing in Windows Write or spreadsheets created in Excel. This section covers the mouse techniques, and the next section covers keyboard techniques.

Mouse Terminology

The following terms are used throughout this book to describe the ways you can use the mouse to select single or multiple items or to execute commands.

Point   To point the mouse is to move it until the arrow lands on the target. The arrow may then change shape, or the target may become high-

Learning the Windows Interface   75

Click	lighted. For example, if you point to the corner or edges of an active window, the arrow changes to a double-headed arrow, which indicates you can adjust the size of the window. Once you have pointed to an area or item on the screen, you usually click the mouse to select it.
Double-click	Double-clicking on a menu item is the same as pressing the (ENTER) key to select the item or execute a command.
Drag	Dragging is the process of clicking and holding the mouse button while you move across several items or a block of text. The highlight follows the mouse movement. Commands or other actions then affect the highlighted text.

Moving and Sizing Windows With the Mouse

The mouse is the easiest way to move and alter the size of a window. The alternative method is to use the Control menu options with the keyboard, which is cumbersome. If you have a mouse, you probably will use the Control menu rarely.

Note If you rearrange the windows in the Program Manager and want to save those changes for the next session, be sure to mark the Save Changes box on the Exit Windows menu when you quit Windows.

SIZING Windows are sized with the mouse by pointing to the corners or side walls (called *hot spots*) until the mouse pointer turns into a double-sided arrow. You then click and drag the window to the desired size. The following illustration shows the mouse hot spots on the window borders.

Mouse Hot-spots

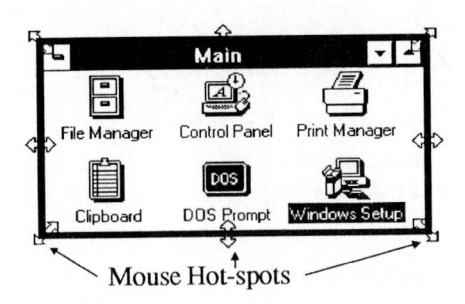

Note If you are resizing Program Manager windows, select Arrange Icons from the Window menu to rearrange the icons in the resized window. You can also choose Auto Arrange on the Options menu to rearrange the icons in the window automatically whenever you resize. This option stays on until turned off.

MINIMIZING, MAXIMIZING, AND RESTORING A WINDOW

You can use the minimize and maximize buttons to reduce or expand a window. A window has three basic sizes that can be controlled with these buttons. Full-screen size is obtained by pressing the (UP ARROW). The window then dominates the entire screen. If a window is maximized, its maximize button converts to a double-arrow button, as shown here:

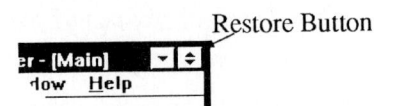

Restore Button

This restore button reduces the window back to its original size. The original size of a window is its size when first opened or the size to which you have adjusted it using the sizing techniques previously discussed.

The down-arrow minimize button is used to reduce a window to its icon. Double-click on icons to restore them to the desktop.

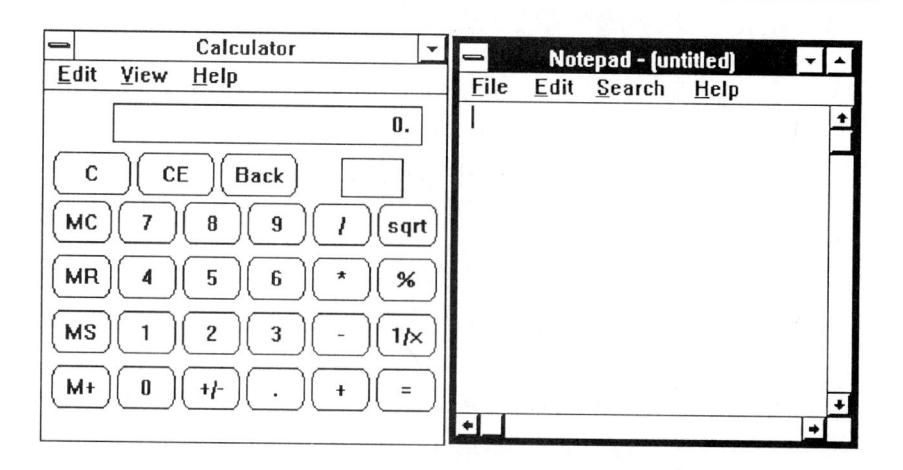

FIGURE 4-11. Two windows moved and resized for side-by-side operation

MOVING A WINDOW To move a window, simply point and click in the title bar, then drag the window to its new location. You may frequently want to resize a window before or after moving it to make way for another window. In Figure 4-11, the Notepad window has been resized and moved next to the calculator for side-by-side operation.

You can also double-click on the desktop, or press (CTRL-ESC) to open the Task List, which can be used to cascade or tile windows. See the last section of this chapter for more details.

CLOSING A WINDOW To close a window with the mouse, double-click on the Control menu selector, which is the small box in the upper-left corner of every window. Note that closing a window is not the same as reducing a window to its icon. When you close a window, the programs or documents in it are removed from memory. Reducing a window to an icon keeps a program available for immediate use.

Scrolling with the Mouse

Scroll bars appear on the right or bottom side of a window if text or objects are not able to fit in the window. In the following illustration, a vertical scroll bar appears on the right and a horizontal scroll bar appears on the bottom.

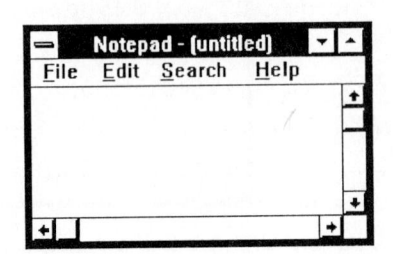

The scroll bar has four mouse hot spots. The first two are the arrows at the top or bottom of a vertical scroll bar and on the left or right of a horizontal scroll bar. You can click with the mouse to move a little, or click and hold to produce a continuous scroll. The third hot spot is the slider box. It can be dragged with the mouse to scroll. The last hot spot is the scroll bar itself. Click just above or below the slider box to move up or down one window of text or items.

Note: It may be easier to scroll text documents using the (UP) and (DOWN ARROW) keys, or the (PG UP ARROW) and (PG DOWN) keys, as described in the keyboard section later in this chapter.

Selecting with the Mouse

Selecting is a process of highlighting an item on a menu, clicking a checkbox, or selecting a block of text. This is easily done with the mouse by pointing and clicking. To select a block of text, point to the beginning of the text, click, and drag through the text you want to select. As you drag the mouse, the text is highlighted.

KEYBOARD TECHNIQUES

If you have a mouse, you probably use keyboard selection techniques rarely, but as mentioned earlier, there may be times when it is faster to use the keyboard than to take your hands off it to grab the mouse. The keyboard techniques described here are basically the same in all Windows applications. You only need to learn the keyboard techniques once.

Menu Selection with the Keyboard

To access the pull-down menus at the top of the active window, first press the (ALT) key. This moves the highlight to the first selection. At that point, you can use one of several methods to access each pull-down menu and its options.

ARROW-KEY METHOD After pressing the (ALT) key, the highlight jumps from the window work area to the menu area. You can use the (RIGHT ARROW) or (LEFT ARROW) keys to then move to the heading of the pull-down menu you want to use. When the heading is highlighted, press the (DOWN ARROW) or the (ENTER) key to display its complete menu. Once a menu is open, you can still use the (RIGHT ARROW) or (LEFT ARROW) to display other menus in the open state. To select an option on the menu, use the (UP ARROW) or (DOWN ARROW) key, and press (ENTER) to execute the selection.

QUICK-KEY METHOD The quick-key method is used to make fast menu selections from the keyboard. The following illustration shows the File menu for the Program Manager, which is very similar to File menus on most other windows:

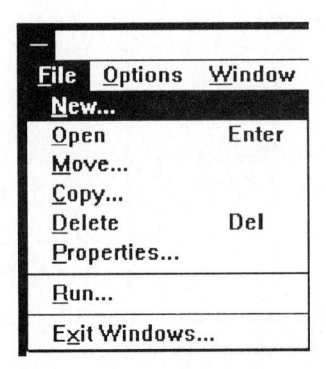

```
 File   Options   Window
 New...
 Open              Enter
 Move...
 Copy...
 Delete            Del
 Properties...
 Run...
 Exit Windows...
```

Notice that each option has one underscored letter; you can type this letter with the window open to execute the selection. When you learn the selection codes in each menu, you can quickly press key combinations, such as (ALT-F-O) to select the Open option in the File menu.

≡Note≡ Press (ESC) to cancel any command, or click in the blank area of another window with the mouse.

DIRECT METHODS Many menus have direct methods for accessing the most used selections. For example, the Edit menu in Notepad lists key combinations to the right of each selection, as shown in Figure 4-12. This screen shows that, among other options, you can press (ALT-BACKSPACE) to undo your most recent operation or (SHIFT-DEL) to cut a selected area.

Many of the options and keys used to access options are the same on most windows, so take the time to learn them. You will learn more about these common commands in the next chapter. As you use the menu, take note of the direct keys used to access the menu options for future use.

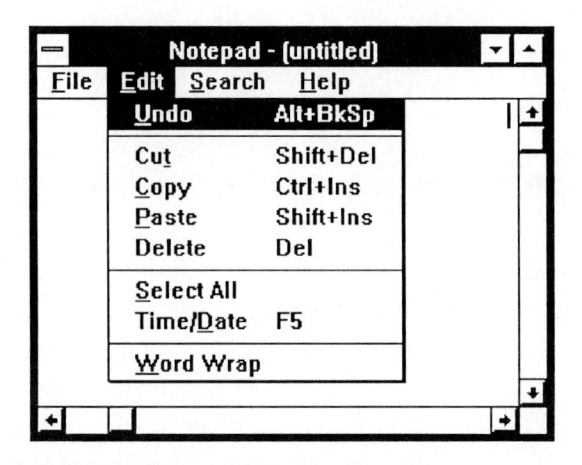

FIGURE 4-12. Some menus list direct access keys on the right

Moving and Sizing Windows With the Keyboard

The Control menu shown here is used to size, move, and close windows.

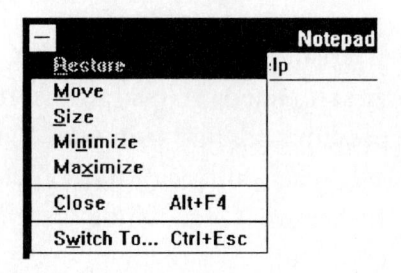

All windows have a Control menu, even those reduced to an icon.

> **Note** If you rearrange the windows in the Program Manager and want to save those changes for the next session, be sure to mark the Save Changes box on the Exit Windows menu when you quit Windows.

The Control menu is accessed in the following ways:

Active window	Press `ALT` and spacebar.
Inactive windows	Press `ALT-ESC` repeatedly until the target window becomes active, and then press `ALT` and the spacebar.
Loaded icons	Icons with active applications have Control menus that can be displayed by pressing `ALT-ESC` until the correct icon is selected, and then pressing `SHIFT-ESC`.
Document windows	For applications that let you open multiple document windows, press `CTRL-F6` until the window becomes active, then press `ALT--` (hyphen).

> **Note** If you are running 386 Enhanced mode, the Control menu for non-Windows applications has additional options to alter the 386 operating mode and to cut and paste between other applications.

THE RESTORE, MINIMIZE, AND MAXIMIZE OPTIONS

When a window is first opened, it has a size determined by Windows or set in a previous session using the Size option. The size of the window can fill any portion of the screen. If you select the Maximize option by typing **X**, the window expands to fill the entire screen. If you select the Minimize option by typing **N**, the window reduces to an icon. To restore the screen to its original size, select the Restore option by typing **R**.

THE SIZE OPTION You may want to reduce or expand the size of a window to see more information or to view two windows side by side, as shown in Figure 4-10. Some windows and most dialog boxes cannot be resized.

To size a window, select Size from the Control menu by typing **S**. A four headed arrow appears. The first arrow key you press selects a corresponding border. You can then press other arrow keys to resize that border. Press the (ENTER) key when you are done.

THE MOVE OPTION Windows can be moved up, down, left, or right on the screen using the Move option on the Control menu. First type **M** to select Move, and then press the arrow keys to move the window in the appropriate direction. When the window is where you want it, press (ENTER). You may want to resize a window before moving it.

You can also press (CTRL-ESC) to display the Task List, which has options for cascading and tiling the windows on the screen. See the last section of this chapter for more information.

THE CLOSE OPTION To close a window, type **C** at the Control menu, or press (ALT-F4). Note that closing the Program Manager window ends your current Windows session.

Using Dialog Boxes with the Keyboard

Dialog boxes appear when a menu command needs additional information, as discussed earlier. The following keys are used to move and select options in dialog boxes:

(TAB)	Moves to different selection areas on the dialog box
(ALT-ARROW)	Opens a drop-down menu box

Arrow keys	Move the highlight to one of the selections in an area
SHIFT-ARROW	Selects more than one item
SPACEBAR	Selects an item
ENTER	Executes the changes made to the dialog box
ESC	Cancels the changes made to the dialog box

CHANGING THE ACTIVE WINDOW

When you have more than one application on the screen, you need a way to quickly get from one to another, especially if one window is completely covered by another. Recall that the active window always appears in the foreground, with inactive windows stacked behind. The keyboard methods are useful to both keyboard users and those with the mouse for switching between windows. The Task List utility is also a convenient tool for switching between windows and is covered in this section.

Switching Windows with the Keyboard

There are two methods for switching to different windows with the keyboard. As you scan through the windows, use the *preview method* to display only the title bar of each one. The *switching method* displays the entire screen of each window. The preview method is much faster because the entire screen is not displayed until you find the window you want.

To begin the preview method, press ALT-TAB. The switching method starts when you press ALT-ESC. To reverse the order of the scan, press ALT-SHIFT-TAB when using the preview method, and press ALT-SHIFT-ESC when using the switching method.

Using the Mouse to Switch Applications

To switch applications with the mouse, simply click anywhere on the inactive window you want to bring to the front. This is only possible, however, if part of the inactive window is showing. Here are some tricks you can use to make this easier:

- Move, resize, and stack your windows so that a small part of each window shows on the desktop.

- Reduce the current window to an icon so underlying windows show.

- Reduce all windows to icons when not in use. This not only saves memory but makes them quickly available at the bottom of the screen.

- Press (ALT-TAB) to scan through the windows, as previously described.

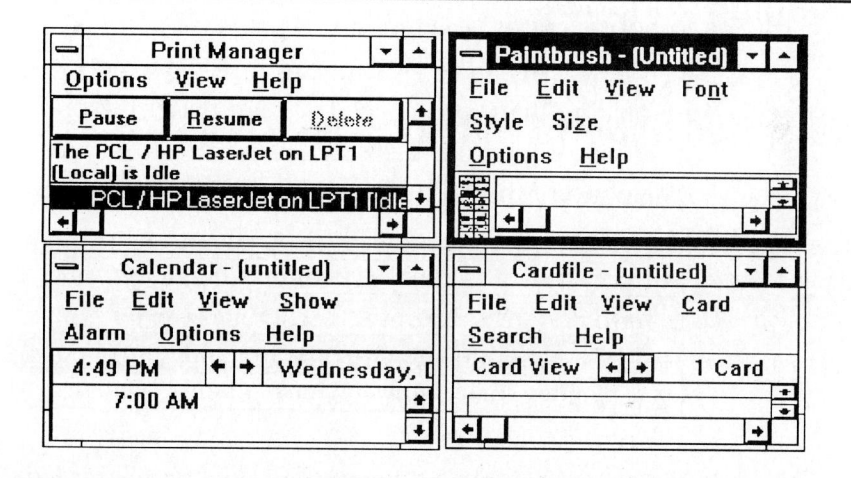

FIGURE 4-13. Tiled windows are placed next to each other and do not overlap

Switching Windows with the Task List Utility

The Task List window appears when you double-click anywhere on the desktop (not a window) or press (CTRL-ESC). You can double-click on a window name to make it active. If you have a mouse, highlight a window name and press (ENTER). The Task List shown here has six different windows to choose from:

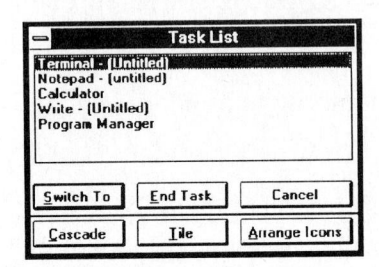

The Task List can also be opened by selecting Switch To from the Control menu of a window.

Arranging Windows

The Task List can be used to rearrange the windows on your screen by placing them in a cascade or tile pattern. Double-click on the desktop to open the Task List, then select either the Cascade or Tile option. The following illustration shows cascaded windows:

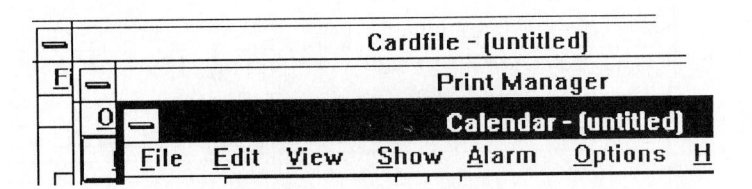

Figure 4-13 shows how windows appear when tiled.

You can use the Arrange Icons button to rearrange the icons on the desktop.

5

WINDOWS APPLICATIONS AND THEIR SHARED FEATURES

The Program Manager
The Main Group
The Accessories Group
Shared Menu Commands
Shared Keyboard Techniques

This chapter introduces you to the applications that come with Windows and explains some of the features they share. Learning the common features, such as editing and file-saving techniques, gives you a head start when it comes to learning more specific topics of these applications covered in Part II of this book. Another benefit of learning those features of Windows that are common to all applications, not just those supplied with Windows, is that you can start using new applications after a minimum of instruction.

Many of the features of Windows applications were introduced in Chapter 1. This chapter explains some of the features of each so you can start planning how you will use Windows as you read through the next few chapters.

THE PROGRAM MANAGER

The Program Manager is your home base in Windows. It rests on the desktop, or can be reduced to an icon while you work on other applications. One of the main uses of the Program Manager is to help you organize your programs and applications into meaningful groups so you can quickly start or access them while working on other applications.

You can also create groups of documents, such as the Budget group discussed in Chapter 1. This example group contains an Excel budget spreadsheet for each of four departments. Since Windows lets you start an application and load a document by clicking on the document itself, it makes sense to place documents in groups.

In fact, your desktop will take on a new look as you go through this book and begin to use Windows regularly. Figure 5-1 illustrates a desktop used by an office manager who creates a company newsletter on a regular basis. Notice the familiar Paintbrush, Notepad, and Write icons have document names, which means they start the program and load the designated document when selected. Take a look at the Daily Activities group. It has an icon named Template, which is a blank Write document with special layouts, tabs, and ruler settings the manager likes to use. Whenever a document is created with Template, it is saved under a different name to retain the template. Two Notebook icons are in the

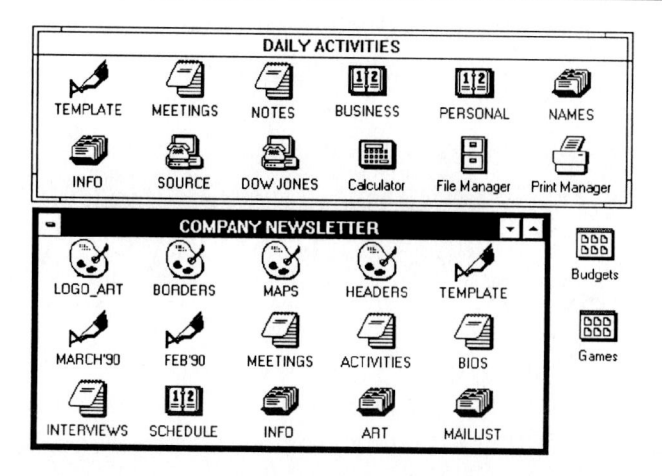

FIGURE 5-1. One way to organize your desktop with Windows

window, one for collecting meeting notes and one for other notes. You also can see that the manager keeps business and personal calendars, and cardfiles for names and general information. A Terminal icon allows you to access Dow Jones. The Calculator, File Manager, and Print Manager icons have been copied to the Daily Activities window for quick access.

The Company Newsletter window has icons used to load Paintbrush art files, a newsletter template, two old newsletters, and notes on meetings, activities, people, and interviews. The Calendar accessory is used to schedule the newsletter, and the Cardfile holds a newsletter mailing list.

You can see by this example that window groups are an extremely flexible way to group programs and documents according to your activities. Since this desktop always appears when Windows is started, the manager has placed the File Manager and Calculator icons on it for quick access. Also notice that the Budget and Games groups are waiting on the side of the desktop, ready for use.

Chapter 10 covers the Program Manager and its organizational techniques in more detail. The next two sections of this chapter explain the applications in the Main and Accessories groups. Following that, you are introduced to common features of applications windows.

THE MAIN GROUP

The Windows SETUP program creates two groups, Main and Accessories, and places the various Windows programs and utilities in them. This section provides a brief overview of the utilities in the Main group.

File Manager

When the File Manager is first opened, it displays a directory tree for the current disk drive. This tree presents in graphic form the directory and subdirectories of the drive, as shown in Figure 5-2.

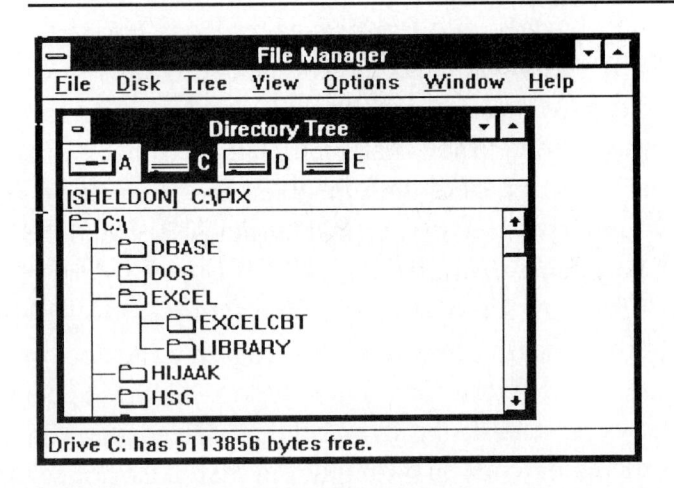

FIGURE 5-2. The File Manager displays a graphic tree of your system's directory structure

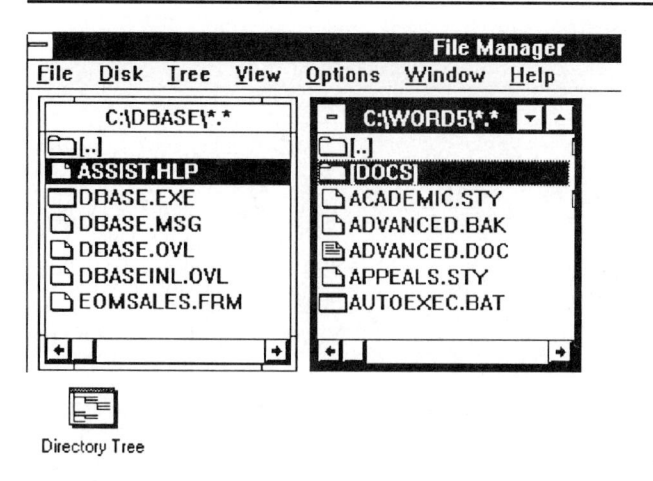

FIGURE 5-3. Two directories can be open side-by-side in the File Manager so you can copy and compare files

> **Note** To learn more about files and directories, refer to Chapter 6.

Notice in Figure 5-2 that the Directory Tree window is subordinate to the File Manager. The menu bar of the File Manager contains commands that affect the active subordinate window. In Figure 5-3, two windows in the File Manager display files from two separate directories. Notice the Directory Tree window itself has been reduced to an icon. When two directory windows are side-by-side, you can easily compare or copy files between them.

Chapters 6 and 7 explain DOS file and directory concepts and explore the features of the File Manager in more detail.

Control Panel

The Control Panel shown in Figure 5-4 contains a set of tools and utilities you can use to alter the way Windows looks and operates. It is discussed in Chapter 9.

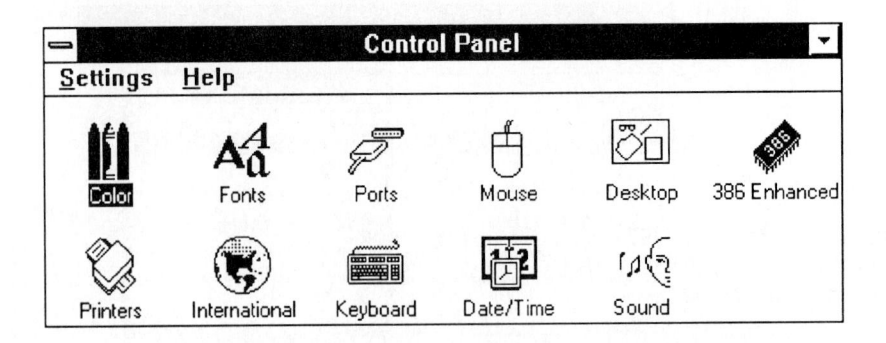

FIGURE 5-4. The Control Panel holds a set of tools for changing the look and feel of Windows

Print Manager

The Print Manager is a print-job management utility that queues documents being printed on your local printer or on a network printer. When you print from a Windows application, the print job is sent to the Print Manager. While it handles the task of sending the job to the printer, you can continue working. The Print Manager can accept several print jobs at once and add them to its queue. By opening the Print Manager window, you can view the queue, remove print jobs from it, or change the order of the queue so one job prints before another. Figure 5-5 illustrates an open Print Manager window with a Write and Paintbrush document waiting in the queue. Chapter 8 discusses printing and the Print Manager in more detail.

Clipboard

As discussed in Chapter 1, the Clipboard is a temporary holding area for blocks of text or graphics that you copy or cut from one document and paste into another. You can open the Clipboard by

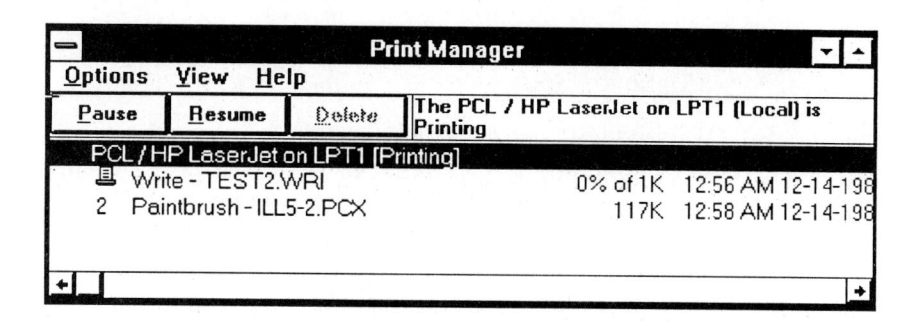

```
┌─────────────────────────────────────────────────────────┐
│ ▬           Print Manager                      ▼ ▲      │
│ Options  View  Help                                     │
│ ┌──────┐ ┌──────┐ ┌──────┐ The PCL / HP LaserJet on LPT1 (Local) is│
│ │Pause │ │Resume│ │Delete│ Printing                     │
│   PCL / HP LaserJet on LPT1 [Printing]                  │
│     🖨 Write - TEST2.WRI           0% of 1K  12:56 AM 12-14-198│
│      2 Paintbrush - ILL5-2.PCX     117K      12:58 AM 12-14-198│
│                                                         │
│ ◄ │                                                   ► │
└─────────────────────────────────────────────────────────┘
```

FIGURE 5-5. The Print Manager manages print jobs in the background

double-clicking on its icon to view the current contents. The Clipboard only holds one object at a time, so the most recent cut or copy overwrites the Clipboard contents. You can open the Clipboard, however, and save its contents to a file. The Clipboard is covered in more detail later in this chapter, since it is a utility shared by most applications.

DOS Prompt

The DOS Prompt icon is used to load a copy of the DOS command interpreter so you can run commands in the DOS environment. You will usually use the Run option in the File Manager to do this, but sometimes you may find it easier to use the DOS prompt, especially if you need to execute a number of commands.

Windows Setup

The Windows Setup utility is used to make alterations to your current setup, or to automatically add new software groups or programs to the Program Manager. The Windows Setup screen shown in Figure 5-6 lists the current settings of the author's system. To change the system settings or to set up new applica-

```
=============================================
|  =        Windows Setup                 ▼  |
| Options  Help                              |
|  Display:    VGA                           |
|  Keyboard:   Enhanced 101 or 102 key US and Non US |
|  Mouse:      Microsoft, or IBM PS/2        |
|  Network:    No Network Installed          |
|  ----------------------------------------  |
|  Swap file:  Permanent (3061 K bytes on Drive C:) |
=============================================
```

FIGURE 5-6. The Windows Setup utility lets you view and alter the installation

tions, you can select the Options pull-down menu. The Windows Setup utility is covered further in Appendix A.

THE ACCESSORIES GROUP

The Accessories group contains productivity tools you will use every day. If you are familiar with previous versions of Windows, you can start using these tools right away. Even if you are not, you can start the applications and explore their features. This section briefly describes each tool, and Part II of this book covers them in more detail.

Calculator

Windows has two types of calculators, standard and scientific. Either mode can be selected by changing the View option on the Calculator menu. The scientific calculator allows you to work with decimal, hexidecimal, octal, and binary numbers, and to convert among them. It also provides advanced statistical, trigonometric, and other functions. The calculators can be operated by clicking their buttons with the mouse, or using various keyboard combinations, as described in Chapter 12.

Calendar

The Calendar provides typical month-at-a-glance features and daily appointment scheduling. You can view the entire month, and then click on any day to view or edit your daily schedule. Daily schedules can have increments of 15, 30, or 60 minutes. You can also insert a specific time if it does not match the intervals. Calendar also has an alarm feature that can alert you of a preset appointment or activity with a flashing message box.

Here is an example of a Calendar window.

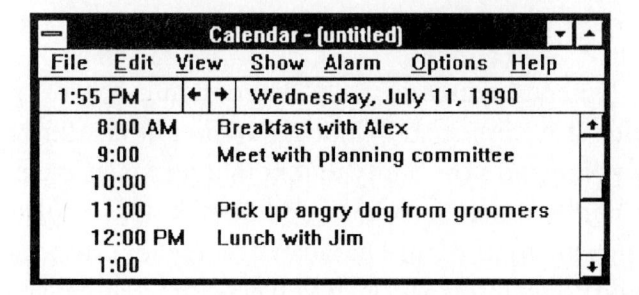

```
┌─────────────────────────────────────────────────┐
│ ─          Calendar - (untitled)          ▼ ▲  │
│ File  Edit  View  Show  Alarm  Options  Help   │
│ 1:55 PM      ← →   Wednesday, July 11, 1990    │
│      8:00 AM    Breakfast with Alex          ↑ │
│      9:00       Meet with planning committee   │
│      10:00                                     │
│      11:00      Pick up angry dog from groomers│
│      12:00 PM   Lunch with Jim                 │
│      1:00                                    ↓ │
└─────────────────────────────────────────────────┘
```

Cardfile

Cardfile mimics an index card filing system. The top line is used for index information and the bottom of the card is used for text or graphics information. You can sort and search cards and create as many index card sets as you want; each is stored on disk with a unique name. Here is an example of a music index.

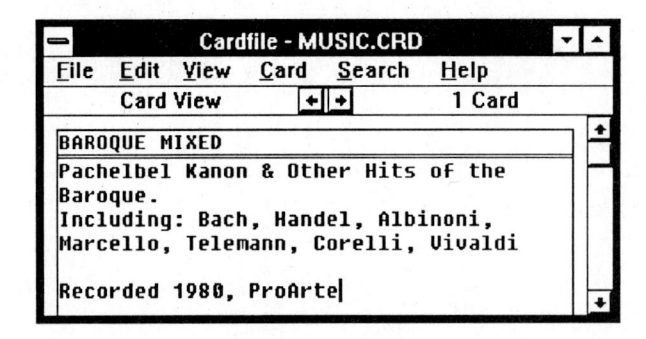

```
        ┌─────────────────────────────────────────┐
        │ ─      Cardfile - MUSIC.CRD        ▼ ▲  │
        │  File  Edit  View  Card  Search  Help   │
        │        Card View      ← ║ →     1 Card  │
        ├─────────────────────────────────────────┤
        │ BAROQUE MIXED                         ▲ │
        │ Pachelbel Kanon & Other Hits of the     │
        │ Baroque.                                │
        │ Including: Bach, Handel, Albinoni,      │
        │ Marcello, Telemann, Corelli, Vivaldi    │
        │                                         │
        │ Recorded 1980, ProArte                ▼ │
        └─────────────────────────────────────────┘
```

The visible card lists the contents of an album of baroque music.

Clock

The analog or digital Clock displays the time on the screen. The Clock can be displayed as a full screen by clicking its maximize button.

Notepad

The Notepad editor is a tool for creating short notes and documents. It is similar to Windows Write but has far fewer features. With Notepad you can type text that wraps at the end of the line and perform text searches. You cannot apply special formats or change the fonts of the characters. Notepad is designed for quickly jotting down information. If you need more advanced features, use Write. Notepad is covered in more detail in Chapter 12.

Paintbrush

Paintbrush is a drawing tool that has many advanced features. You can use it to draw images and copy them to your other Windows applications. For example, the chess piece in Figure 5-7 could be copied to a chess club newsletter.

Paintbrush comes with a set of tools for drawing lines, boxes, and circles and a set of tools for painting with a roller, brush, and

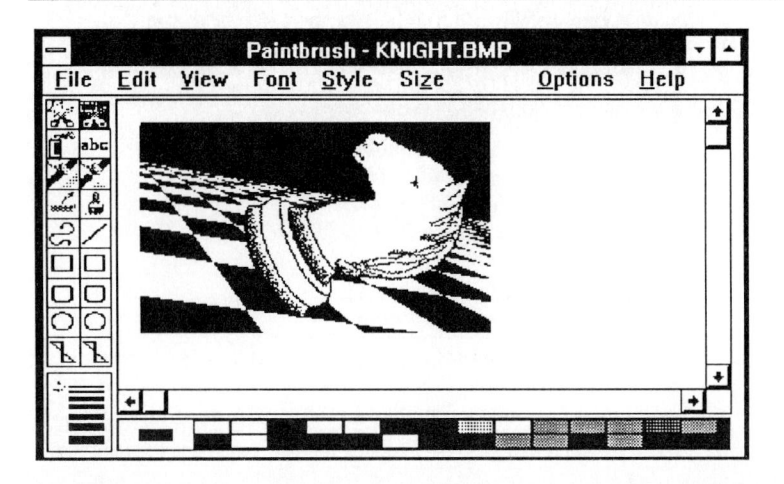

FIGURE 5-7. Windows Paintbrush creates black and white or color images that you can copy to other applications

spray can. You also can cut from any location and paste anywhere else. A full set of fonts is available for creating captions. And if your hand isn't steady, you can zoom in on your work and draw one bit at a time, as shown here:

The true image size is in the upper-left corner.

PIF Editor

The PIF (Program Information File) Editor is used to supply Windows with startup information about non-Windows applications. You must use the PIF Editor only for applications that are

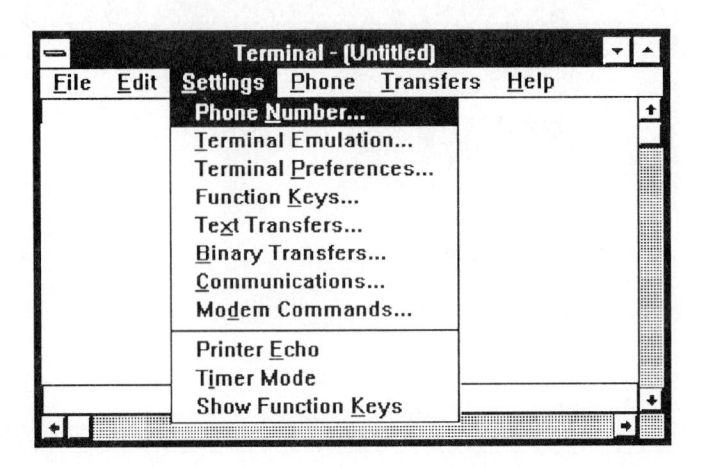

```
          Terminal - [Untitled]
File  Edit  Settings  Phone  Transfers  Help
            Phone Number...
            Terminal Emulation...
            Terminal Preferences...
            Function Keys...
            Text Transfers...
            Binary Transfers...
            Communications...
            Modem Commands...

            Printer Echo
            Timer Mode
            Show Function Keys
```

FIGURE 5-8. The PIF Editor provides Windows with information to run non-Windows applications

not recognized by SETUP during installation, including many small utility programs or commands you use on a regular basis. As you can see by the PIF Editor screen in Figure 5-8, you supply the directory and name of the executable program file, along with the name that will appear in its window and any optional parameters it needs when started. You can also specify the amount of memory it needs and whether it should run in a window or a full screen.

Recorder

The Recorder is a unique tool you can use to record a sequence of keystrokes and mouse movements for instant replay at a later time. Any set of commands you must repeat later is a candidate for recording. When keystrokes and mouse movements are recorded, they are converted to a *macro*. A set of macros is saved to a file. You can have more than one macro file, which means you can open one set of macros when working on Microsoft Excel and open another when working in Windows itself. The BOOK.REC macro set used to write this book is shown here:

```
Recorder - BOOK.REC
File  Macro  Options  Help
ctrl+F1                    Open Paint
ctrl+F2                    Rearrange Icons
```

Recorder is covered in detail in Chapter 12.

Terminal

Terminal is a communications program you can use to connect with other computer systems or information services. It requires a Hayes-compatible modem, a free serial communication port, and connection to the telephone system. Figure 5-9 shows a Terminal window with its Settings menu open. Terminal is an extensive program that is covered in more detail in Chapter 15.

Write

Windows Write is a word processing program that offers many of the features of more extensive programs like Microsoft Word. Write has commands for finding and changing text, aligning paragraphs, indenting, printing headers and footers, and altering the tab settings. You can also switch fonts and apply other text formats, as shown in Figure 5-10. Write is a suitable substitute for many more expensive word processors, unless you need features more advanced than those discussed here. For example, Microsoft Word for Windows offers a spell checker, thesaurus, style sheets, and more elaborate font, character, paragraph, and document formats, among other advanced features. Since Write and Windows operate in the same way, you can use Write now and upgrade to Word later without the need to learn an entire new program.

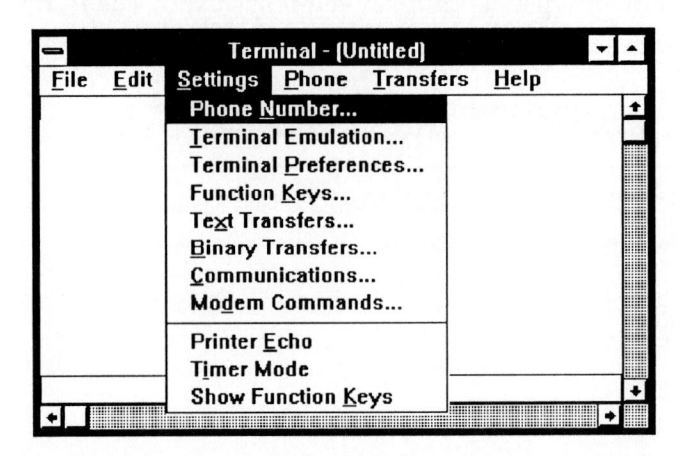

FIGURE 5-9. Windows Terminal is a full-function communications program

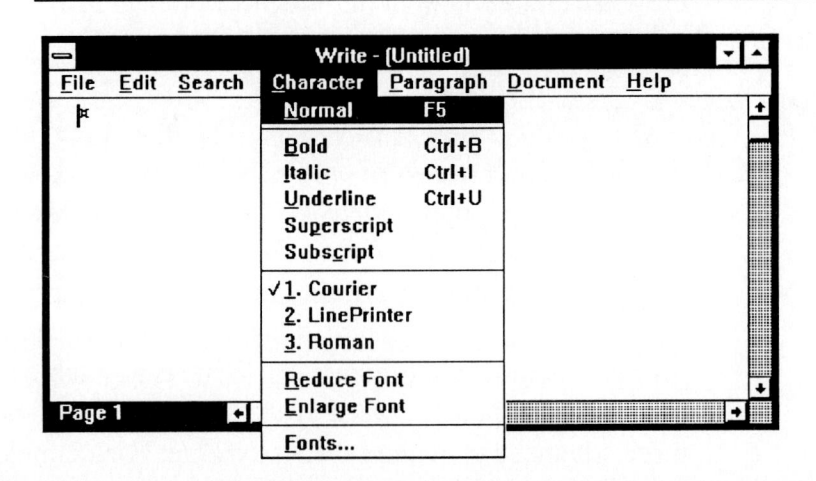

FIGURE 5-10. Windows Write is a word processing program with text formatting features

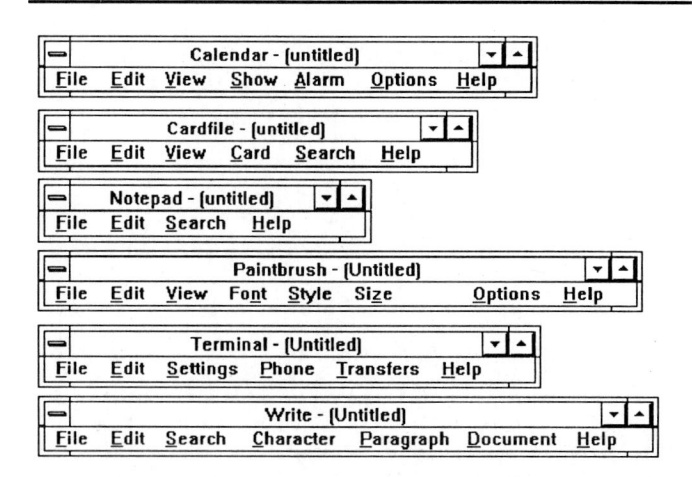

FIGURE 5-11. Many Windows applications have similar menu commands

SHARED MENU COMMANDS

Most applications written specifically for Windows have similar menu headers, menu options, and dialog boxes. You can see this in Figure 5-11, which shows the menu bars of six different Windows applications.

The most common menu headers are File, Edit, and Help, which appear on almost all windows. Other common headers are View, Font, Search, and Options. This section shows you how to use the most common options on these menus, which includes commands for opening and saving files, cutting and pasting, and printing.

The File Pull-Down Menu

The most common menu options on the File menu are shown here.

```
 File   Edit   View
 New
 Open...
 Save
 Save As...
 Print...
 Page Setup...
 Printer Setup...
 Exit
```

Keep in mind that some File menus may have additional features, which will be covered in later chapters that deal with the specific application.

THE FILE/NEW OPTION The New option is used to clear the screen of any existing work and begin a new file. If the existing work has not yet been saved, Windows asks if you want to save it before opening the new file.

THE FILE/OPEN OPTION The Open option is used to open an existing file. A dialog box similar to Figure 5-12 appears. This

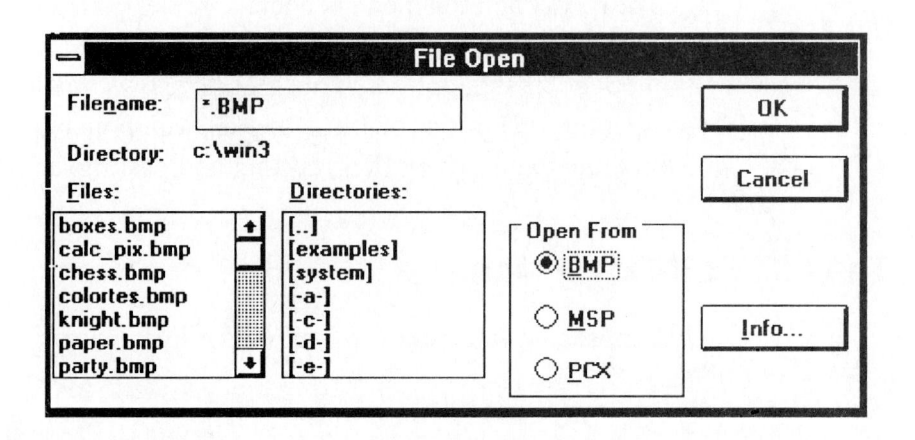

FIGURE 5-12. The File Open dialog box

is the Open window for Paintbrush. Note that the Open From field does not appear on other Open windows; this option is used to select a particular type of graphics file in Paintbrush.

To use the Open menu, first make sure the correct directory for the file you want is selected in the Directory field. In Figure 5-12, the current directory is C:\WIN3. If you need to change the directory, point to a selection in the Directories box.

Note If you are unfamiliar with the concepts and terminology of directory structures, refer to Chapter 6.

The Directories box lists the parent directory name, subdirectories, and other drive names. In Figure 5-12, the parent directory is represented as [..]. You can double-click on this to move up one directory. You can switch to the subdirectories, [EXAMPLES] and [SYSTEM], by double-clicking on their names. To move to another drive, double-click on the drive letter.

Tip If you need to move to a directory on another branch, click the double-dot [..] until you get to that branch, and then click on the target directory name.

When you switch drives or directories, a new list of files appears in the Files box. You can scroll through the list using the scroll bar. When you see the file you want, double-click on it.

An alternative method of opening a file is to type its full path and filename in the Filename box.

THE FILE/SAVE OPTION Use the Save command if you have previously saved a file and it already has a filename. Keep in mind that the Save command saves the changes you have made without asking you to verify. There may be times when you want to save a changed file under a different name, in which case you should use the Save As option discussed next. If you attempt to

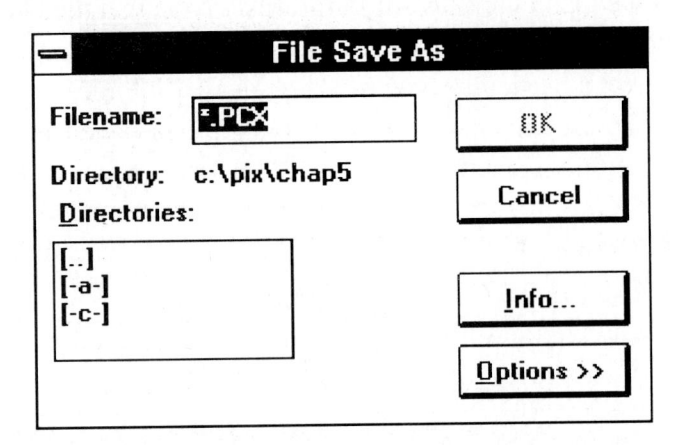

FIGURE 5-13. The File Save As dialog box

save a file the first time with Save instead of Save As, the Save As dialog box is opened.

THE FILE/SAVE AS OPTION The Save As option is used the first time you save a file. As with the Open option, you can switch directories with Save As. To save a file in another directory, click on the items in the Directories box until the correct directory appears. For more information, refer to the previous section, "The File/Open Option."

The File Save As dialog box shown in Figure 5-13 has an Options button. This button appears only on the Paintbrush File Save As dialog box and is used to select the graphics file type. See Chapter 14 for more details.

THE FILE/PRINT OPTION The Print option is used to send a file directly to the printer without specifying additional setup options. It assumes you have already selected the correct printer

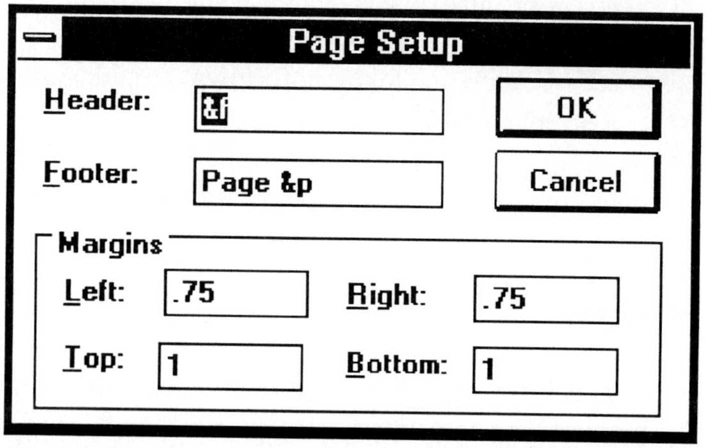

FIGURE 5-14. The Page Setup dialog box

and print method on the Page Setup and Printer Setup dialog boxes from a previous printing or that you are using the default printer.

THE FILE/PAGE SETUP OPTION The Page Setup dialog box does not appear in all File menus, because with some applications its functions are part of other menus. Figure 5-14 illustrates the Page Setup dialog box for the Notepad, Paintbrush, Calendar, and Cardfile accessories.

You can create headers and footers for your documents by typing text in the Header and Footer boxes. In addition, you can type the following codes in the header or footer, by themselves or combined with text, to perform the tasks listed:

&d   Inserts the current date
&p   Inserts the page number
&f   Inserts the current filename

&l   Left justifies the text that follows
&r   Right justifies the text that follows
&c   Centers the text that follows (default setting)
&t   Inserts the current time

For example, you can type the following in the Header or Footer box:

Page &p

This prints "Page" followed by the page number. You can create more elaborate headers or footers by combining text and several codes. For example, you could type the following to print a title on the left and page number on the right:

&l January Sales Report &r Page &p

The Margins box is used to set the margins on all sides of the paper. The application warns you if you enter a margin that is too small.

THE FILE/PRINTER SETUP OPTION   The Printer Setup box shown here is used to select the printer to use if more than one is available.

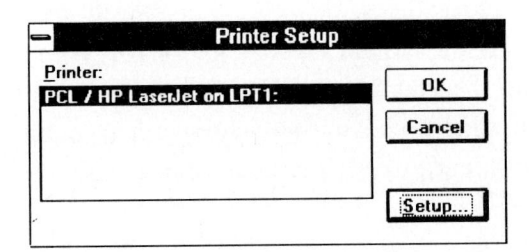

```
┌─────────────────────────────────────┐
│            Printer Setup            │
│ Printer:                            │
│ PCL / HP LaserJet on LPT1:    ┌──OK──┐
│                               └──────┘
│                               ┌Cancel┐
│                               └──────┘
│                                     │
│                               ┌Setup.┐
│                               └──────┘
└─────────────────────────────────────┘
```

You can also press the Setup button to change the configuration of the selected printer. Setup options are covered in Chapter 8.

THE FILE/EXIT OPTION The Exit option is used to quit the application. If files are open and have not been saved, a message box appears asking if you want to save before exiting.

The Edit Pull-Down Menu and the Clipboard

The most common menu options on the Edit menu are shown here:

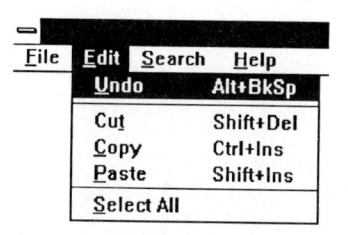

```
File  Edit  Search  Help
      Undo         Alt+BkSp
      Cut          Shift+Del
      Copy         Ctrl+Ins
      Paste        Shift+Ins
      Select All
```

Keep in mind that some Edit menus may have additional features, which will be covered in later chapters that deal with the specific application.

THE EDIT/UNDO OPTION The Undo option is used to undo the last editing change you made. If you deleted text or part of a graphic, or if you change the format of a block of text, it will be restored when you select Undo.

THE CLIPBOARD OPTIONS The Cut, Copy, Paste, and Select All options are called the *Clipboard options* because they are used to place text or graphics on the Clipboard and Paste the Clipboard contents. The Clipboard options are the same for all Windows menus and have the following effects:

Cut   Removes the selected text or graphic and places it on the Clipboard. The quick-key combination is SHIFT-DEL.

Copy Makes a copy of the selected text and places it on the Clipboard. The quick-key combination is `CTRL-INS`.

Paste Copies the contents of the Clipboard to the currently active window, usually at the insertion point. The quick-key combination is `SHIFT-INS`.

Select All The Select All option is used to select all text or graphics objects, whether they are visible in the window or not. This option is not available on all menus.

Typically, you cut or copy an object or text from one window and then press `ALT-ESC` to switch to the other window where the object or text can be pasted. Clipboard contents are pasted at the insertion point.

Note Chapter 11 covers how to transfer information between non-Windows applications.

The Clipboard is a powerful tool for transferring information between applications, because it allows the receiving application to convert the Clipboard contents to a format it understands. This conversion takes place in the background automatically.

COPYING A WINDOW OR THE ENTIRE SCREEN

At times you may want to copy an entire screen or one of its windows for pasting elsewhere. When this book was written, many screens were copied into Paintbrush, where they were edited and saved. The techniques described here take a bit-mapped snapshot of the screen. This picture can then be pasted in Paintbrush and other supporting applications.

- *To copy the entire screen.* Make sure the information you want is on the screen, and then press the (PRTSC) key. You can use the Paste command to place the screen in another application. If this method does not work, you may have an old keyboard. Press (ALT-PRTSC) or (SHIFT-PRTSC) instead.

- *To copy a window.* Make sure the window you want to copy is active, and then press (ALT-PRTSC) to place it on the Clipboard. With an old keyboard, you may need to press (SHIFT-PRTSC).

USING THE CLIPBOARD WINDOW You can open the Clipboard by double-clicking its icon on the Main window. Here, the Clipboard window is open so you can see its contents:

The menu options let you save an image into a special Clipboard file for later use. Other options are

File/Open	Opens a previously saved Clipboard image
File/Save As	Saves the image on the drive or in the directory of choice
Edit/Delete	Clears the Clipboard
Display/Auto	Clipboard allows the receiving application to automatically convert the image to its own format
Display/Bitmap	Clipboard enforces the bitmap format

Using Windows Help

Most Windows menus have a Help heading in their menu bar. Help offers a quick way to look up information about the application you are using without referring to the manual. If you select any of the items on the Help menu, a Notepad Help screen similar to the following appears with information about that category.

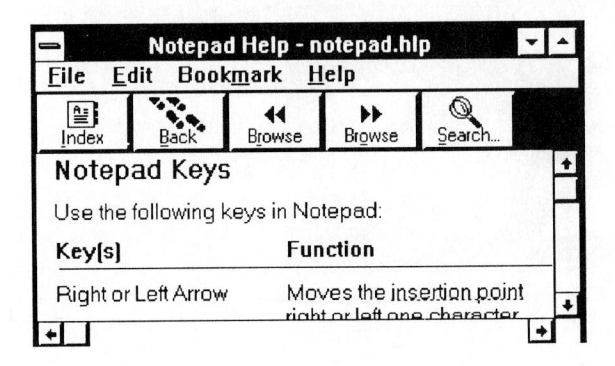

As you scroll through the items, you can point to underlined items and click the mouse to see information related to those topics. If you are using the keyboard, press the (TAB) key to select underlined items. When you are done, press the Back button to return to the previous text. You can also press the Index button to see a complete index of help items.

The Browse buttons are used to scroll one window's worth of text either up or down, and the Search button is used to search for text. The Search dialog box contains a text box where you can type keywords to use in a search, or you can select from a list.

There are several menus on the Help menu bar you can open to print the Help text, open another Help menu, annotate your own Help text, or create a bookmark.

To annotate your own text to the current Help screen, click on Annotate in the Edit menu. A dialog box appears in which you can type the text to be added. When you save the annotation, a paperclip icon appears to the left of the area where it was added. Later, when reading through the Help text, you can click on the annotation marker to display the added text.

The Bookmark feature is used to place bookmarks on topics you want to refer to later or use frequently. Move to the area of the Help text you want to mark and select Define from the Bookmark menu. Type a name for the bookmark and click on OK. To jump to the bookmark at a later time, open the Bookmark menu and select the name of the bookmark, which will appear on the menu itself.

SHARED KEYBOARD TECHNIQUES

The keys listed in this section are necessary if you have a keyboard, but even if you have a mouse you will find them useful, because they are sometimes superior to mouse movements. Note that these keys are the same in most Windows applications. You may want to make copies of these pages and post them near your machine.

The insertion point is a flashing bar that follows your text as you type. You can move the insertion point to previously typed text, and then insert or delete text at that point.

Correcting Typing Mistakes

Typing mistakes are corrected by moving the insertion point just beyond the point where text is to be corrected, and then pressing BACKSPACE to remove the unwanted text. You can then insert new characters if necessary. You can also place the insertion point in front of the text to be deleted and press the DEL key. The following section explains how to get to other text areas when you need to make alterations.

Moving the Insertion Point

The keystrokes listed here are used to jump to different parts of the text to make corrections or insert new text.

Arrow keys	Scroll in any direction, one character or line at a time
`CTRL-RIGHTARROW`	Jumps to the next word
`CTRL-LEFT ARROW`	Jumps to the previous word
`PG UP` or `PG DOWN`	Scrolls up or down one window full of text or options
`CTRL-PGUP`	Scrolls left one window
`CTRL-PGDOWN`	Scrolls right one window
`HOME`	Jumps to the beginning of a line
`END`	Jumps to the end of a line
`CTRL-HOME`	Jumps to the beginning of a document
`CTRL-END`	Jumps to the end of a document

Selecting Text

Text must be selected before you can perform an operation on it, such as deleting or formatting. All the key combinations listed here extend the selection from the position of the insertion point, so you may want to reposition it before pressing the selection keys. The insertion point acts as an anchor for the highlight.

Note: None of the following key combinations use the `ALT` key. The `ALT` key is used throughout Windows to select the menu bar. This may help you remember more easily the key combinations listed here.

SHIFT-DOWN ARROW	Extends the selection to the next line
SHIFT-UP ARROW	Extends the selection to the previous line
SHIFT-END	Extends the selection to the end of the line
SHIFT-HOME	Extends the selection to the beginning of the line
SHIFT-PG DOWN	Extends the selection down one window
SHIFT-PG UP	Extends the selection up one window
CTRL-SHIFT-RIGHT ARROW	Extends the selection to the next word
CTRL-SHIFT-LEFT ARROW	Extends the selection to the previous word
CTRL-SHIFT-END	Extends the selection to the end of the document
CTRL-SHIFT-HOME	Extends the selection to the beginning of the document

Cut and Paste Shortcut Keys

You probably will delete a lot of text as you work with Windows applications. If you use the correct keys, you can control where deleted text goes in case you want to use it again. The following key combinations are substitutes for using the Clipboard commands on the Edit menu.

DEL or **BACKSPACE**	Performs a destructive deletion; you cannot recover the text
SHIFT-DEL	Deletes the highlighted text to the Clipboard
CTRL-INS	Copies the highlighted text to the Clipboard
SHIFT-INS	Pastes the text on the Clipboard into the document
ALT-BACKSPACE	Undoes the previous editing operation

6

DOS CONCEPTS FOR WINDOWS

File Concepts
Directory Concepts

If your use of Microsoft Windows is your first experience with computers, you're in luck. But before you read on, spend a few moments in silence for all the computer users who have come before, those who trudged through the arcane world of DOS commands and text-only screens, those users who learned cryptic commands or wrote them on Post-It notes to tag on the side of their screen, and of course, those users who lost data or messed up some program because they couldn't figure out how to use the system.

Fortunately, Microsoft Windows is here to make it easy for you to use computers. Since Windows has a graphics interface, you can grasp basic concepts easily and start using your system quickly. Most of the tasks normally performed at the DOS level with obscure and nearly extinct commands can be performed with a few clicks and drags of the mouse in Windows. And it is easy to remember how to perform an operation because the pull-down menus are always there to remind you.

This chapter introduces you to some of the basic concepts you must know when you work with files and directories in subsequent chapters.

FILE CONCEPTS

It is important to understand file concepts when working with DOS and Windows. There are different types of files and unique ways of naming them. Files also "live" in the directories of your system. These concepts are covered here.

A file is a collection of information initially created in the memory of your system and then stored on disk with a corresponding filename. Files have the following characteristics:

- *Unique names.* No two files in the same location on a disk can have the same name.

- *Program code.* Program files are written by programmers and contain code your computer can understand.

- *Text/Data.* Files can contain standard alphanumeric characters, readable by humans.

- *Portability.* Files can be copied from one disk to another and from one computer system to another.

- *Changeability.* Files are not static. They can shrink and grow in size or be completely deleted. DOS manages files and the space where they are stored as they go through these changes. The life cycle of a file is shown in Figure 6-1.

- *Location.* Files are stored on floppy disks or hard drives. Files may be placed in unique directories on a disk. Directories are subdivisions of disk storage used to separate groups of files.

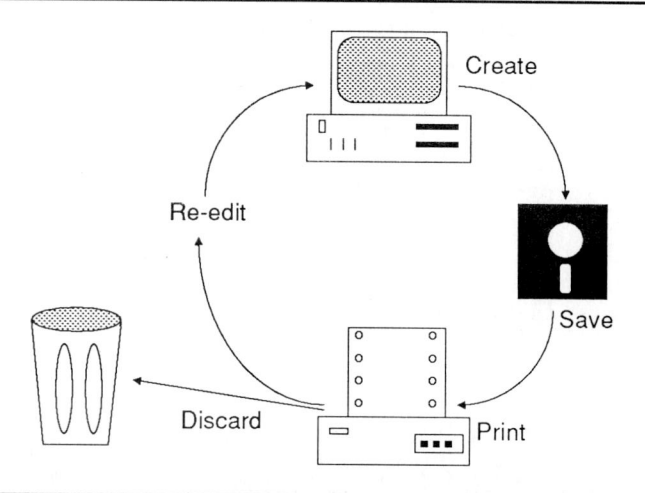

FIGURE 6-1. The life cycle of a file

File Types

The types of files used by Windows and non-Windows applications are listed and described here.

PROGRAM FILES Program files contain computer-readable code written only by programmers. You cannot interpret the information in the file with special debugging tools. A program file under DOS has the extension .COM or .EXE and can be executed by typing its name at the DOS command line or by using the run command in Windows.

SUPPORT FILES Many files exist as auxiliary files to program files. Although they cannot be executed directly, they are read by program files. Files of this nature have extensions such as .OVL (overlay), .SYS (system), and .DRV (driver).

TEXT FILES Text files contain information that can be read by listing the file to the screen. The standard format used in the PC world is ASCII, which assigns a specific code number to characters, symbols, and numbers. This numeric representation is recognized by all DOS-based systems so ASCII files can be copied and used on other PCs.

GRAPHICS FILES Graphics files may contain bit-mapped information, which is basically a representation of the dots on the screen. Another method of storing graphics is in the GDI (Graphics Device Interface) format, which represents drawings by the commands used to create them.

DATA FILES Data files contain information, usually created by a database program like Ashton Tate's dBASE or by a spreadsheet program like Microsoft's Excel. Information in data files is separated in various ways to form the fields of a database or the cells of a spreadsheet. Common formats are comma- delimited files for databases and SYLK (SYmbolic LinK) or DIF (Data Interchange Format) for spreadsheet data. Refer to your program manual for more details.

Naming Files

Each file must have a unique name within the same directory on a disk. In some cases, creating a new file with the same name as an existing file will overwrite the existing file (Windows warns you before overwriting files). When naming files, you must follow the convention discussed here. Also suggested here is a filenaming strategy you should follow.

The convention for naming files is illustrated in Figure 6-2. The name portion of the file cannot exceed eight characters, and the extension cannot exceed three characters. When typing the filename and extension, place a period between them as a separa-

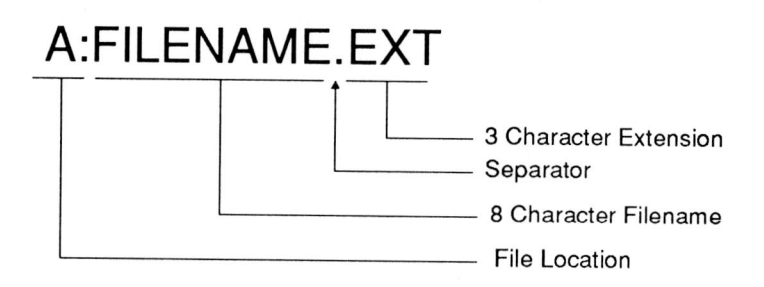

```
        A:FILENAME.EXT
         │        │   │
         │        │   └──── 3 Character Extension
         │        └─────── Separator
         │     └────────── 8 Character Filename
         └──────────────── File Location
```

FIGURE 6-2. Filenaming conventions

tor. The extension is optional, but highly recommended. As you will see later, many applications add their own extension so all you have to do is type the filename. You will need to add the drive letter when referring to files on another drive. In fact, the complete name of a file includes its drive and directory locations, but you do not need to specify them if you are logged onto the drive and directory where the file is located. Directories are discussed in a later section.

The following characters cannot be included in a filename:

/	(slash)	"	(quotation mark)	:	(colon)
\	(backslash)	[ ]	(brackets)	;	(semicolon)
|	(bar)	=	(equal sign)	,	(comma)

You cannot use a period in a filename except to separate the filename from the extension. The following reserved DOS device names also cannot be used as filenames.

CON	LPT2	COM2	NUL
LPT1	COM1	PRN	COM4
AUX	LPT3	COM3	

FILENAMING STRATEGIES To keep your files organized and to help you keep track of what is in the files, you need to develop a filenaming strategy. This strategy involves using the filename and extensions to describe a file's contents, the program that created it, and possibly the type of data in the file (text, graphics, numbers). Many programs automatically add an extension. Table 6-1 lists extensions created by the Windows accessory programs. Notice that Paintbrush is capable of creating three different types of files and corresponding extensions.

Table 6-2 lists several other extensions you can use when creating files with the Windows accessories or any other program. Keep in mind, however, that most programs suggest an extension of their own that describes the creating program and type of file. For example, Excel spreadsheets have the extension .XLS, and Lotus 1-2-3 spreadsheets have the extension .WKS. Extensions should help you locate the files created by a particular program.

Program	Extension	Meaning
Paintbrush	.BMP	New Paintbrush bit-map image
Paintbrush	.MSP	Older Paintbrush bit-map image
Paintbrush	.PCX	PC Paintbrush bit-map image
Calendar	.CAL	Calendar file
Clipboard	.CLP	Saved Clipboard image
Cardfile	.CRD	Index card file
Program Manager	.GRP	Group Information File
PIF Editor	.PIF	Program Information File
Recorder	.REC	Set of Recorder macros
Notepad	.TXT	Notepad text file
Write	.WRI	Windows Write text file

TABLE 6-1. Filename Extensions Assigned by the Windows Accessories

Extension	Usage
.BAK	Added by a file editor to the backup of an edited file
.BAT	Reserved extension for DOS batch file
.DAT	Free-form extension for data files
.DTA	Another free-form data file extension
.DOC	Free-form extension for any document file
.HLP	Commonly used extension for Help files
.MNU	Free-form extension for menu files
.MSG	Message file
.TMP	Free-form extension for temporary files

TABLE 6-2. Common Filename Extensions

The filename itself can describe and categorize the contents of files. Try to create filenames that make sense to you and others. Names like NOTE.TXT and FILE.DOC are meaningless if you create additional notes and files. Although you can use simple names like JANREPRT.TXT to describe a report for January, consider the following filename strategy for differentiating among monthly report files created with Microsoft Excel:

    RA90130.XLS
    RB90130.XLS
    RC90130.XLS
    RA90228.XLS
    RB90228.XLS
    RC90228.XLS

At first these filenames may seem cryptic, but consider the naming procedure. The R designates the files as reports; budget files might begin with B. The second letter indicates the type of report; in this example, three separate reports are created at the end of each month

(A, B, and C). The report date is then included in the filename, and .XLS is added as an extension by Excel.

LISTING FILES WITH WILDCARD CHARACTERS A *wildcard character* is a stand-in for any letter or group of letters in a filename. The question mark (?) is used to represent a single letter, and the asterisk (*) is used to represent two or more letters. Wildcards are typically used to list files. Windows allows you to specify wildcards to alter the way files are listed in a window of the File Manager.

Using the report files previously discussed, you can use File Manager to list files, as shown in the four examples in Figure 6-3. Notice that the title bar of each window shows how the file list is displayed. The files are located on drive C in the DATA directory. In the upper-left example, all files that begin with "RA" are listed. In the upper-right example, all files that begin with "R" and have a "1" in the fifth position (January files) are listed. In the lower-left example, all A files for 1990 are listed. This example assumes files for other years may be in the directory. In the lower-right example, the A file for January is listed.

```
C:\DATA\RA*.*              C:\DATA\R???1*.*
RA90130.XLS                RA90130.XLS
RA90228.XLS                RB90130.XLS
                           RC90130.XLS

C:\DATA\?A90*.*            C:\DATA\RA??1*.*
RA90130.XLS                RA90130.XLS
RA90228.XLS
```

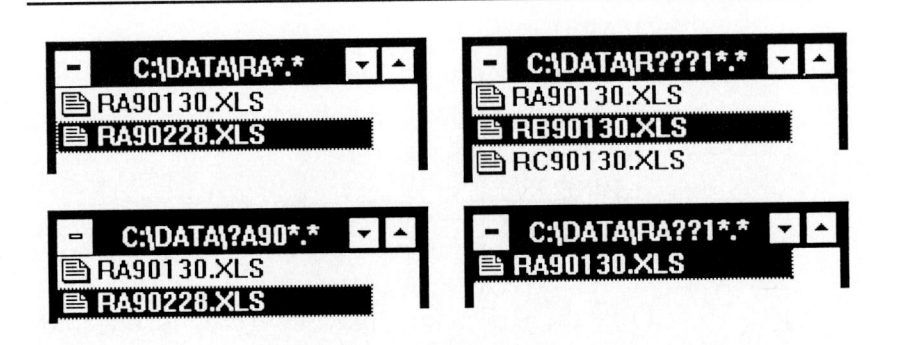

FIGURE 6-3. Windows File Manager can be used to view different sets of files using wildcard characters

Notice how the question mark serves as a place marker. Any character may occupy its position. The asterisk designates a group of letters and the extension in the listings. In Figure 6-3, asterisks replace the ending letters in the filename and allow any characters to be used in the extension. Using the File Manager to change the view of the file list is discussed in Chapter 7.

DIRECTORY CONCEPTS

Directories separate files on hard drives in much the same way you organize paper files in a filing cabinet. Figure 6-4 illustrates the file drawer analogy. The drawer itself is like a directory and hanging folders are like subdirectories. Each subdirectory holds individual files. You might think of a complete bank of filing cabinets as your hard drive.

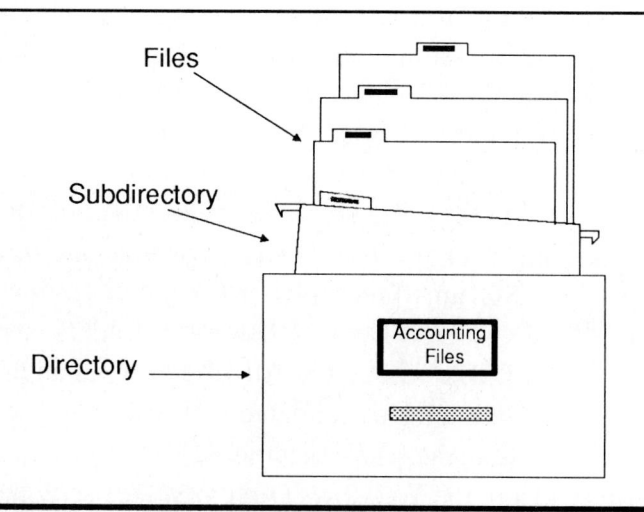

FIGURE 6-4. A file cabinet analogy for a hard disk filing system

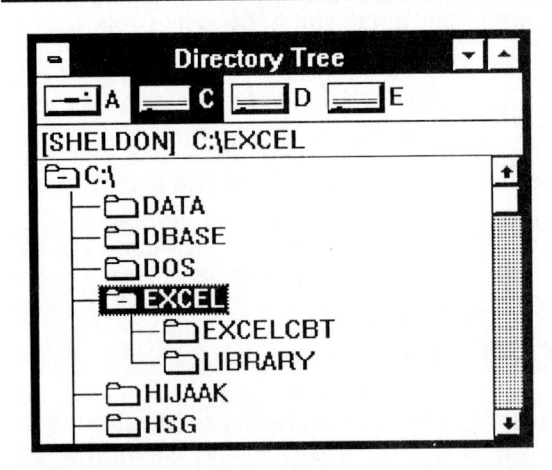

```
┌─────────────────────────────────────────┐
│ ▬           Directory Tree        ▼ ▲   │
│ ┌─┐    ┌─┐   ┌─┐    ┌─┐                 │
│ │ │A   │ │C  │ │D   │ │E                │
│ └─┘    └─┘   └─┘    └─┘                 │
│ [SHELDON]  C:\EXCEL                     │
│ ┌─┐ C:\                              ▲  │
│ └─┘  ├─ ┌─┐ DATA                     █  │
│      ├─ └─┘                          █  │
│      ├─ ┌─┐ DBASE                       │
│      ├─ └─┘                             │
│      ├─ ┌─┐ DOS                         │
│      ├─ └─┘                             │
│      ├─ ┌──┐ EXCEL                      │
│      │  └──┘                            │
│      │     ├─ ┌─┐ EXCELCBT              │
│      │     │  └─┘                       │
│      │     └─ ┌─┐ LIBRARY               │
│      │        └─┘                       │
│      ├─ ┌─┐ HIJAAK                      │
│      ├─ └─┘                             │
│      ├─ ┌─┐ HSG                      ▼  │
│         └─┘                             │
└─────────────────────────────────────────┘
```

FIGURE 6-5. The Windows File Manager Directory Tree window

Now consider Windows' view of your hard drive. Figure 6-5 illustrates a partial directory tree for a typical hard drive, C in this case. You need to view this graphic representation of a hard drive filing structure as an inverted tree. The folder on the top left is referred to as the *root directory* because all other directories branch from it. You can see this by following the lines that branch to each directory. Notice that the root directory is called C:\. The backslash is used to refer to the root directory in filenames.

Directories that branch from the root directory are listed below it. In Figure 6-5, DATA, DBASE, DOS, EXCEL, HIJAAK, and HSG are directories that branch from the root directory. The EXCELCBT and LIBRARY folders are *subdirectories* of the EXCEL directory. All directories can have subdirectories and subdirectories can have their own subdirectories. Files are stored within these subdirectories. The following illustration has been cut from the Windows Directory Tree screen. It shows several layers of directories and subdirectories.

```
     ┌─┐A ┌─┐C ┌─┐D ┌─┐E
[SHELDON]  C:\DATA\LOTUS\DIV-2
📁 C:\
 └─📁 DATA
      └─📁 LOTUS
           ├─📁 DIV-1
           └─📁 DIV-2
```

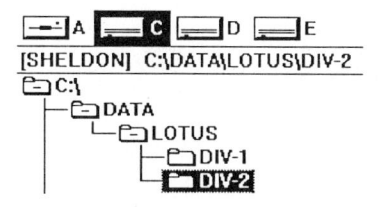

Notice that the current drive is highlighted at the top.

Below the drive icons is the name of the current directory, including its full path. The path to the DIV-2 subdirectory starts at the root directory, goes through the DATA directory, and finally branches from the LOTUS directory. When referring to files in this directory while working in others, you must specify this path. For example, the full name of a file called JANBUDG.WKS in the DIV-2 directory would be

C:\DATA\LOTUS\DIV-2\JANBUDG.WKS

In most cases, you need not type out such long names when manipulating files. With Windows File Manager, you can open two windows side-by-side to copy files from one to the other, as shown here:

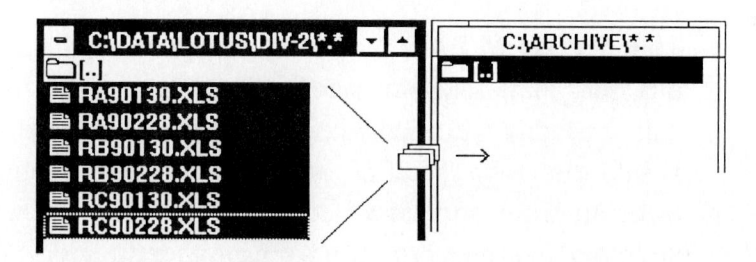

```
┌─ C:\DATA\LOTUS\DIV-2\*.* ▼ ▲    C:\ARCHIVE\*.*
 📁[..]                            📁[..]
 📄 RA90130.XLS
 📄 RA90228.XLS
 📄 RB90130.XLS          ┌─┐
 📄 RB90228.XLS          │ │ →
 📄 RC90130.XLS          └─┘
 📄 RC90228.XLS
```

The selected files in the left window are dragged to the window on the right. The File Manager lets you copy or move files. When you move files, they are deleted in the old location.

Organizing with Directories

Directories are used to keep program files and data files separate. Always create separate directories for each of your programs, because it is possible that program files for one might overwrite the files of the other. It is also a good idea to store your data files in their own directory, not in the directory of the program that creates them. This prevents the data files from getting mixed up with the program files and makes it easier to keep track of them.

Not only is it important to separate data and program files, but you may also want to separate different types of data files to organize them. Backup becomes easier too, since you can simply backup an entire directory at once. In the following illustration, program files for Microsoft Excel are stored in a directory that branches from the root called EXCEL:

```
├─ EXCEL
│   ├─ BUDGETS
│   ├─ EXCELCBT
│   └─ LIBRARY
```

Branching from the EXCEL directory are three data directories that hold different types of Excel files.

THE SYSTEM PATH The *system path* is a list of program directory names where executable programs can be found. The path is usually specified when your system is started. If a program is in a directory specified on the system path, you can run that program from another directory. You can switch to any data directory and run a program from another directory. All files then are stored in the data directory. Specifying program directories on the path in this way is important to the data directory strategy previously discussed.

Each program directory should be specified by the PATH command in the AUTOEXEC.BAT file, which is the batch file automatically run by your computer when it starts. You can edit this file with the Notepad editor discussed in Chapter 12. The structure of the PATH command for the examples described in this chapter is shown here:

PATH C:\DOS;C:\WORD5;D:\EXCEL

Note that each directory is preceded by its drive letter and full path. Use a semicolon to separate each directory in the list. When searching for programs, DOS follows the path in the order shown, so you may want to place the most used program directories first.

7

WORKING WITH THE FILE MANAGER

A Quick Introduction to the File Manager
Working with Directory Trees
Using Other File Manager Options
Manipulating Files
Other Program Manager Techniques

The File Manager is a new addition to Windows that replaces the MS-DOS Executive of previous versions. It has a new graphics oriented interface that makes many file-management functions easy to understand and execute. For example, copying a file is as simple as dragging its icon from one place to another. At the same time, the File Manager lets you view your files in new ways. You can open a window on several directories at once to view their contents and to perform file operations. This is impossible to do at the DOS level. The File Manager lets you view the entire directory tree or zoom in on a particular branch.

The File Manager makes it easy for you to organize your hard-disk filing system, because you can see exactly what the directory structure is. You can quickly locate the directory you want to work in by clicking its icon on the Directory Tree window.

The organization methods discussed in Chapter 6 are easy to implement because the File Manager helps you organize your files into special data directories. The directories can branch from the directory of the program that creates them or from other directories. The File Manager makes it easy to see and find these directories, so you don't have to worry about lost or misplaced files. Since the File Manager can run in a window separate from your current application, you can easily switch to it and create a new data directory or move a file from one directory to another while your other application is running.

A QUICK INTRODUCTION TO THE FILE MANAGER

This section gives you a brief overview of the File Manager so you can plan how you will use it as you learn its features.

To start the File Manager, double-click on the file cabinet icon that appears on the Program Manager's Main window. The most striking feature of the File Manager is the Directory Tree window, shown on the left in Figure 7-1. The Directory Tree window displays a graphic representation of the hard drive directory structure. In Figure 7-1, note that the branches of the DATA directory have been "opened" to show the LOTUS directory and its subdirectories.

Another feature of the File Manager is its *directory windows,* of which there can be many. In Figure 7-1, two directory windows are open and visible on the right. The top window is labeled C:\TEMP*.*, and the bottom window is labeled C:\DATA\RA*.*. These windows display the files in the selected directories. Directory windows provide a unique way to view one or more directories simultaneously and to copy files between them.

[Figure 7-1 shows the File Manager window with labels pointing to: File Manager window, Directory windows, Directory icons, and Directory tree.]

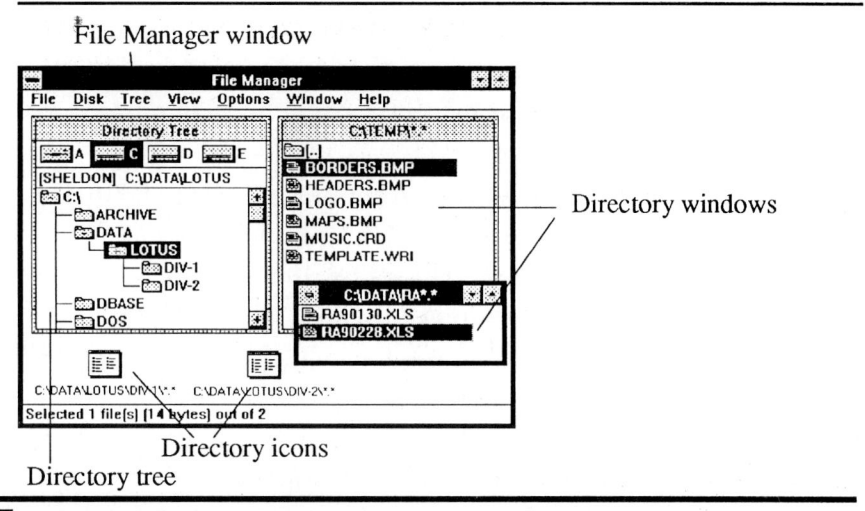

FIGURE 7-1. The File Manager and its Directory Tree window

Two other directory windows have been reduced to icons and are visible at the bottom of the screen. Directories reduced to icons are as important as open directory windows and are referred to as *directory icons* in this book. You can copy files to directory icons in the same way you copy them to open directory windows. In this way, you can have as many directory icons as will fit on the desktop if you ever need to reorganize or clean up your filing system.

The File Manager Menu Bar

The File Manager menu bar contains several options for working with files, formatting disks, arranging the directory tree, selecting the file view, and altering features of the File Manager. Each menu heading is discussed in the sections that follow. Keep in mind that many of the functions on the menu are meant for those using the keyboard method. If you use a mouse, you often can skip the menus by using various point and click methods discussed here.

As you read through the following sections, click on the menu heading to pull down each menu and experiment with the options.

Windows won't let you do anything wrong without first giving you plenty of warning, unless you change the Confirmations field on the Options menu.

FILE The File menu options are divided into five groups according to how they affect files, directories, and the selection of files and directories. The Open option opens the currently selected directory or attempts to open a file if it is associated with a program. The Associate option links a file to the program that created it so both will open when the file is clicked.

The Run option allows you to start a command or program, and the Print option prints the selected file, assuming it is a text file that can be created with Notepad. The Search option can locate a file anywhere on your hard drive.

The Move, Copy, Delete, and Rename options all do exactly what their names imply. The Move option copies a file to a new location and then removes the original file; Copy leaves the original intact. The Change Attributes option can be used to protect a file from being altered or deleted. It can also hide a file, alter its archived status, or make it a system file. You can use the Select All option to select files for any of the previously mentioned operations.

The Create Directory option creates a subdirectory branching from the currently selected directory or a directory with the path you specify.

DISK The Disk commands are used to work with floppy diskettes and network drives. The Copy Diskette option copies the contents of one diskette to another, and the Label Disk option places a name on a diskette. The Format Diskette and Make System Diskette options initialize diskettes. You use the Network options to connect or disconnect to a network, which is covered in Appendix C.

TREE The Tree options expand or collapse the branches of the directory tree. You use this menu only if you do not have a mouse, because the tasks are easier to perform by clicking on the directory icons.

VIEW The View menu contains powerful options for changing the way files are listed in directory windows, as discussed in the last chapter and shown in Figure 6-1. You can change the order of the listing or specify that only certain files be listed. Wildcard characters are used to create specific lists. You also can specify that certain files not be displayed, such as program files and documents. These listing options can be useful when you organize or optimize your system.

OPTIONS The Options menu lets you change the operating characteristics of the File Manager. For example, you can specify no warning when deleting files or directories. You can also alter the way File Manager windows look or the way they display items.

WINDOW The Window option is used to rearrange the windows on the screen in cascade or tile format or to close all directory windows. If you do not have a mouse, the names of windows or icons are listed in the Window menu. You can open the Window menu to make another window active.

HELP To learn how to use the Help menu, refer to Chapter 5 or use the instructions in Help itself. Remember, Help is a shared menu item that operates the same on most menus in Windows.

WORKING WITH DIRECTORY TREES

This section explains how to operate directory trees. The mouse or menu options can be used to control your view of the hard-disk filing system and to help you switch to other directories. If you are at your system, experiment with the directory and subdirectory icons as you read.

Changing Drives

The first thing you may want to do when the Directory Tree window first appears is to change drives. This can be done by pointing on the drive of your choice or by pressing CTRL and the letter of the drive you want to view.

Viewing the Directory Tree

As mentioned in the last chapter, all folders on the directory tree branch from the root directory, which is on the top. Each directory folder can have its own branching subdirectories and can hold files. Initially only the first level of directories is visible. Subdirectories that branch from root directories are not visible until you make them so.

CHANGING DIRECTORIES To select a different directory, click on it with the mouse or use the arrow keys to move up and down through the directory icons. In addition, the scroll bar or any of the following keys can be used to move around in the list:

Key	Action
HOME	Moves to top of list
END	Moves to bottom of list
RIGHT ARROW	Moves to subdirectory if open
LEFT ARROW	Moves to parent directory
PGUP	Moves up one window
PGDN	Moves down one window
First letter of directory	Moves to a specific directory name

EXPANDING DIRECTORIES When you land on a directory icon that has a plus sign (+), you can type (+) to expand the directory. If you have a mouse, simply click on the directory to expand it. You can also type an asterisk (*) to expand the entire subdirectory structure if it is more than one level deep.

To expand all branches in the directory tree from the root level down, press (CTRL-*).

COLLAPSING DIRECTORIES When a directory is expanded, a minus sign (–) appears in its directory icon. You can land on the icon and type (-) or click on the directory with the mouse to collapse the directory. Collapsing directories saves window space and reduces the amount of memory in use by the File Manager. Be sure to close all unnecessary windows for this reason.

Working with Directory Windows

When you land on a directory you want to use, you can open its directory window to view the files within the directory, along with the names of its subdirectories, if any exist. This section explains how to work with directory windows.

OPENING A WINDOW ON A DIRECTORY To open a directory window, double-click on the appropriate icon with the mouse, or press (ENTER) if the highlight is on the directory. The directory window opens on the top of the desktop, with the Directory Tree window and the File Manager behind. To open a window for a directory on another drive, first click on the icon for the drive and then double-click on the directory.

All directory windows and the Directory Tree are subordinate to the File Manager. Thus, the menu options on the File Manager menu bar affect the currently active subordinate window. Each

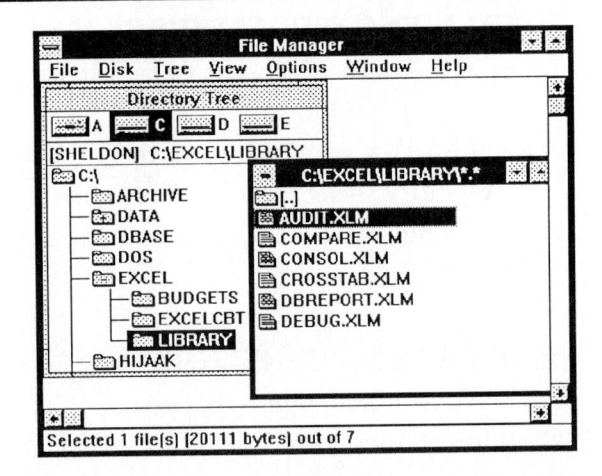

```
                              File Manager
   File  Disk  Tree  View  Options  Window  Help
                 Directory Tree
         A        C        D        E
   [SHELDON] C:\EXCEL\LIBRARY
       C:\                      C:\EXCEL\LIBRARY\*.*
          ARCHIVE         [..]
          DATA            AUDIT.XLM
          DBASE           COMPARE.XLM
          DOS             CONSOL.XLM
          EXCEL           CROSSTAB.XLM
              BUDGETS     DBREPORT.XLM
              EXCELCBT    DEBUG.XLM
              LIBRARY
          HIJAAK

   Selected 1 file(s) (20111 bytes) out of 7
```

FIGURE 7-2. Directory names appear in the directory icon, the path listing at the top of the Directory Tree window, and in the title bar of the directory window

directory window you open acquires the name of the directory it represents. In Figure 7-2, notice that the name of the highlighted directory icon, the pathname in the directory tree, and the menu title of the directory window all share the same name.

THE CONTENTS OF A DIRECTORY Once a directory is open, the files in it are listed. Windows uses icons to represent files, so you can easily locate the one you want. Since a directory may have its own subdirectories, you may see the familiar directory icon as well. The icons are illustrated in Figure 7-3 and are described here:

- *Parent directory icon.* All subdirectories branch from *parent directories,* which are represented by the directory folder icon and a double-dot title. You can select or double-click on this

Icon	Label	Type
📁	[..]	Parent Directory
📁	[EXAMPLES]	Subdirectory
▫	CALC.EXE	Program File
📄	BOOK.REC	Associated Document
📄	ALIEN.HSG	Normal File

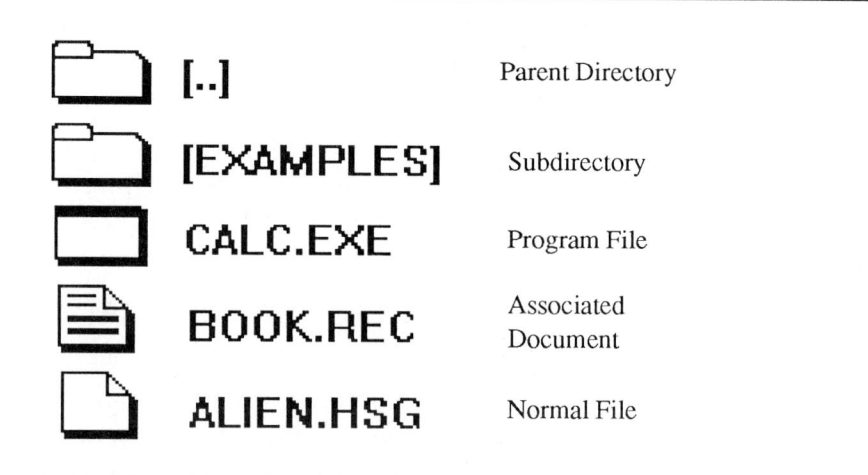

FIGURE 7-3. The icons used to represent directories, programs, and files in the File Manager

icon to move back towards the root directory. The root directory is the only directory without this icon.

- *Subdirectory icon.* A directory icon appears for each subdirectory that branches from the current directory. The name appears to the right of the icon. Selecting or double-clicking on the icon displays the new directory's contents in the window.

- *Executable program icon.* The program icon represents an executable file with the extension .COM, .EXE, .PIF, or .BAT. You can double-click on the icons to start the program or application.

- *Associated document icon.* The associated document icon represents a file associated with an application. You can double-click on these icons to start the associated application and load the contents of the selected file into its workspace.

- *Normal icon.* This icon is used for all other files.

MAKING ANOTHER DIRECTORY WINDOW ACTIVE To make another directory window active, you can either click on it with the mouse or choose its name from the Window menu. If you want to use the click method but cannot see the menu, choose Cascade or Tile from the Window menu to rearrange the windows on the screen.

DISPLAYING A PARENT OR SUBDIRECTORY You can easily display the contents of another directory located up or down the list by selecting the parent icon or subdirectory icons in the directory window. Figure 7-4 displays the contents of the Lotus directory, which has a parent directory and subdirectories of its own. You select the parent icon to display the contents of the DATA directory. Select the DIV-1 subdirectory icon to display its contents.

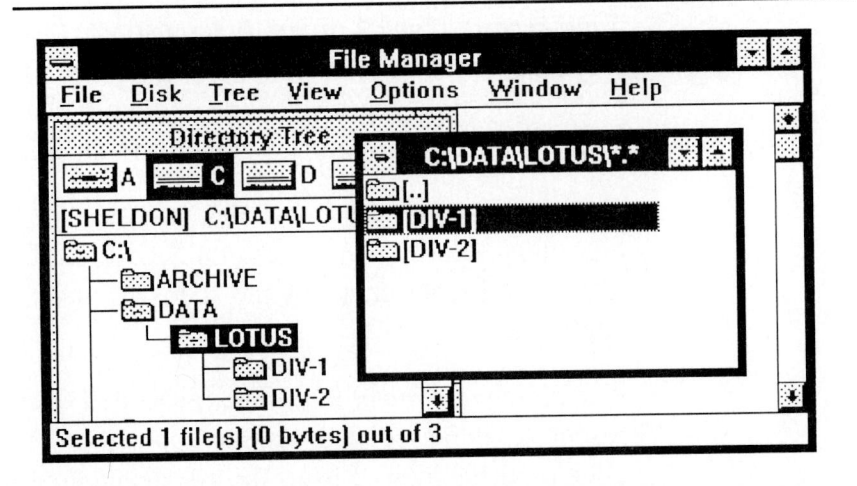

FIGURE 7-4. A subdirectory branches from its parent directory and can have subdirectories of its own

Whether a new window is opened or the new directory listing replaces the contents of the existing window depends on whether you check the Replace on Open option from the View menu. Switching to a directory that already has an open window does not open a new window but rather brings to the front the existing window.

DISPLAYING MORE THAN ONE DIRECTORY WINDOW

At any time, you can click on the Directory Tree window to choose another directory for display. To display the new directory window and keep the existing directory window on the desktop at the same time, make sure the Replace on Open option from the View menu is not checked. When more than one window is open, you can resize them and place them side-by-side. You then can compare files, perform copy operations, and delete files based on the contents of other windows. This is demonstrated later.

REPLACING DIRECTORY WINDOWS   As was mentioned previously, you should check the Replace on Open option from the View menu if you want only one directory window on the screen at a time. When you select a new directory, its file listing replaces the contents of the window.

REDUCING A DIRECTORY WINDOW TO AN ICON   In Figure 7-5, two previously open directory windows have been reduced to icons, and a new window is open. The directory icons stay at the bottom of the screen until you want to use them. To reduce a window to an icon, click on the minimize button. To reopen it, double-click on its icon.

Note that the menu title of the open directory window in Figure 7-5 is only partially visible. When you reduce a window to a smaller size, ellipsis appear after the first few letters of the menu title if the full name cannot fit.

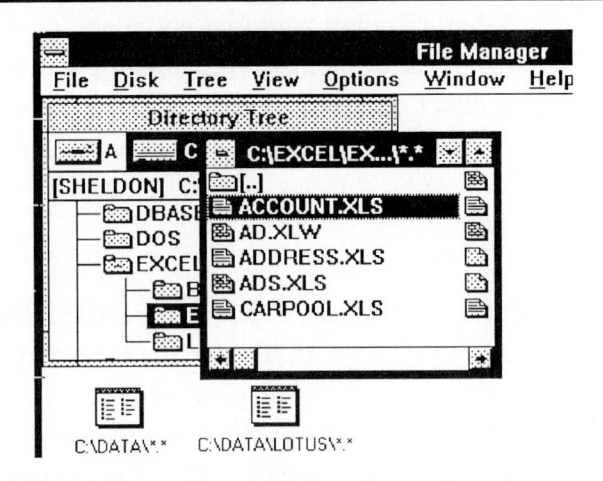

FIGURE 7-5. Directory windows reduced to icons are named after the directories they represent

Changing the Way Files Are Listed

The View menu is used to alter the way files are listed on the active directory window or all windows subsequently opened. Altering the way files are listed is referred to as altering the *view*.

The View menu has three groups that control how files are listed. The first group controls whether extended file information is listed or not, the second group controls the sorted order of the files, and the third group lets you specify the type of files to list. You can use wildcard characters or other methods to extract only the files you want. Wildcard characters are discussed in Chapter 6.

If you have more than one directory window open, the view is only altered on the active window, not the inactive one. However, you can make the new view the system default, and all subsequently opened windows will imitate it.

Note that changing the sort method when the Directory Tree window is active causes that sorting method to be applied to any new directory windows you open, but not those already open.

If you reduce a window that uses a wildcard file-extraction method, the icon displays the directory and the type of files listed, as shown here:

C:\EXCEL\EXCELCBT*.CBT   C:\WIN3*.BMP

The View menu is shown here, and each option is covered in the sections that follow.

```
View
√ Name
  File Details
  Other...
√ By Name
  By Type
  Sort by...
  Include...
  Replace on Open
```

VIEW/NAME OPTION When a window is first opened, only the filenames are listed. To display additional information about the files, like the size and creation date, you must use the File Detail option.

Click on the Name option to revert back to name-only listing if you have previously selected the File Detail option.

VIEW/FILE DETAIL OPTION When File Detail is selected, the statistics of the files are displayed. This information includes file sizes, creation or last modification dates, creation times, and attribute information. If this option is set, you may need to scroll down to see the complete file list.

File attributes are set with the Attributes option on the File menu, which is described later in this chapter. The following attributes are included.

- *R (read-only)*. The file cannot be altered or erased.

- *A (archive)*. Files are marked with the archive flag if they have been modified. An archive flag is an indication to the DOS BACKUP and XCOPY commands that a file needs to be backed up. See your DOS manual for more details.

- *H (hidden)*. Hides the selected file. You must select Show Hidden/System Files from the Include dialog box to display files that have been hidden.

- *S (system)*. System files are hidden. You must select Show Hidden/System Files from the Include dialog box to display them.

Note File information can be important when comparing files or trying to determine the most recent file in a set. The time information on a file listing can prove useful if you need to check the validity of a save operation.

VIEW/OTHER OPTION The View Other dialog box shown here

is used to specify the type of information displayed when the File Detail option is selected. You can turn off the display of some information to save room or prevent screen clutter in the file listings.

 Check the Set System Default box if you want to make the changes apply to all windows. If this box is left blank, the changes apply only to the currently active window. If you check this box, you then can save the setting for your next File Manager session by checking the Save Settings box when exiting File Manager.

VIEW/BY NAME SORTING OPTION The By Name option is selected automatically when you open a new directory window, unless you selected another sorting method. The By Name option displays the file list in alphabetical order by filename. Click it to restore name order if you had previously selected another option.

VIEW/BY TYPE SORTING OPTION If you select By Type from the View menu, the file list in the current directory window is sorted on the filename extensions. If you want all new windows to be sorted by type, select the option when the Directory Tree window is active.

Since extensions are normally added to files by the program that creates them, you can use the By Type option to sort files in program order. If you are using data directories, as discussed in Chapter 6, all the files in the directory probably have the same extension, so you may be better off selecting the By Name option. The By Type option is preferred when you are working in a directory with mixed files.

VIEW/SORT BY OPTION Clicking the Sort By option opens the following dialog box.

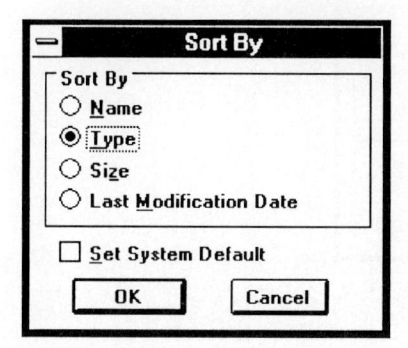

This option lets you choose two additional sorting methods, and make one of them the system default, if necessary. Note that the first two options are repeats of the By Name and By Type options available from the View menu. The Size option lists files according to their file size, which may be useful when you want to determine the most recent copy of a file or to delete old files. The Last Modification Date option displays files according to their date. This option is extremely useful when you are cleaning up your system, since the date gives you information on the age and validity of a file.

> **Note** To actually see the size and last modification date information, click on the View menu's File Details option.

If you want the sort order you selected in the Sort By dialog box to affect all open windows, click in the Set System Default dialog box. If you want to save these changes for the next File Manager session, be sure to click the Save box when you exit the File Manager and Windows.

VIEW/INCLUDE OPTION When you click on the Include option, a dialog box similar to the following appears.

This shows the wildcard specification used for the upper-right listing in Figure 6-3. You can type any name in the Name box, using any combination of wildcard characters, which are discussed in Chapter 6.

The Include dialog box allows you to include or exclude the following file types, which are related to the file icons listed in Figure 7-3.

Directories	Shows the parent and subdirectory icons
Programs	Lists files with the .COM, .EXE, .PIF, and .BAT extensions
Documents	Lists files associated with applications
Other Files	Lists all other files

Think of the File Type checkboxes as a means of extracting files from the list to more easily see a certain type of file. Remove the checkmark from a box to extract its file type from the list. For example, you could check only the Program and Document boxes to view executable files.

Hidden and system files are hidden from view to prevent erasure or alteration. These files also may be hidden to prevent other users from tampering with your system. To show these files, click on Show Hidden/System Files.

If you want the changes in the Include box to affect all open windows, click on the Set System Default box. If you want to save these changes for the next File Manager session, be sure to click the Save box when you exit the File Manager and Windows.

VIEW/REPLACE ON OPEN OPTION As mentioned earlier, you open new windows when you click on a parent or subdirectory icon. To replace the contents of an existing window with a new directory listing, click on the Replace on Open option from the View menu. The option stays active until you click it off.

USING OTHER FILE MANAGER OPTIONS

The File Manager has several menus for controlling how the directory tree and directory windows are displayed and the kind of information they list.

Changing Display Options

You can use the Options menu to set the following characteristics of the File Manager windows:

Lower Case	Displays file listing in lowercase
Status Bar	Appears at the bottom of the Program Manager window to display information about the number of files selected and the amount of disk space they require
Minimize on Use	Causes the File Manager to shrink to an icon when a program is executed

Arranging and Updating Directory Windows

The Window menu has the following options for arranging directory trees and directory windows, refreshing the screen, and closing all windows. You can also select from a list of open windows.

Cascade	Arranges windows so that only the title bar of each is visible, making it easier to select other windows in the stack. Each window is resized to an acceptable size to accommodate file details.

Tile	Prevents overlapping windows by shrinking each window to fit in a tile-like pattern on the screen. This option will probably make your windows too small, but you can increase the size of the File Manager window to allow more room. Use Tile if you want to place two windows side-by-side for comparisons and copies.
Refresh	Manually updates the contents of a window if the automatic feature does not work properly. This may be the case when connected to network drives.
Close All Directories	Closes all directory windows, including directory icons.

MANIPULATING FILES

This section explains the File menu options you use to manipulate files in various ways. Since we will be creating, copying, renaming, and deleting files in the following pages, you should be sitting at your system.

Selecting Multiple Files For an Operation

You already know that a file must be highlighted before an operation can be performed on it. You can use the techniques described here to select more than one file for an operation. Files may be selected as a *contiguous group,* in which the files are next to each other, or as a *noncontiguous group,* in which files are scattered in the window.

> **Note:** To select all files in a directory window, press `CTRL-/` or choose Select All from the File menu. If files have similar names, you can use the View option to display only those files you want to work on, as described later in this chapter.

The techniques used to make both contiguous and noncontiguous selections can be confusing. The following guidelines, which apply to both the keyboard and mouse methods, should help you.

- All group selections have an *anchor file,* which is the first file to be selected.

- Use the `SHIFT` key to extend a selection from its anchor point when you select contiguous files.

- Noncontiguous selections are "bridged" with the `CTRL` key if you use a mouse, or by pressing `SHIFT-F8` if you use the keyboard.

- If you use the keyboard method, use the spacebar to select each noncontiguous file as you scroll through the list, or to "drop" an anchor when you select additional noncontiguous groups.

The following sections explain how to use these techniques to select files or groups of files.

> **Note:** Since contiguous groups are easiest to select, you may want to rearrange a file list in name or extension order, using the options on the View menu before beginning.

SELECTING A CONTIGUOUS GROUP OF FILES If you have a mouse, click on the anchor file, press the `SHIFT` key, and then click on the last file in the group. The highlight extends through all the files in between.

If you are using the keyboard method, press the arrow keys to locate the first file in the group, and then press the (SHIFT) key as you press the arrow keys until you get to the last item in the group.

SELECTING SCATTERED FILES You usually want to select single files here and there on the screen. If you are using the mouse, simply click on each file you want highlighted as you press the (CTRL) key to bridge your selections.

To use the keyboard method, press the (SHIFT-F8) bridge keys, and then press the spacebar on each file you want to include in the group as you move through the list with the arrow keys.

SELECTING SCATTERED GROUPS OF FILES To select scattered groups, you must combine the anchor and extend technique with the bridge technique to tie groups together.

Using the mouse, select the first group by clicking on the anchor file. While pressing (SHIFT), click on the last file in the group. Press (CTRL) to create a bridge to the next group and then, while continuing to press (CTRL), press (SHIFT) and click on the last file of the second group. Continue this method until you have selected all groups.

If you are using the keyboard, press (SHIFT-F8), and, as you scroll through the list with the arrow keys, press the spacebar to anchor each new group. Then press (SHIFT) and the arrow keys to extend each group. To select the next group, let up on the (SHIFT) key, press the arrow keys to locate its anchor file, and then press (SHIFT) again while you move through the group using the arrow keys. Continue this method until you have selected all groups. Finally, press (SHIFT-F8) again to finish selecting.

CANCELING SELECTIONS You may need to remove items from a selection, either because you selected them by mistake or because they were included as part of a group selection. It is sometimes preferable to select a large group and then remove one or two files you don't want.

Using the mouse, click on each selection while pressing the CTRL key. With the keyboard, press SHIFT-F8, and then move to each item to be deselected and press the spacebar. When done, press SHIFT-F8 again.

Creating Directories and Files

As you work with Windows, you will need to occasionally create a new directory where files can be stored. Directories can be subdirectories of the current directory, or they can branch from another directory. This section shows you how to create both types of directories, how to create files, and how to copy and move files between directories using various examples.

Before beginning, click on the Close All Directories option from the Window menu.

Note: The following examples and illustrations assume your directory for Window is called WIN3. Substitute your directory name if it is different.

CREATING A BRANCHING DIRECTORY Directories can be created as subdirectories of your current directory if you do not specify another path. For this example, click on the WIN3 directory in the directory tree to make it the current directory. The directory expands, revealing the WIN3\SYSTEM directory.

Choose Create Directory from the File menu, and then type **TEMP** in the Name field of the Create Directory dialog box. A new directory icon named TEMP is added as a subdirectory of your WIN3 directory in the directory tree. In a moment, you will add a file to this directory.

CREATING A ROOT-LEVEL DIRECTORY Another way to create directories is to specify their full path, if they are to branch from the root of other directories. While still located in the WIN3 directory, create a directory called EXAMPLES that branches from the root directory. You'll use this directory later when copying files.

Choose Create Directory from the File menu and type **\EXAMPLES** in the Name field of the dialog box. The new directory will be created at the root level because you have typed the backslash character, which signifies that the path starts at the root level, not the current directory.

CREATING A NEW FILE Now that you have created the directories, you can create a file to copy to them using the Notepad accessory. Start Notepad by double-clicking its icon on the Program Manager's Accessory window. You may need to temporarily reduce the File Manager to an icon or press (ALT-ESC) to reveal the Program Manager. Once you have started Notepad, type anything you want, such as **This file was created as a test**, and then select the Save As option from the File menu. When the File Save As dialog box appears, type \WIN3\TEMP\TEST in the Filename box. This specifies that the file should be saved in the WIN3\TEMP directory with the name TEST. Notepad assigns the extension .TXT to the filename. If you cannot save the file, make sure you have typed the directory names correctly. Your directory for Windows may have a different name.

Now you have a file to work with and manipulate in a number of ways. Exit Notepad by double-clicking its Control menu selector or by choosing Exit from the File menu. Restore the File Manager to the screen if you minimized it.

Viewing Files

To view the new file in the WIN3\TEMP directory, double-click the TEMP directory icon on the directory tree. A directory window similar to the following should appear, with the new TEST.TXT file as part of its listing.

```
C:\WIN3\TEMP\*.*
[..]
TEST.TXT
```

If you want to read the file, double-click on its filename or select Open from the File menu. Notepad starts, and the contents of the file are displayed on the screen. You can close Notepad again when you are done viewing the file.

Do not assume that every file on your system can be read in this way. Windows knows to open the Notepad accessory when TEST.TXT is selected because it has the extension .TXT, which is associated with Notepad. Interestingly, if you change the name of TEST.TXT to TEST.BAK, Windows displays an error message saying it does not know what application to associate with the file. This points out that the association is in the filename extension.

Moving and Copying Files
Using Menus

When it comes to moving and copying files, the mouse is clearly superior to the keyboard, but there are times when the keyboard method is faster. For example, rather than opening two side-by-side windows to copy a file using the mouse-drag method (described later), it may be easier to use the Copy dialog box and type the name of the destination directory.

You can move and copy directories as well as files. For example, you can click on one directory and drag it to another to make it a subdirectory of that directory. All files in the directory then move with the directory to its new location. This feature is a powerful and convenient way to reorganize your system.

DUPLICATING A FILE IN THE SAME DIRECTORY It is often necessary to make a duplicate of a file in the same directory. For example, you may want to keep one version of a file and edit another. The following example explains how to duplicate the file TEST.TXT to a new file called TEST2.TXT.

Make sure the WIN3\TEMP directory window is still active and highlight the TEST.TXT file. Choose Copy from the File menu. The Copy dialog box appears with the TEST.TXT filename in the From field. Type TEST2.TXT in the To field, as shown here:

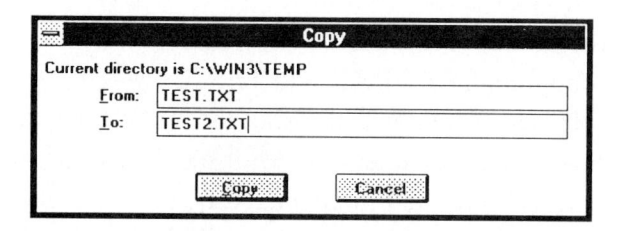

```
                    Copy
Current directory is C:\WIN3\TEMP
    From:  TEST.TXT
    To:    TEST2.TXT

           Copy        Cancel
```

Press (ENTER) or the Copy button. The new file appears in the directory window.

You can quickly duplicate more than one file by using wildcard characters. Choose Copy from the File menu and press (ALT-F) to move to the From field. (The "F" in "From" is underlined in the menu display to indicate it is an (ALT) key.) Type **TEST*.TXT** in the From field, and then tab to the To field and type **TEST*.BAK**. The WIN3\TEMP directory window appears with four files, as shown here:

```
            C:\WIN3\TEMP\*.*
 [..]
 TEST.BAK
 TEST.TXT
 TEST2.BAK
 TEST2.TXT
```

The wildcard characters in the command let you specify a group of files to copy; in this case, all those that had TEST as the first four letters and .TXT as an extension. These files are then copied to new files with the same filename but the .BAK extension.

Note that the .TXT files are labeled with the Associated icon since Windows associates .TXT files with Notepad. Since the .BAK files have a new extension that Windows does not recognize, they are labeled with a normal icon.

COPYING AND MOVING FILES TO OTHER DIRECTORIES Copying and moving files to other directories is a simple matter of first selecting one or more files to copy and then using the Copy or Move option on the File menu to designate the destination directory. Recall that Move deletes the source files after they have been copied to the destination.

To copy the TEST.BAK and TEST2.BAK files to the EXAMPLES directory, select both using the techniques described in the previous section, "Selecting Multiple Files for an Operation." Select Copy from the File menu. Notice that the names of the files appear in the From field of the Copy dialog box as shown in Figure 7-6. Type the destination directory in the To field and press (ENTER).

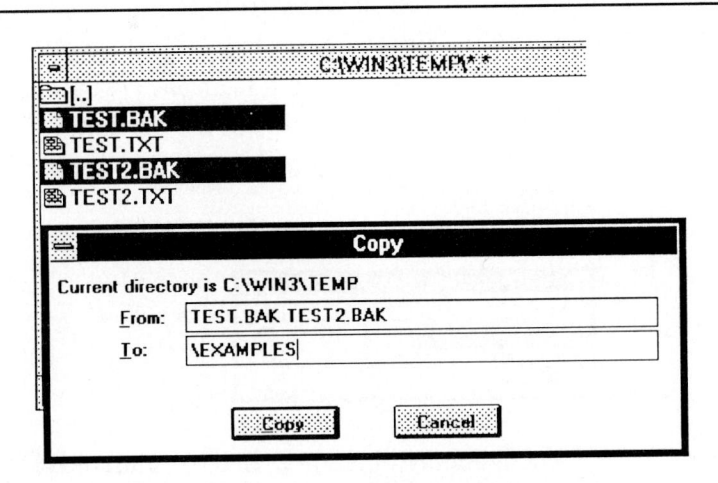

FIGURE 7-6. The Copy dialog box

The operation to move files is the same except the Move command is selected.

Since TEST.BAK and TEST2.BAK have the same file extension, you could have typed ***.BAK** in the From field of the Copy box instead of selecting the files on the directory window. You also use the From field to copy files from a directory other than the one displayed in the directory window.

COPYING AND MOVING DIRECTORIES You can copy or move an entire directory to another directory. This makes the copied directory a subdirectory of the destination directory. All files in the directory are copied with it. Open the Copy or Move command and type the full path of the source directory in the From field. Type the full path of the destination directory in the To field and press (ENTER). If the destination directory already has a subdirectory with the same name as the source, the files in the source are copied into it and no new directory is created.

Moving and Copying Files Using the Mouse

When you copy or move files with the mouse, the source directory must be open as a window and the destination directory must be visible in the directory tree, as shown in Figure 7-7. You can also open a window on the destination directory.

To copy files, the destination directory must be visible so you can drag the icon from the source to the destination. Since you select files in the source directory, you must open a window on it.

To copy files, hold down the (CTRL) key as you drag the selected files from source to destination. If you copy to another disk drive, you do not need to press (CTRL) since Copy is the default mode when dragging between drives.

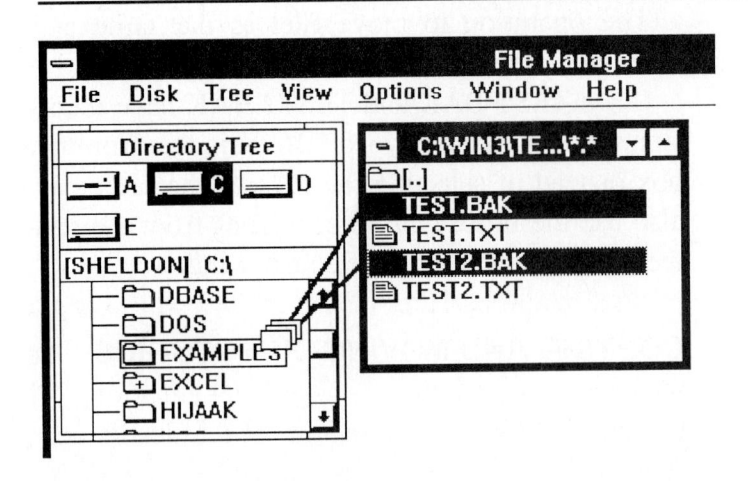

FIGURE 7-7. To copy from a directory window to another directory, make the destination directory visible in the Directory Tree window

By default, Windows moves files rather than copying them when dragging between directories on the same drive. To *move* files to a different drive, hold down the (ALT) key.

Figure 7-7 shows how the two .BAK files in the TEMP directory are copied to the EXAMPLES directory. To perform this operation, select the files in WIN3\TEMP, and then drag them to the EXAMPLES directory icon while pressing the (CTRL) key. As you drag the highlighted files, an icon appears as shown in Figure 7-7, and a box appears around the EXAMPLES directory icon when it is selected.

Note If the files already exist in the directory, Windows displays a warning message that the files will be copied over if you continue.

Remember, you can open windows for directories on other drives and copy or move files between them by dragging from one window to another.

COPYING AND MOVING DIRECTORIES An entire directory can be moved or copied with the mouse by dragging its icon onto the icon of the destination directory. Remember that Move is the default when working with directories on the same drive. If you want to copy a directory to another directory and leave the original intact, press the (CTRL) key. Copy is the default when working between drives. To remove a directory from one drive and move it to another, press the (ALT) key while dragging.

When a directory is dragged from one place to another, it becomes a subdirectory of the destination directory. If a subdirectory already exists with the same name, the files in the source directory are copied to the destination and no new directory is created.

Renaming Files

You can rename files using the Rename option from the File menu. Select the file or files to be renamed in the directory window, and then choose the Rename option. In the To field, type the new filename. If several files are selected, use wildcard characters to specify the portion of the filename you want to keep.

To try the next example, double-click on the EXAMPLES directory icon in the directory tree to open a window on its files. Select the two files with the .BAK extension, and then select Rename from the File menu. When the Rename dialog box opens, note that both selected files are listed in the From field. In the To field type ***.DOC** and then press (ENTER). Your screen will look similar to this:

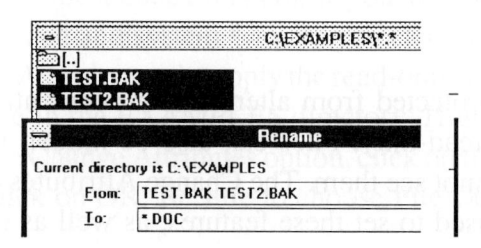

and in a moment your file listing should look similar to the following:

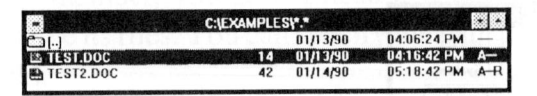

```
              C:\EXAMPLES\*.*
[..]                      01/13/90    04:06:24 PM    —
TEST.DOC            14    01/13/90    04:16:42 PM    A—
TEST2.DOC           42    01/14/90    05:18:42 PM    A-R
```

Notice the A and R flags are set for the TEST2.DOC file. You can set flags for multiple files by selecting more than one file at a time.

CREATING TEMPLATE FILES A *template file* is a file with premade settings you use on a regular basis. For example, you may want to create a blank file with tabs and margins set a certain way to fit a form you use on a regular basis. By marking this file with the read-only attribute, you can load and edit the file, but Windows forces you to save it with a different name, thus preserving the original template for future use. This is covered further at the end of the next section.

Associating a File with a Program

The Associate option on the File menu lets you link a file with an application. When you double-click on an associated document, the program then starts and loads the file into its workspace. The Associate option provides you with a way of organizing your system around your data files rather than programs. For example, if you create a regular company newsletter, you could store all the files used for this newsletter in a special directory, even though the files may have been created by different programs. With all the files in the same directory, it becomes easy to view the files used to create the newsletter. Double-clicking on the file starts the application without the need to know the name of the application or its directory.

The Associate dialog box is shown on the following page.

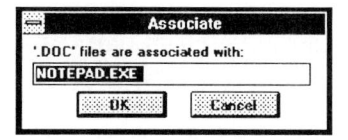

```
┌─────────────────────────────┐
│ ═            Associate      │
├─────────────────────────────┤
│ '.DOC' files are associated with: │
│ ┌─────────────────────────┐ │
│ │NOTEPAD.EXE              │ │
│ └─────────────────────────┘ │
│    ┌──────┐    ┌──────┐     │
│    │  OK  │    │Cancel│     │
│    └──────┘    └──────┘     │
└─────────────────────────────┘
```

To associate the files in the EXAMPLES directory with the Notepad accessory, you must first select the files and then choose Associate from the File menu. Type **NOTEPAD.EXE** in the dialog box as shown, and then click on OK. You can then double-click on either file to start Notepad and load the file into its workspace.

Recall that the files in the EXAMPLE directory are copies of files originally created by Notepad. You might wonder why they are not still associated with Notepad. Since the extension was changed from .TXT, which Windows normally associates with Notepad, to .DOC, the association was lost.

> **Note:** If a program you want to associate with a file is not in a directory specified in the system path, type the directory name in front of the program name in the Associate box.

In the last section TEST2.DOC was marked read-only. Now that you have associated the file with Notepad, double-click on it to load it into the workspace. Make any changes you want, and then try to save it using the Save option, not Save As. The following dialog box appears.

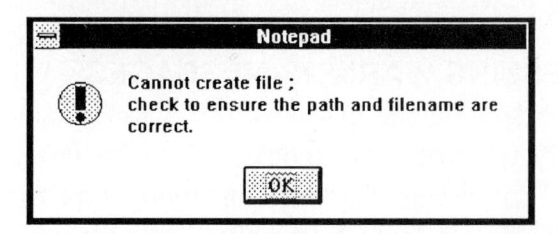

```
┌─────────────────────────────────────────────┐
│ ═                Notepad                    │
├─────────────────────────────────────────────┤
│         Cannot create file ;                │
│  (!)    check to ensure the path and filename are │
│         correct.                            │
│                                             │
│              ┌──────┐                       │
│              │  OK  │                       │
│              └──────┘                       │
└─────────────────────────────────────────────┘
```

Windows does not let you save the file since it is read-only, but the File Save As dialog box appears after you click on OK, allowing you to save it under a different name and thus preserve the original. This feature can be used to create and preserve template files as discussed previously.

Deleting Files and Directories

Now that you have copied, renamed, printed, and associated the example files, it's time to bid them farewell. You can use the Delete option on the File menu to remove both files and directories; however, a better way is to highlight the files to be deleted and press the (DEL) key. The Delete dialog box appears to confirm the deletion. Remember, you cannot delete TEST2.DOC until you remove its read-only attribute.

Keep in mind that you can use wildcard characters to remove multiple files if the need arises. To remove a directory, highlight its icon and press (DEL). After deleting all the files in the EXAMPLES directory, you can click the EXAMPLE icon on the directory tree and press (DEL) to remove it.

Note: Use caution when deleting files while an application is running. Certain applications create temporary files that are removed after the application is terminated. Removing these files beforehand may unnecessarily destroy information. Temporary files begin with a tilde (~) and have the extension .TMP.

SUPPRESSING WARNING MESSAGES Windows confirms each deletion one-by-one with a warning dialog box. If you are already sure you want to delete files, this box may become a nuisance. To prevent the warning dialog box from appearing, choose Confirmation from the Options menu. The dialog box appears on the next page.

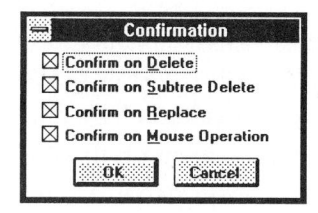

You can choose to turn confirmations off for each type listed by not checking the box.

OTHER PROGRAM MANAGER TECHNIQUES

Other tasks you can perform with the File Manager include searching for files, running commands, and working with diskettes. These are covered in the following sections.

Searching for Files

If you cannot remember where you stored a particular file, you can use the Search option on the File menu to locate it. The Search dialog box has a field where you enter a filename or partial filename. You can use wildcard characters to specify a partial name for the file for which you are searching. If you want to search the entire disk, not just a particular volume, click the Search Entire Disk box.

For example, typing **TEST*.*** in the Search field produces this Search Results screen:

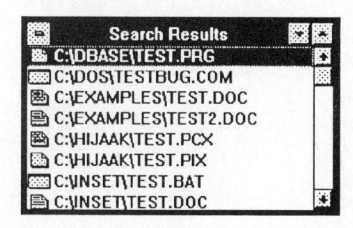

Notice that the list includes all occurrences of files with TEST as the first four characters of the filename. Some of these are program files or associated files that you can execute by double-clicking on their icons. In this way you can use Search to quickly locate files or programs you want to run. You can also use it in Copy and Move operations.

Running DOS Commands

You can start any program by double-clicking on its filename or using the Run command on the File menu. The Run dialog box has a Command Line field where you can type the path and filename of the program you want to run. A checkbox called Run Minimized causes the File Manager to be reduced to an icon when the application starts, thus reducing memory usage and removing screen clutter.

You also can start an application and load one of its document files simultaneously by dragging the document file onto the program file. Use this method if a file has not been associated with a program.

The Run option is not meant to be the way you should start programs on a regular basis. If you have a program you need to start frequently, add it to a Program Manager window as an icon so you can simply double-click to start it. This is covered in Chapter 10.

For more information on starting and running applications, refer to Chapter 11.

Formatting Diskettes

You can format diskettes using options on the File Manager Disk menu. You can use the Format Diskette option to create a data diskette. The Make System Diskette option copies the DOS system files to a previously formatted diskette, thus making a disk you can use to start a DOS-based system.

Remember, formatting erases all information on a disk, so make sure you want to do this before continuing. When you select the Format Diskette option, an instruction dialog box appears. You can click the Format button if you want to specify the creation of a high-capacity diskette or you want to copy the system files as part of the formatting process.

Refer to your DOS manual for more information about formatting and diskette capacities.

Labeling Diskettes

The Label Disk option on the Disk menu adds a label to a diskette or hard drive or changes its existing label. Select the icon of the drive to be changed, and then select the Label Disk option from the Disk menu. Type the new name and click on OK.

Copying Diskettes

The Copy option on the Disk menu makes a duplicate of a diskette in the A or B drive. You must have two diskettes of the same capacity. The source diskette is placed in the A drive and the destination diskette is placed in the B drive. If you have only one drive, place the source diskette in the drive first. The command prompts you for the destination diskette when it needs it.

The Copy option is similar to the DOS DISKCOPY command. It formats the destination diskette, so you should make sure it does not contain valuable files.

8

WORKING WITH PRINTERS

Printer Setup and Configuration
Fonts
The Print Manager
Handling Printer Problems

This chapter covers aspects of printing you may need to refer to as you use Windows. If your printer is already installed and working fine, you may want to just skim the topics, move on to Chapter 9, and refer to this one only when necessary.

There are four main considerations when it comes to printing under Windows. The first is to make sure the printer is installed on the proper output port of your computer and that the software drivers are installed and configured. While most of this should have been done during the installation, you may need to change the setting or install a different printer. This is covered first in this chapter.

The next topic of interest is fonts. Windows comes with a set of its own fonts, but you may want to install special fonts purchased from a third party. This is common with most laser printers.

Third is the Print Manager, which manages the print jobs you send to your printer or network printers, if they are available. It places print jobs in a *queue,* or waiting line, and then sends them one-by-one to the printer. You can open the Print Manager and change the order of print jobs in the queue, or remove a print job altogether. The Print Manager is not used when printing from non-Windows applications.

The last topic to consider is whether you are connected to a network. If so, you can refer to Appendix C for additional information after you have gone through this chapter.

PRINTER SETUP AND CONFIGURATION

When you ran the Windows SETUP program, you were given a chance to install a printer. If you put that task off until now, or if you are referring to this section during the installation, you will find detailed information in this section to help you. If you want to add a new printer or change a current printer installation, you can refer to the discussion of the Printers option on the Control Panel in this section.

Because there are so many different types of printers, the Printers option on the Control Panel offers extensive on-line help, depending on the type of printer you are installing. Once you select a particular printer, you should click on the Help button to read the most current information and instructions for your printer.

The most important part of installing and configuring a printer is copying the correct printer driver for your printer from the Windows diskettes. A driver file gives Windows the special instructions it needs to interact with your printer, such as the control codes to change font sizes and styles.

If your printer does not appear on the list of available printer drivers in the Printers window, you may need to do the following:

- Check your Windows documentation for a list of compatible printers.

- Check your printer manual to see if you can make it emulate a printer that is on the list.

- Choose the Generic/Text Only option on the printer driver list. This driver prints text only and does not support font changes, but will suffice until you can get a correct driver from your printer manufacturer or Microsoft.

Copying a New Printer Driver From Diskette

If you are installing a new printer or installing a new printer driver for your existing printer, read this section to learn how to copy a driver file from the Microsoft Windows diskettes or other diskette to your hard drive.

First, open the Control Panel by double-clicking on its icon in the Main window of the Program Manager. When the panel appears, double-click on the Printers icon. In a moment, the Printers dialog box appears, as shown in Figure 8-1. If you previously installed a printer, its name appears in the Installed Printers list box. To add the new printer, click on the Add Printer button. A list of known printers appears at the bottom of the dialog box. You can scroll through this list, or type the first letter of the name of your printer to get closer to it in the list. With the printer highlighted, click on the Install button.

Follow the instructions for inserting the diskette that contains the correct printer driver file for the printer you selected. You may

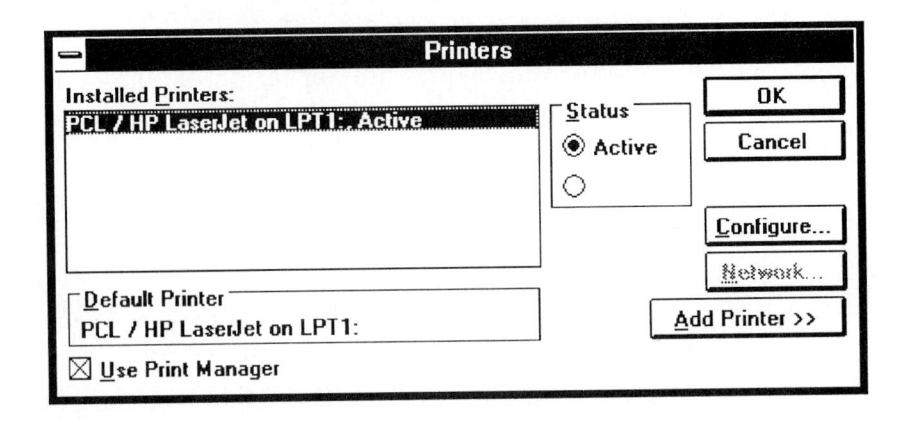

```
Installed Printers:
PCL / HP LaserJet on LPT1:, Active
```

FIGURE 8-1. The Printers dialog box

also be asked to insert font diskettes. The Installed Printers box displays something like this:

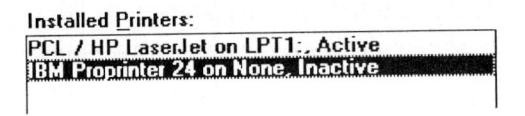

```
Installed Printers:
PCL / HP LaserJet on LPT1:, Active
IBM Proprinter 24 on None, Inactive
```

The new printer, in this case an IBM Proprinter, is listed as Inactive and with None as the port assignment.

Setting the Printer Port

Once the new printer driver appears in the Installed Printers box, you must assign it to one of your computer's output ports. Click the Configure button on the Printers dialog box. The following dialog box appears.

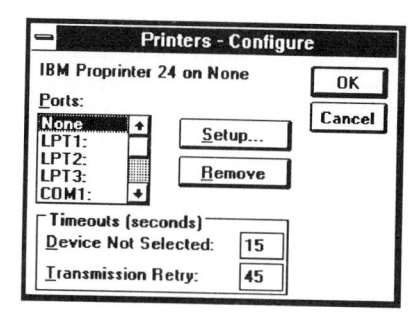

The least you must do to get the printer working is assign it one of the ports listed in the Printers-Configure dialog box. Remember that LPT ports are for parallel printers and COM ports are for serial printers.

PARALLEL AND SERIAL PORTS Generally, printers in the world of PC-DOS are connected using parallel cables and protocols. Modems are serially connected. In some cases, a printer is connected serially to take advantage of longer computer-to-printer distances. Check your printer manual to determine which type of port it uses.

In a parallel connection, signals travel over a multitude of wires in parallel, much like a freeway, but the distance of this freeway is limited to about 12 feet, after which you start to lose synchronization in the signals. The protocols for parallel connections in the DOS world are well established, and you won't need to configure the port any further. Select LPT1 if this is the first parallel printer, LPT2 if this is the second, and LPT3 if this is the third.

Serially connected devices can extend for much greater distances than parallel devices, depending on the type and shielding of the cable used. Such devices are connected to the communications ports of your PC, which are COM1, COM2, and in some cases COM3 and COM4. If you have a modem or other serial device connected, be sure to determine which port it is using and connect your printer to another.

If your printer is connected serially, you must set various communications parameters, such as the baud rate (speed). Windows does a good job of making the best settings, but you need to make sure they match the settings of your serial printer. You can either use the Ports icon on the Control Panel to set Windows to match your printer, or you can set the dip switches on your printer to match Windows. Ideally, you should refer to your printer manual for the best configuration. Refer to Chapter 9 for more information on the Ports utility.

TIMEOUT OPTIONS The Timeout options specify how much time Windows waits before sending messages about printer problems. Device Not Selected is concerned with the off-line status of the printer, and Transmission Retry is concerned with the failure of the printer to receive any transmissions from your computer (in other words, your computer is turned off).

The default settings usually are adequate, but you may need to extend them if you are getting errors from your printer when they are not appropriate. For example, some graphic images take longer to prepare and send to the printer than text images. Also, you may need to account for delays on network printers.

Configuring New Printer Drivers

A few minor details must be taken care of before you begin printing. Click on the Setup button of the Printers-Configure dialog box to display a screen similar to that shown in Figure 8-2. Depending on the printer you have installed, your screen may look quite different from the one in Figure 8-2, which is for an IBM

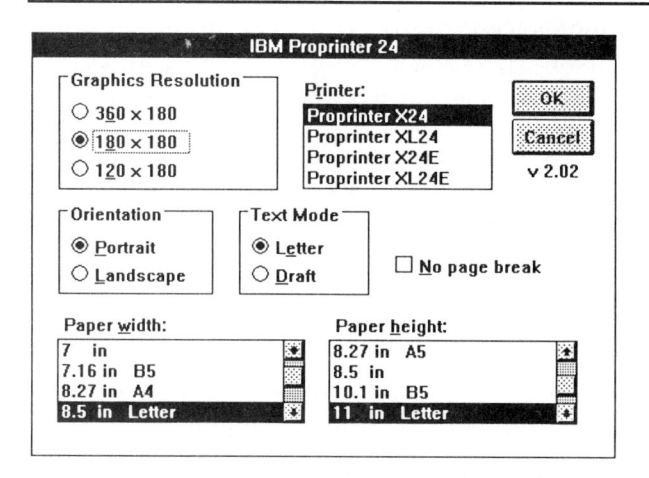

FIGURE 8-2. An example of a printer configuration dialog box

Proprinter. A similar box is shown in Figure 2-5. The options for each printer are similar and are described here:

Printer	Must be set to the exact printer you are using.
Paper Source/Feed	Choose Tray or Bin for cut-sheet paper. Choose Tractor for tractor-fed paper.
Paper Width/ Paper Height	The paper size you will be using can be selected in these boxes.
Memory	Specifies the amount of memory your printer has for downloadable fonts.
Orientation	Laser printers allow normal *portrait orientation* or sideways *landscape orientation*. Choose the option you want to use for this printer.

Graphics Resolution	Normally high, medium or low. Higher resolutions print slowly but produce high-quality output.
Cartridges	Printers that support font cartridges will have a list box where you can select the cartridges installed in your printer.
Fonts	Select this option to install additional fonts, as discussed later in this chapter.
Text Mode	If your printer supports it, you can choose to print in draft mode or letter quality mode.
No Page Break	Turns the Page Break option off.

Some printers have additional boxes for installing fonts and other options as shown in Figure 2-5. Remember to refer to the Help option on the dialog box for specific information about your printer.

After you have made all the proper selections, be sure to click on OK in the dialog box to save your settings. You will need to cycle back through each dialog box you left and click on OK to completely install the printer.

Selecting the Active And Default Printers

If you have more than one printer installed on the same port, use the Status box on the Printers menu to make one of the printers active on the port. Remember that each printer has its own set of drivers. If you change the printer on the port, Windows needs to know which driver it should use.

You can also set one of your printers as a default printer. All print jobs are sent to the default printer. This lets you control when print jobs should be printed on the second printer. For example, if you print long accounting reports at the end of each month, you can ensure they are printed on a dot matrix printer instead of a default laser printer by opening the printer setup dialog box on your application and manually setting the dot matrix printer active for the current job.

FONTS

This section explains how to load and manage fonts used by Windows and your printer. The Fonts icon on the Control Panel is used to install additional fonts at some point after you have already installed a printer. A selection to install fonts also appears during initial printer setup and when selecting the Printers icon on the Control Panel. Either method produces the same results. This section shows you how to use the Fonts utility.

Fonts are important to the appearance of your printed sheets, and to some extent, to the appearance of text on the screen. Every printer has at least one built-in font, usually Courier or some derivative of it. Most popular printers include additional fonts in the Roman and Modern categories that can be enhanced in various ways, such as by boldfacing, italicizing, or scaling. To access these additional fonts, you must install the correct printer driver for your printer, as discussed in the previous section. In this way, Windows knows how to switch to each font or style using the formatting changes you apply to your documents.

Why Add New Fonts?

If your printer is capable of handling additional fonts, add them to improve the quality of your printed documents. You can add fonts by purchasing additional font cartridges or by purchasing software fonts on disk that are copied to the memory of your printer before printing.

Most popular printers today support the addition of other font sets. These fonts may come in cartridge form or on diskette. For example, the Hewlett-Packard LaserJet series printers have two slots for extra font cartridges. The number of available font cartridges to fit these slots has increased dramatically in the last few years, not only from Hewlett-Packard, but also from other manufacturers.

Disk-based *soft fonts* must be downloaded from your computer system to the memory of the printer. They offer a cheaper alternative to cartridges, but additional memory is often required. It may also take more time than you like to download each font set from computer disk to printer memory. Some of the new third-party font cartridges offer the best buy in font upgrades for your printer. You can often buy a large set of fonts on one cartridge for the price of a single Hewlett-Packard cartridge.

> **Note** A font is a single typeface with a variety of sizes. Since fonts must be customized for a particular printer, you should use the fonts designed for your printer only.

How Fonts Are Used in Documents

The height of fonts is measured in points, with a single point being 1/72 of an inch. Some font sets come in a preset variety of sizes—10-point, 12-point, 14-point, and 16-point—that look best on the designated printer. You can often scale the font to any size you wish; however, scaling a font to a size that is not recommended may not produce the best results if a font was created to look best at only a few set sizes.

Once you install a font, its size and style can be adjusted from within your applications. In Figure 8-3, the Fonts dialog box for Windows Write is displayed on the screen. The dialog box lets you pick the font for the currently highlighted text. Notice the Sizes box has a list of recommended sizes, but you can specify a point size of your own in the Point Size box. In this example, 16-point

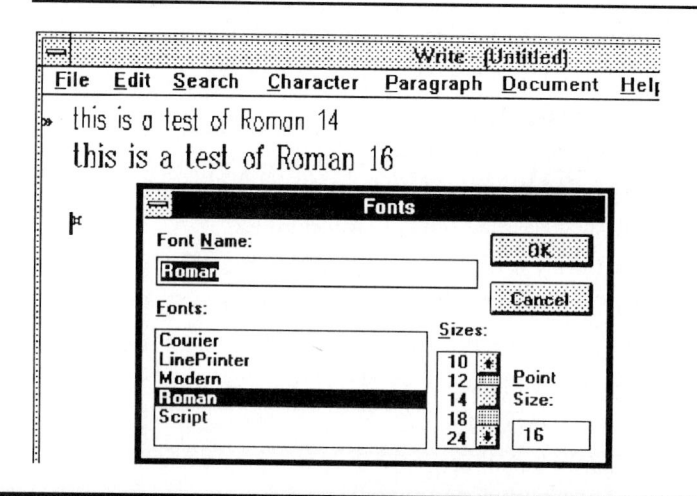

FIGURE 8-3. Characters are formatted using the font-selection dialog boxes in most Windows applications

was applied to the second line of text in the document. Notice also that the screen mimics the actual printed results as best as possible.

Figure 8-4 shows the font-selection dialog box for Microsoft Windows Word, which is a high-performance word processing program. When this dialog box is opened, you can control all aspects of the selected text, including its character spacing. The font and point size can be selected by pulling down the text boxes at the top. Other features can be set by clicking in checkboxes. This type of dialog box is representative of the method used to control fonts in Windows applications.

How Fonts Are Displayed and Printed

Fonts are not always displayed on the screen the way they will appear on your printed output. In most cases, the final printed

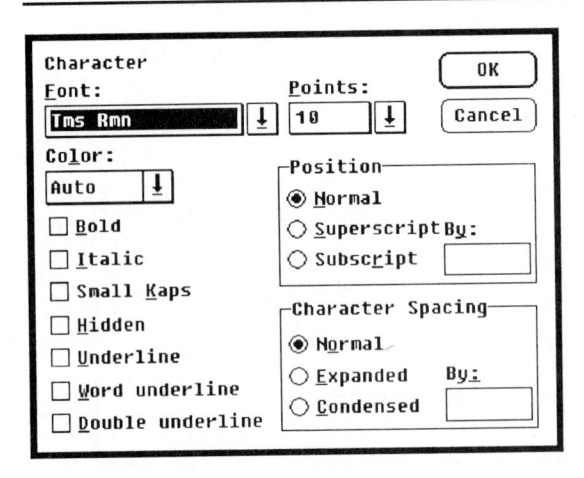

FIGURE 8-4. The font-selection dialog box for Microsoft Word for Windows

output exceeds the quality on the screen. Windows tries to make the screen fonts appear as close to their final printed quality as possible, but often all you see is an approximation of the size and style. This approximation should suffice, because it gives you an idea of the placement of characters on the final printout. Since the characters are scaled to their approximate size, the left-to-right character count and the number of lines should accurately match the point size selected.

When fonts are printed, the description of the font in the printer or font cartridge is used to produce the best results. Remember that the printer driver produces a list of recommended font sizes when you format the text of your document. If you use sizes that are not recommended, the output on the printer may become rough or jagged. This has to do with the way a character is designed.

Raster fonts contain bit-mapped renditions of each character that must be resized when you select a different point set. These renditions can be designed to retain their qualities when expanded or contracted to the recommended sizes, but may not hold their quality if you pick an off size. *Vector* or *stroke fonts* do not consist of a set of predrawn characters. Instead, a description of the appearance of each font is supplied in the font set. These fonts can then be changed to any size without distortion. Although vector fonts may sometimes look better than raster fonts, the trade-off in the amount of time it takes to print them may not make their use worthwhile.

Windows comes with a set of basic raster fonts it uses to display fonts on the screen. Although mainly designed for screen display, these fonts are used by some dot matrix and ink jet printers. When you install a printer, the printer driver file provides Windows with information it needs to use the built-in or cartridge fonts on your printer. But not all printer drivers have a set of fonts to display on the screen that match what will be printed. In this case, Windows substitutes a font that resembles the selected font as closely as possible. You should contact the font manufacturer to obtain the companion screen fonts, if they are available.

Adding Fonts

You use the Fonts icon on the Control Panel to install additional fonts for your printer. Open the Control Panel and double-click on the Fonts icon to display the currently installed fonts in their recommended sizes. If the font is a vector font, it is displayed in only one size since it is a scaleable font.

To add a new font, click on the Add button. The dialog box requests the name of the file to be installed. Be sure to specify the drive name if it is located on diskette.

THE PRINT MANAGER

The Print Manager is a print job manager that allows you to continue working while it sends print jobs to the printer. The Print Manager only works with Windows applications. Non-Windows

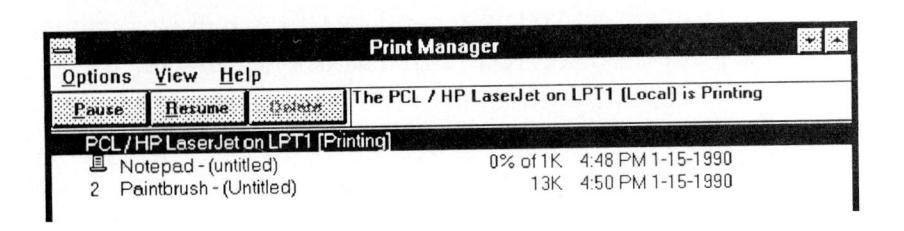

FIGURE 8-5. The Print Manager window

applications print as they normally do without going through the Print Manager queue.

As the Print Manager receives each file to be printed, it places them in a queue, or list, where they await printing. The Print Manager holds the files in the queue if the printer is off or out of service and prints them at the next available time. If you end your Windows session, the queue is discarded.

You can view the files in the Print Manager queue, as shown in Figure 8-5. You can also change the order of the queue if you want one file to print before another. Additionally, files can be removed from the queue.

The Print Manager is started by double-clicking on its icon in the Main menu of the Program Manager.

Note: You may need to activate the Print Manager for the current printer. Open the Control Panel and click on the Printers icon, and then click on the Use Print Manager option.

The Print Manager Menu Options

The Print Manager has two important menus. The Options menu lets you change the priority and features of the Print Manager. The

View menu provides options for turning the display of certain file information on or off, and for working with network queues.

OPTIONS MENU OPTIONS The following options are located on the Options menu:

Low Priority	Your running applications are given more processor time than the print jobs.
Medium Priority	Your running applications may show some slowdown as printing is given more time.
High Priority	Applications will run much slower as print jobs are given high priority.

As you can see, the priority settings are used to control how much time the Print Manager gets to print each file in the background as you work with other applications. In any multitasking environment, each running application is given a slice of the processor's time. The number of slices you give the Print Manager is determined by setting low, medium, or high priority to the print job.

How you use the priority options depends on your current activity. For example, you may be more interested in getting a print job done, but still want to have access to an application such as Notepad if the phone rings. The High Priority option is useful for this type of situation.

These message options are available on the Options menu:

Alert Always	Messages are displayed immediately.
Flash if Inactive	If the Print Manager is reduced to an icon, this option causes the icon to flash until you expand the window to read the messages. If the Print Manager window is inactive, the title bar flashes until you activate the window.

Ignore if Inactive   This option causes messages to be ignored if the Print Manager window is inactive or reduced to an icon.

If you are connected to a network, the Network option is available on the Options menu. It displays the Network Options dialog box, which has two checkboxes. If Update Network Display is set to off, the status of network queues is ignored. If Spool Net Jobs Direct is checked, print jobs are sent directly to the network printer and the Print Manager is ignored.

VIEW MENU OPTIONS The View menu has two options of interest in this section. The Time/Date Spooled option turns the time-and-date information on or off, and the Print File Size option turns the file-size information on or off. You may want to remove this information from the screen for clarity.

The remaining options on the View menu are covered in Appendix C, which discusses using Windows with a network.

Print Manager Activities

The activities discussed in the following sections can be performed when the Print Manager window is open and files are waiting to be printed in the queue. When a file first starts printing and is sent to the queue, the Print Manager icon appears on the desktop. You can double-click on the icon to see the contents of the queue and the status of the file.

PAUSING, RESUMING, AND CANCELING PRINTING The Print Manager menu has three buttons that allow you to quickly pause and resume a print job, or remove it from the queue completely. First, select the file to be affected, and then press one of the buttons.

If you cancel the printing of a file that is printing in Graphics mode, you may have to reinitialize the printer by turning it off and on again.

CHANGING THE ORDER OF THE PRINT QUEUE   If a file has not yet begun to print, you can change its position in the queue. This applies only to a job being printed on your local printer, not a network printer. To change the position of a file in a local print queue, drag the file up or down in the print queue using the file selection techniques discussed in Chapter 7.

With a mouse, click on the file and drag it to its new location. With the keyboard, first select the file to change, and then press CTRL while pressing the up or down arrow key.

HANDLING PRINTER PROBLEMS

Not every printer problem is caused by a lack of power. The cable may be defective or you may be using the wrong printer driver. If you use a parallel printer you are not likely to experience any connection problems, but if you use a serial printer, you may experience problems in getting the serial communications setting correct.

The first thing to do if your printer won't print at all is to run a self-test of the printer. If it runs as expected, you probably have a bad cable or connection port. The next thing to try is sending a file to your printer directly from DOS. Exit Windows or any other application and type the following lines at the DOS prompt, replacing LPT1 with the device name for the port the printer is attached to (LPT2, COM1, COM2 etc).

COPY CON LPT1

THIS IS A TEST

Then press **F6** and **ENTER**.

If your printer prints the text, you know the connection is correct. On some laser printers, you will need to press the Paper Feed button to eject the sheet. If you have a serial printer and it prints garbled text, you should check the baud rates and other communications parameters in the printer and your computer. Refer to your printer manual for more details, and check the communications settings using Ports and Printers on the Control Panel.

If you are having printing problems from within Windows and not in applications you are running outside of Windows, you should make sure the correct printer driver is installed. In most cases, this is the problem. If fonts do not print, make sure you have selected them properly when setting up the printer.

9

CUSTOMIZING WINDOWS WITH THE CONTROL PANEL

Color
Date/Time
Desktop
Fonts
International
Keyboard
Mouse
Network
Ports
Printers
Sound
386 Enhanced

The Control Panel is used to set and alter various operating characteristics of Windows. You use its options shortly after installing Windows to set features and then periodically to alter those features as you see fit or as applications demand.

When you open the Control Panel by double-clicking on its icon in the Main window of the Program Manager, the following display appears:

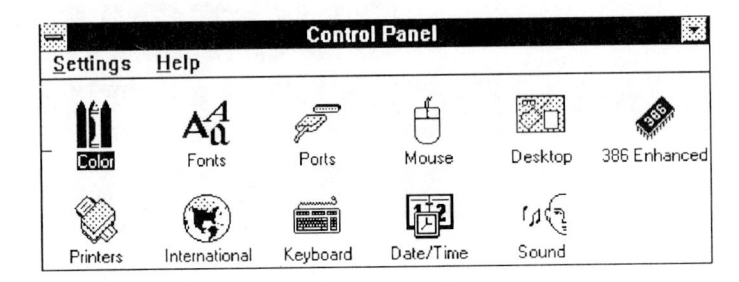

The printer-related options were covered in Chapter 8. Other options are used to set the screen, keyboard, mouse, and desktop features. Each option is covered in alphabetical order in the following sections.

COLOR

The Color option changes the color elements of Windows, including borders, title bars, and workspace and background colors, among others. Windows comes with a full set of predefined color schemes you can select, or you can change these schemes to fit your own taste using a predefined color palette. You can even create your own custom colors. These topics are covered in the following sections.

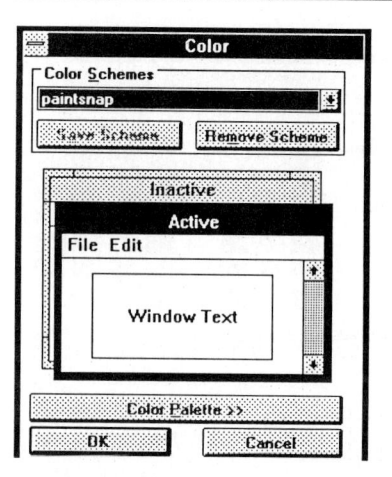

FIGURE 9-1. The Color dialog box

Selecting Existing Color Schemes

The dialog box shown in Figure 9-1 appears when you double-click on the Color icon on the Control Panel. The Color Schemes drop-down list box at the top of the dialog box shows the name of the current color scheme. The middle of the screen shows a representation of each window's elements and its color. The bottom of the screen has three buttons. The Color Palette button is used to create custom color schemes and is covered in the next section.

Click on the down arrow in the Color Schemes list box to pick a different scheme. A list of those supplied with Windows appears. Select each one to see the color combinations. Click on the OK button when you find a color scheme you like. The new color scheme is used even if you exit Windows and return to it later.

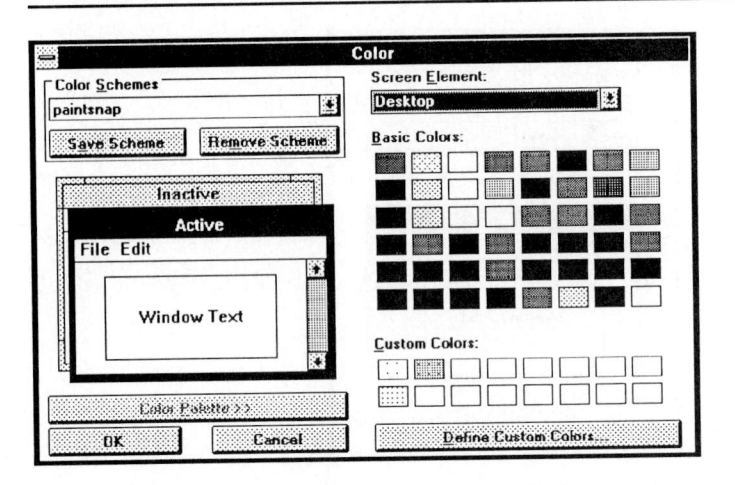

FIGURE 9-2. The Color dialog box expanded to show the custom color scheme options

Changing Existing Color Schemes

If you find a color scheme you like, but you want to change one or two of its colors, click on the Color Palette button. The Color dialog box expands to its full extent, as shown in Figure 9-2.

On the right of the expanded dialog box is the Screen Element drop-down list box, which shows the name of the current window element you want to change. Under it is the Basic Colors area, which includes a set of predefined colors. Below that is the Custom Colors area, which is discussed in the next section.

To define a custom color scheme, select each screen element you want to change, and then select a new color for it. Screen elements are selected using either of the following methods.

- Click on the element you want to change in the windows representation on the left of the dialog box. Its name then appears in the Screen Element list box.

- Click on the down arrow of the Screen Element list box to reveal each window element name, and then select the name you want to change. Some elements, such as the window frame, can be selected only by using the Screen Element list box.

When the name of the appropriate element appears in the Screen Element box, click on a new color in the Basic Colors section (or in the Custom Colors section, if any have been defined). The new color appears in the screen representation on the left of the dialog box.

You can continue to work and rework the color scheme until you get it the way you want. At that point, you can click on the Save Scheme button to save the scheme. If you do not save the scheme, Windows continues to use it, even if you exit Windows and return. If you make another change or choose an existing scheme, Windows then discards the unsaved color scheme.

The Remove Scheme button removes any color scheme, including those supplied with Windows. You may want to shorten the list by removing those schemes you do not like.

Creating Custom Colors

The Define Custom Colors option lets you create a new color by defining its luminosity, saturation, and hue as well as its red, green, and blue components. Click on the Define Custom Colors button to open the Custom Color Selector dialog box shown in Figure 9-3.

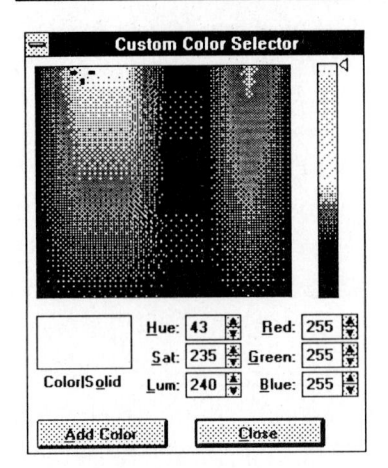

FIGURE 9-3. The Custom Color Selector dialog box

Notice in Figure 9-2 that up to 16 new colors can be defined and added to the Custom Colors section of the expanded Color dialog box. You can define colors on the Custom Color Selector dialog box using either of two methods: You can move the cursor around in the Color refiner box, which is the color block on the upper left, or you can enter exact numbers in the Hue, Sat, Lum, Red, Green, and Blue boxes. These color components are described here:

Hue	The horizontal position of the cursor in the Color refiner box.
Sat	Saturation is the vertical position of the cursor in the Color refiner box.
Lum	Luminosity is the brightness of the color on a scale of black to white. This is the scale just to the right of the Color refiner box. It has a slider that can be moved up and down with the mouse.

> **Note:** Luminosity takes precedence over saturation, and saturation takes precedence over hue.

CREATING A NEW COLOR Creating a new color is as simple as moving the mouse around in the Color refiner box and adjusting the Luminosity bar to the right of it until the color you want appears in the Color/Solid box. The Color/Solid box shows two versions of your custom color. The right side of the box displays a solid color that is the closest your video monitor can come to your custom color. The color on the right includes a pattern component that simulates the luminosity in your selected color. If you do not like the pattern component, double-click (or press `ALT-O`) on the solid color.

You can also enter numeric values in the Hue, Sat, Lum, and color boxes, or you can click on their up or down arrows to add or subtract the component. As you do so, the Luminosity bar and the Color/Solid box change accordingly.

When the color is the way you want, click on an unfilled box in the Custom Colors area of the Color dialog box, and then click on the Add Color button in the Custom Color Selector dialog box to add the color to your custom color set. You also can click on a box that already has a color to replace the existing color. If you do not click on a box in the Custom Colors area but click on Add Color anyway, Windows adds the color to the first box on the left.

When you are done with the Custom Color Selector dialog box, click on its Close button to return to the Color dialog box. You can then continue creating custom window color schemes. Although new custom colors always are saved, be sure to click on Save Scheme if you want to save a new color scheme, and then click on the OK button to confirm your changes and exit the dialog box.

DATE/TIME

Your computer system probably has its own clock for keeping track of the date and time. The current date and time is added to the information stored with each new file you create and is displayed when you list those files.

> Note: If you need to change the format used to display the date and time, see the "International" section later in this chapter.

To change the clock in your computer system, double-click the Date/Time icon on the Control Panel. The dialog box shown here appears:

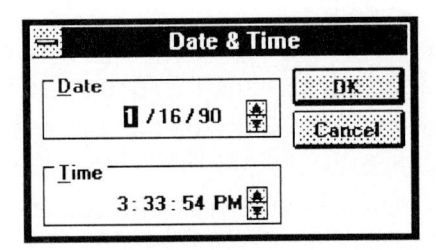

```
┌─ Date & Time ──────────────┐
│ ┌Date─────────┐  ┌──OK──┐  │
│ │  1/16/90 ▲▼ │  │Cancel│  │
│ └─────────────┘  └──────┘  │
│ ┌Time─────────┐            │
│ │ 3:33:54 PM▲▼│            │
│ └─────────────┘            │
└────────────────────────────┘
```

To change the time or date, highlight the part to change with the mouse and type the new value. Alternatively, you can click on the up- or down-arrow button to increase or decrease the values. When the date and time are set correctly, click on the OK button to save the changes.

DESKTOP

The Desktop icon on the Control Panel opens the dialog box shown in Figure 9-4, which has the following options.

FIGURE 9-4. The Desktop dialog box

Pattern	The desktop pattern underlies all your windows. It can be altered to help you differentiate between each window or for esthetic reasons.
Wallpaper	The Wallpaper option lets you select a bitmap graphics image, which is usually created in Paintbrush from a file list. This image then lies under all your windows. You can create your own or use those supplied with Windows.
Cursor Blink Rate	The cursor blink rate can be adjusted from slow to fast.
Sizing Grid	The Sizing Grid box has two options. Granularity lets you select the grid a window "snaps to" when it is resized. The Border Width option lets you change the size of window borders.

Altering Desktop Patterns

Recall that all your windows and icons rest on the desktop. You can change the pattern of the desktop to provide a unique background for your windows. To change the desktop pattern, open the Desktop dialog box, shown in Figure 9-4, by double-clicking on the Desktop icon in the Control Panel.

To choose an existing pattern, click on the down arrow on the Pattern Name list box to reveal a list of current selections. Highlight the pattern you want and click on the OK button. The new pattern appears on the desktop. Keep in mind that some patterns may make the titles of icons hard to read.

EDITING OR CREATING A DESKTOP PATTERN You can change an existing pattern or create your own custom pattern by clicking on the Edit Pattern button. A Desktop-Edit Pattern dialog box appears, similar to Figure 9-5. You can edit or draw patterns by clicking in the large bit pattern box in the center of the dialog box. If you click on a white bit, it turns black. If you click on a black bit, it turns white.

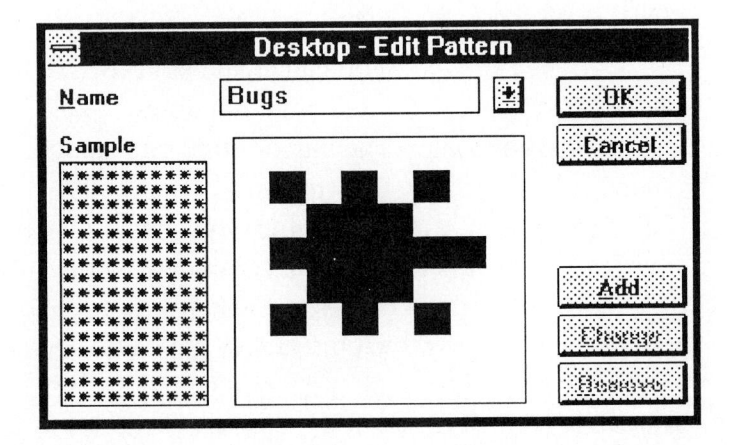

FIGURE 9-5. The Desktop-Edit Pattern dialog box

To edit an existing pattern, first click on the down-arrow button in the Name list box and choose the pattern you want to change. You then can edit the pattern in the bit pattern box. As you draw, notice that the Sample box displays an actual-size image of the pattern. When you have the pattern the way you want, you can click on the Change button to save the edited pattern under the same name, or you can type a new name in the Name box and click on Add.

To create a new pattern, simply start clicking in the bit pattern box. When you have the pattern the way you want, type a name in the Name box and click on the Add button.

When you are done editing patterns, click on the OK button to return to the Desktop dialog box. You can then make the new pattern your desktop pattern using the methods just described.

Selecting a Wallpaper

Like the wallpaper you use to decorate a room, the Wallpaper option lets you add a graphics image to your desktop. Windows has a complete set of premade images, or you can create your own.

Wallpaper images must be files with the .BMP extension that exist in the Windows program directory. You can create these images with Windows Paintbrush or any drawing program that creates .BMP files. Images can even be those scanned from color photographs.

How images are placed on the desktop depends on their size. If an image is larger than the screen, it can be centered. If it is smaller than the screen, it can be tiled, which causes the image to be repeated from the top left. For example, if you create a one-inch square box shape and tile it, the desktop becomes a checkerboard pattern of the squares. The Center or Tile option is selected by clicking on the appropriate button in the Wallpaper box in the Desktop dialog box.

To select a new wallpaper, open the Desktop dialog box and click on the down-arrow button in the Wallpaper File list box.

Choose one of the images, and then click on the Center or Tile button. Click on the OK button on the Desktop dialog box. You may need to experiment to find a pattern you like. In addition, you can change any of the wallpaper image files that appear in the pull-down box by loading them into the Paintbrush workspace.

> **Note** Wallpaper patterns overlay desktop patterns.

Keep in mind that wallpaper uses more memory than desktop patterns, so if you are running short on memory, you may need to remove your wallpaper.

Changing the Cursor Blink Rate

The cursor blink rate can be set slower or faster by changing the appropriate option on the Desktop dialog box. To change the rate, first open the Desktop dialog box by double-clicking on the Desktop icon on the Control Panel. When the dialog box appears, move the slider bar in the Cursor Blink Rate box, using the blinking bar below it as a guide. When the blink rate is set, click on the Desktop OK button to save the change.

Changing Granularity

Granularity is the size of the pattern in the invisible grid that windows will "snap to" as you resize them. The default granularity is 0, which turns off this "snap to" effect. Using any size above 0 can make it easier to resize windows to the same size for esthetic or other reasons. The grid affects the size and position of windows.

To set a different grid spacing, first open the Desktop dialog box by double-clicking on the Desktop icon on the Control Panel. When the dialog box appears, type a number in the Granularity field, or click on the up- or down-arrow button to increase or decrease the number. The range is from 0 to 49, with each increment equal to 8 pixels. Click on the Desktop OK button when the setting is the way you want it.

Changing the Border Width

The border width of windows is changed by increasing or decreasing the number in the Border Width field of the Desktop dialog box. To change the settings, double-click on the Desktop icon, and then type a number in the Border Width box. You can also click on the up- or down-arrow button to increase or decrease the number. The allowable range is from 1 to 49. Click on the Desktop OK button when the setting is the way you want it.

FONTS

You use the Fonts option to install additional fonts you purchase for your printer. Refer to Chapter 8 for a complete discussion of fonts and how to install them.

You can double-click on the Fonts icon to see samples of the current fonts installed in your system for your printer. A list of installed fonts is displayed on the screen. You can scroll through the list and click on one, and the sample appears in the box at the bottom of the dialog box.

INTERNATIONAL

The International option sets the time, date, currency, number, keyboard, and measurement formats of your system. To change any settings, double-click the International icon on the Control Panel. The International dialog box appears, as shown in Figure 9-6. Changes are made by selecting from list boxes or clicking on Change buttons to open dialog boxes. You should explore each feature to find those you want to change. On each pull-down list

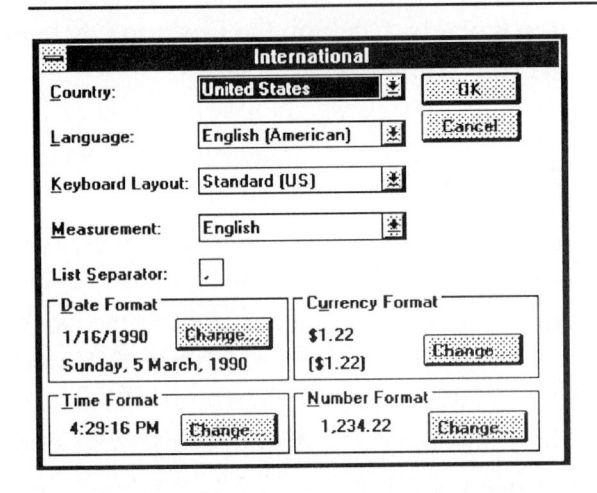

FIGURE 9-6. The International dialog box

box, you should click on the item you want to select. On items with Change buttons, click on the buttons to open their dialog boxes, make any changes you want, and then click on the OK button. When you have the settings you want, click on the OK button of the International dialog box.

The following items appear on the International dialog box:

Country
: Specifies the country. The standards normally used in the country you select are set in other options on the International dialog box where appropriate.

Language
: Specifies the language to use. Windows then makes language-specific settings in many of its programs and utilities.

Keyboard Layout
: Specifies the keyboard layout of your computer. A particular layout has special characters and symbols you may need.

Measurement
: Lets you select the metric or English system of measurement.

List Separator	Specifies the list separator you want to use in list boxes.
Date Format	You can specify short or long form. Click the Change button to see a dialog box of possible settings.
Time Format	You can specify 12- or 24-hour format, and you can specify the separator as well as leading zeros. Click the Change button to see a dialog box of possible settings.
Currency Format	Offers several currency format options. Click the Change button to see a dialog box of possible settings.
Number Format	Offers number format options. Click the Change button to alter the separator and leading zero format.

KEYBOARD

The keyboard repeat rate can be changed by opening the Keyboard dialog box. The repeat rate determines how fast a key repeats when you hold it down. To open the Keyboard dialog box, double-click on the Keyboard icon on the Control Panel. This dialog box appears:

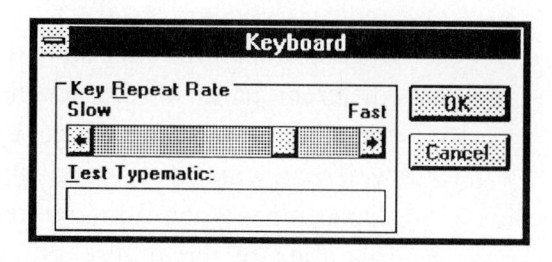

Move the Key Repeat Rate slider bar left or right to adjust the rate. If you want to test the new rate, position the highlight in the Test Typematic box and press any key. When you have set the rate, click on the OK button to save the new setting and close the dialog box.

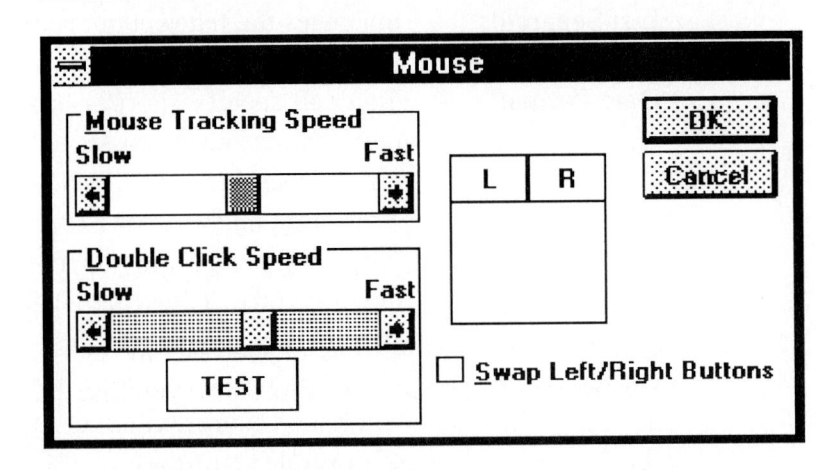

FIGURE 9-7. The Mouse dialog box

MOUSE

The operating characteristics of the mouse can be set by opening the Mouse dialog box, shown in Figure 9-7. The options on the dialog box let you change the following:

Tracking speed	Determines how fast its arrow moves across the screen in relation to the mouse movement. If you are coordinated, you can turn this option all the way up to quickly access different parts of the screen. If you are creating precise drawings in Paintbrush, you may want to slow it down.
Double-click speed	Determines when Windows registers a double-click of the mouse. Slow this option down for more control.

Left/right You can reverse the action of the buttons on the mouse, depending on which hand you use.

To change the setting of an option, move the slider bar left or right. Mouse tracking can be tested by moving the mouse around anywhere on the screen. Click speed can be tested by double-clicking in the TEST box. If you want to change hands with the mouse, click in the Swap Left/Right Buttons checkbox.

Experiment with several settings until you find the one you like. If you are using a mouse for the first time, you may want to set the tracking and click speeds to their slowest settings, and then turn it up later when you are familiar with it.

NETWORK

The Network icon appears on the Control Panel if you have installed and are running a network. Using Windows with a network is discussed in Appendix C.

PORTS

The Ports icon is used to specify the communication settings for serial (COM) ports. You can specify settings for baud rate, data and stop bits, parity, and flow control. You may need to change these settings when you install either a modem for telephone communications or a serially connected printer. In some cases, you may need to make port adjustments when connecting a mouse.

To change serial port settings, double-click on the Ports icon on the Control Panel. An initial dialog box appears with an icon for each port, either COM1, COM2, COM3, or COM4. Click on the

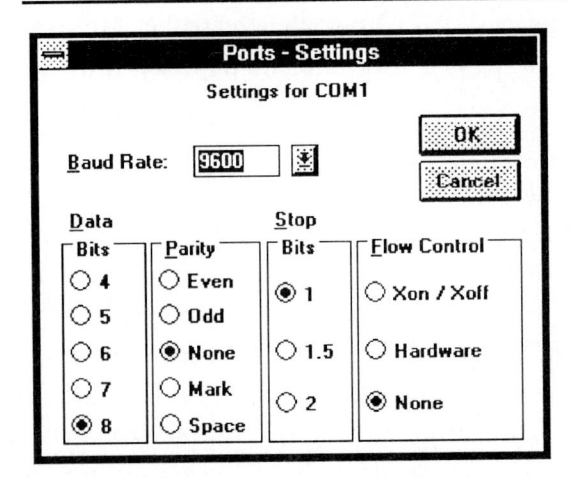

FIGURE 9-8. The Ports dialog box

port icon you want to change and click on the Settings button. The dialog box in Figure 9-8 appears.

Note Your system may not physically have all of the ports listed on the initial Ports dialog box.

What settings you use depends on the communications parameters your modem requires or the settings of the printer, if you are connecting a printer to the port. Click on the appropriate settings for the port, and then click on the OK button to save them. You should refer to the manual of the device you are connecting for the appropriate settings, which are described here:

Baud Rate	The speed at which information is transferred through the port
Data Bits	The number of data bits in each packet of information

Parity	The error-checking method used
Stop Bits	The delay between stop bits
Flow Control	The handshaking method used

Communications settings are covered in Chapter 15.

PRINTERS

You use the Printers icon on the Control Panel when you install new printers and alter the settings of those already installed. You can make the following settings for an installed printer:

- Make the printer the default printer

- Turn on or off its use of the Print Manager

- Make it active or inactive for a port

- Connect or disconnect it from network printers

- Change the configuration of a printer

The setup and configuration of printers is covered in detail in Chapter 8.

SOUND

The Sound icon turns Windows' warning beep on and off. Double-click on the Sound icon to open the Sound dialog box. Click in the Warning Beep box to turn sound on, or remove the checkmark to turn sound off. Click on the OK button to save your changes.

386 ENHANCED

The 386 Enhanced icon appears if you are running Windows on an Intel 80386-based system. The dialog box lets you manage such things as device contention and resource allocation when Windows applications and non-Windows applications are running under Windows. Refer to Chapter 21 for more details on this option.

10

GETTING ORGANIZED WITH THE PROGRAM MANAGER

Working with the Program Manager
Arranging Windows and Icons
Creating Groups

The Program Manager can be considered the main menu for the Windows program. Its purpose is to run your applications and to organize those applications within its windows. You use this window to start applications, and you return to it when you exit applications. The Program Manager continues to run in the background as you work in applications, and it allows you to start other applications and switch among them. In this way, the Program Manager is essential to starting a multitasking session.

The original appearance of the Program Manager window can be seen in Figure 3-1. If you have been reading through this book, your desktop may no longer appear this way, because Windows allows the resizing and rearrangement of windows to be saved for the next session. Instead, you may have your own window arrangement in use. This is appropriate because the Program Manager is designed to be a tool you use to organize the layout of your Windows desktop. This chapter introduces you to techniques for enhancing your Windows desktop using Program Manager.

WORKING WITH THE PROGRAM MANAGER

The Program Manager is an icon-oriented application. You can create icons for your most-used applications, then start those applications by clicking their icons. In addition, you can create icons for the document files you use often and add them to a window. By double-clicking on the document icon, the program associated with the file is started and the file is loaded into the program workspace. You are already familiar with this concept from Chapter 7. Documents that appear in a File Manager directory window can be associated with an application and loaded in the same way.

In the Macintosh world, the process of clicking on an application to start it or to load a document is often referred to as *launching* the application. This term is also appropriate for Windows and is used in this book.

You can get organized with group windows in several ways. For example, you can create a window called Utilities to hold a set of icons that start your public domain utility programs. You can also create group windows for documents. For example, you could create a window called Templates that holds a set of template files, like those discussed in previous chapters. A template file is basically a blank file with preset parameters you use every day, like tab settings, margins, headers, footers, page number schemes, and other common formats. You load a template when you want to create a new document with these settings and formats. The document is always saved under a different name to preserve the template settings for future use. You could have several different template files for writing letters, creating reports, and formatting tables located within the same group window.

Another Look at the Program Manager

Taking another look at Figure 3-1, you can see the basic arrangement of the Program Manager window. Inside the window are group icons and other windows. Any window opened in the Program Manager is a subordinate window. You cannot move it out of the Program Manager onto the desktop. When all the windows are closed within the Program Manager, a set of group icons remains.

Group icons are the elementary unit of organization in the Program Manager. Each group icon holds a set of icons, which can be program and document icons. The basic set of group icons that Windows creates when first installed is summarized here:

- *Main group.* Holds the utilities you can use periodically to manage Windows.

- *Accessories group.* Holds the accessories that come with Windows, like Write and Paintbrush. You can add your own programs to this group or create a similar group.

- *Games group.* Stores the games you play on your computer. Windows comes with two games.

- *Windows Applications group.* Created by SETUP to store programs that are Windows "aware."

- *Non-Windows Applications group.* This group contains programs that will run under Windows, but possibly only in full-screen mode, not in a window on the desktop.

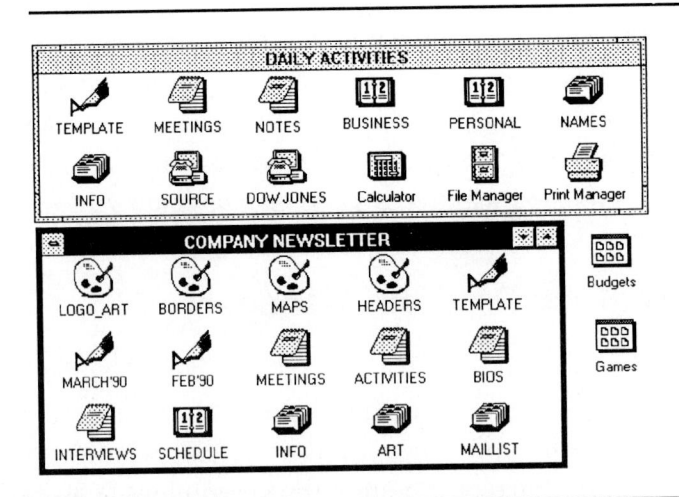

FIGURE 10-1. The Windows desktop may be rearranged to fit your own needs

These groups are completely optional. As you will see later in this chapter, you can create your own groups and copy the icons in these groups into groups of your own design. Figure 10-1 illustrates the desktop that was discussed in Chapter 5. In this example, a company manager has placed document icons used to create a company newsletter into a group window called Company Newsletter and icons used on a daily basis into a window called Daily Activities. The Budgets and Games group icons appear on the side. The Daily Activities window contains document icons that load files such as meeting notes, name indexes, and business calendars. Also included are the File Manager, Calculator, and Print Manager icons, which have been copied from the Main and Accessories windows.

Recall from Chapter 4 that groups, windows, and icons take several shapes in the Program Manager and on the desktop. These are listed here:

- *Group windows.* Used to organize icons. They are created using options on the Program Manager File menu and can be given names that help you organize your programs and files, as shown in Figure 10-1. Group windows can be resized and placed beside other group windows in the Program Manager window, but they are always subordinate to the Program Manager window and cannot be moved to the desktop.

- *Group icon.* A group window that has been reduced to an icon. It appears within the Group Manager window only and cannot be moved to the desktop.

- *Unloaded icons.* Icons within group windows are unloaded programs and documents waiting to be loaded into your system's memory. Unloaded icons are created to make the launching of programs easier. The Windows documentation refers to these as *program item icons.*

- *Active group window.* Think of an active group window as a launching pad. Programs are started by clicking on any unloaded icon within the window. While the program is running, you can switch back to the Program Manager and start additional programs. In this way, the Program Manager coordinates multiple launches and is the coordinator of multitasking activities in Windows.

- *Inactive window.* If you switch from an active window back to the Program Manager or to a window that is running another application, the window becomes inactive.

- *Loaded icon.* If a window is inactive, you may want to minimize it, thus reducing it to a *loaded icon.* The program and document in the reduced window remain in your system's memory but do not continue to run, unless you are multitasking in Windows 386

Enhanced mode. When a window is reduced to an icon, less memory is used. Loaded icons provide a quick means of switching between multiple applications.

It is important to note that loaded icons are placed on the desktop, not in the Program Manager window, but a loaded icon may look just like the unloaded icon in the Program Manager window. A loaded icon includes the name of the document currently in the application's workspace. In this way, the Program Manager allows you to run another copy of a loaded program by selecting its icon on the Program Manager window. You may want to do this when transferring data between documents.

Opening and Minimizing Group Windows

To open any group window, simply double-click on its icon at the bottom of the Program Manager screen. The window will open to reveal the unloaded icons available for use. To close a group window, click on its minimize button. Its group icon will then appear at the bottom of the screen.

The next section explains how to rearrange the windows and icons in the Program Manager window.

ARRANGING WINDOWS AND ICONS

The techniques used to rearrange the windows within the Program Manager allow you to organize your programs and documents.

Moving and Sizing Windows

You can resize a group window and place it alongside another group window so that you can display the icons you use most. You may also want to copy Windows ready-made icons to a new custom group.

To resize any group window, use the sizing techniques already discussed in Chapter 4. Move the mouse cursor to the corner or edge of any window and resize it as necessary. Click in the title bar to drag a window to any location within the Program Manager window.

> **Note** Windows automatically rearranges icons in windows as they are resized if you click on the Auto Arrange option on the Options menu. This is discussed in the next section.

It may help to maximize the Program Manager window before you begin arranging the subordinate windows within it. The arrangement in Figure 10-1 was achieved by first maximizing the Program Manager window. The Daily Activities window was then resized and moved to the top. Then the Company Newsletter window was resized and placed under it. Finally, the Program Manager window was resized around the two inner windows.

Arranging Windows and Icons

The Program Manager menu bar includes the Options and Window menus. These menus provide options for rearranging the icons and windows in the Program Manager.

ARRANGING ICONS AUTOMATICALLY The Auto Arrange option on the Options menu is important to check when resizing windows. It causes the icons in the window to automatically rearrange themselves to fit the new window's size, which helps you determine how large the window needs to be during resizing. Of course, you can make a window any size you want; if the icons do not fit, a scroll bar appears at the bottom or side of the window so you can view icons not visible in the window.

ARRANGING ICONS MANUALLY You can move icons around with the mouse to arrange them in any style you like. Then at any time you can select the Arrange Icons option on the Window menu to "square-up" the icons in an orderly manner. The Arrange Icons option is really used for esthetic reasons. If you like the icons to look neat and orderly, it saves you the trouble of trying to line them up with the mouse.

ARRANGING WINDOWS The Window menu has two options for rearranging the windows within the Program Manager. Click on the Cascade option to rearrange the window in a cascading fashion with only title bars showing. Click on Tile to arrange the windows side-by-side. When you select Tile, windows may shrink to an unacceptable size, but you can click the maximize button of the window you want to use to bring it to full size on the screen. When done, you can click on the resize button to restore the menu in the tile arrangement. In this way, open windows can be easily selected and do not overlap one another.

Saving Your Changes

When you finally achieve the screen arrangement you like, you can save the changes for your next Windows session by clicking the Save Changes checkbox as you exit Windows. When you restart Windows, the screen arrangement will be restored to the screen.

CREATING GROUPS

This section explains how to create new groups and add program and document icons to them. You will see that there are several methods for adding icons to groups. You have already seen one method if you let the Windows SETUP program create groups for your Windows and non-Windows applications. You can run SETUP at any time to add new items to groups. The New option on the Program Manager File menu is another method for adding group items. Still another way is to open the File Manager and copy a program or document file from a directory to a group window. Finally, you can copy icons that already exist in one group window to another group window.

It doesn't matter which method you use because they all accomplish the same thing. The number of new items you want to add and the current status of your screen play a part in the method you choose, as you will see in the following discussions.

Creating a Group Window

If you plan to reorganize your Program Manager window in a way that matches the way you work, the first thing you will probably do is create a new group icon. This is done by choosing New from the File menu. The New Program Object dialog box appears, as shown in Figure 10-2.

Select Program Group from the dialog box, and the Program Group Properties dialog box appears, as shown here:

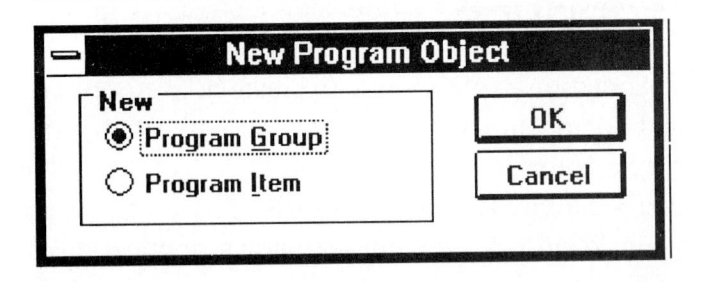

FIGURE 10-2. The New Program Object dialog box

Type the description for the group in the Description box. This is the name that appears in the group window title bar and with the group icon. You do not need to type a name in the Group File box because Program Manager automatically creates a file with the extension .GRP. Click on the OK button when you are done. The new group appears as a window on the screen, with the title of the group in the window's title bar.

CHANGING A GROUP NAME If you want to change the name of a group, you can click on its icon or window and then select the Properties option from the File menu. The Program Group Properties dialog box, similar to that shown in the previous illustration, appears. Type the new group name in the Description field and press the OK button.

DELETING A GROUP If you want to delete a group, click on its icon or window and choose Delete from the File menu. The Program Manager asks for confirmation that you want to remove the group and the icons in it.

> **Note:** Before deleting a group entirely, you may want to copy some of its icons to other groups.

Adding Items to a Group

As mentioned previously, you can add items to a group in several ways. These items can be programs or documents associated with programs.

ADDING PROGRAM ICONS To add a program icon to a group, first open the window for the group to which you want to add the icon. This is important so Windows knows you are creating a program icon, not a group icon. Choose New from the Program Manager File menu. The New Program Object dialog box appears, as shown in Figure 10-2. Select Program Item from the dialog box and click on the OK button. The Program Item Properties dialog box appears as shown here:

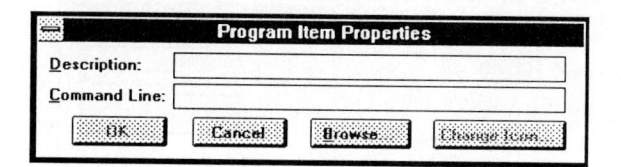

```
┌─────────────────────────────────────────────┐
│            Program Item Properties          │
│  Description:  [                         ]  │
│  Command Line: [                         ]  │
│    [ OK ]  [ Cancel ]  [ Browse ] [Change Icon]│
└─────────────────────────────────────────────┘
```

This box is similar to the Program Group Properties box but allows you to browse your hard-drive filing system for the filenames of the programs or documents you want to add as an icon. It also lets you select the type of icon graphics to use.

Type the description that will appear in the program icon in the Description box, and then type the command required to start the program in the Command Line box. If the directory where the program is located is not specified in the system path, as discussed in Chapter 3, include the full path as part of the command. For example, the following illustration shows what you would type in the boxes to create an icon for Microsoft Word that is located in a directory called WORD5.

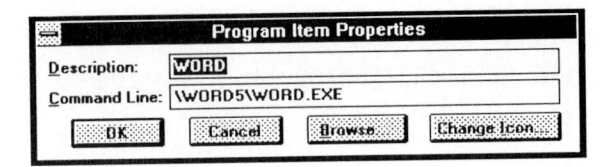

```
┌─────────────────────────────────────────────────┐
│            Program Item Properties              │
│ Description:  [WORD]                            │
│ Command Line: [\WORD5\WORD.EXE]                 │
│   [ OK ]  [ Cancel ]  [ Browse ]  [Change Icon] │
└─────────────────────────────────────────────────┘
```

Notice that the path is specified in the Command Line box, followed by the WORD.EXE command used to start Word.

If you do not know the name of the program you want to add, you can press the Browse button on the Program Item Properties dialog box to display the Browse dialog box, as shown in Figure 10-3. This

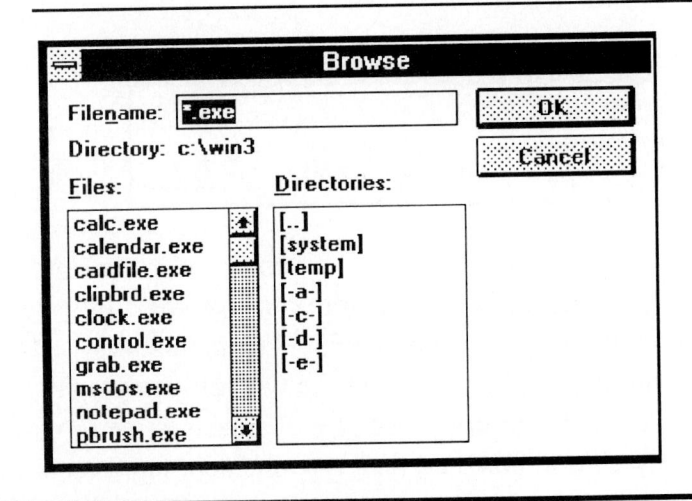

```
┌─────────────────────────────────────────────────┐
│                     Browse                      │
│ Filename: [*.exe]                    [  OK  ]   │
│ Directory: c:\win3                   [Cancel]   │
│ Files:              Directories:                │
│  calc.exe            [..]                       │
│  calendar.exe        [system]                   │
│  cardfile.exe        [temp]                     │
│  clipbrd.exe         [-a-]                      │
│  clock.exe           [-c-]                      │
│  control.exe         [-d-]                      │
│  grab.exe            [-e-]                      │
│  msdos.exe                                      │
│  notepad.exe                                    │
│  pbrush.exe                                     │
└─────────────────────────────────────────────────┘
```

FIGURE 10-3. The Browse dialog box, used to locate programs on your hard drive

dialog box appears after a search is made of the current directory for program files with the .EXE extension.

Select the name of the program from the list. If the program is in a different directory, select it in the Directory box. If the program has a different extension, type it in the Filename box. You can type ***.COM** to see program files with the .COM extension or ***.BAT** to see a list of batch files.

Before clicking on the OK button to create the new icon, you may want to change the graphics image that the Program Manager uses for the icon. Click the Change Icon button on the Program Item Properties dialog box. A dialog box similar to this one appears:

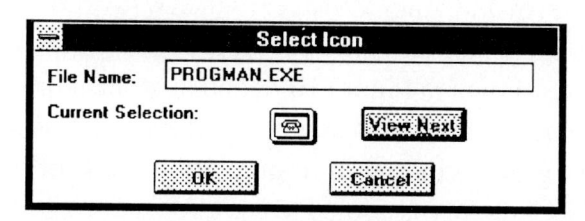

```
┌─────────────────────────────────────────────┐
│                 Select Icon                 │
│ File Name:  PROGMAN.EXE                     │
│ Current Selection:   [icon]  [View Next]    │
│              [ OK ]         [ Cancel ]      │
└─────────────────────────────────────────────┘
```

You can choose different icons to help you differentiate among the items in a group window. When everything is the way you want, click on the OK button to save the changes.

ADDING DOCUMENT ICONS Associated documents and icons are loaded together. If you want to load other documents, you must create separate icons for each. Each of these documents should have a label that distinguishes it from the others.

To create a document icon, follow the same steps outlined for creating a program icon. However, in the Command Line box you must include the path and name of the document you want to load into the program's workspace. In the following illustration, a file in the DOCS directory called TEMP.WRI is loaded into the workspace of Windows Write.

Be sure to type a descriptive name for the icon in the Description field of the Program Item Properties box.

THE FILE MANAGER METHOD   You can add programs or documents to a Program Manager group window by placing a File Manager directory window beside it, and then copying the appropriate file in the File Manager window to the group window. Position the File Manager and Program Manager windows side-by-side, as shown in Figure 10-4, and drag the icon of the program you want from the File Manager directory window to the Program Manager group window. In Figure 10-4, the Cardfile program in the WIN3 directory is copied to a group window called Databases.

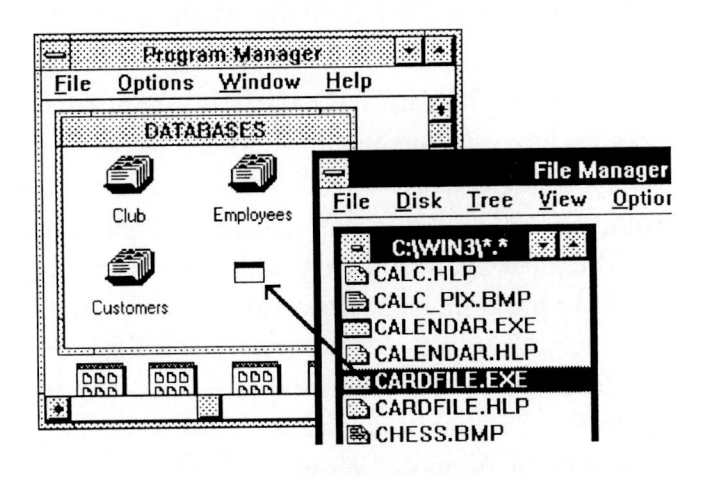

FIGURE 10-4.   The Program Manager and the File Manager can be placed side-by-side for easy copying of programs to group windows

After moving the file, click on its new icon in the group window and then choose the Properties option from the File menu. When the Program Item Properties dialog box appears, rename the icon appropriately in the Description field, and then add the document filename to the end of the text in the command line. In this example, all icons in the Databases window are designed to open different index files in the workspace of the Cardfile program, so you must add the appropriate file.

THE WINDOWS SETUP METHOD You can use the SETUP utility on the Program Manager's Main menu to add program icons to any of your group windows. It has the ability to search your entire drive or individual directories for programs and provides a quick way to set up many programs simultaneously.

Double-click on SETUP to start the program, and then choose Set Up Applications from the Options menu on the Windows Setup dialog box. SETUP asks if you want to search all drives, the path only, or specific drives, as shown here:

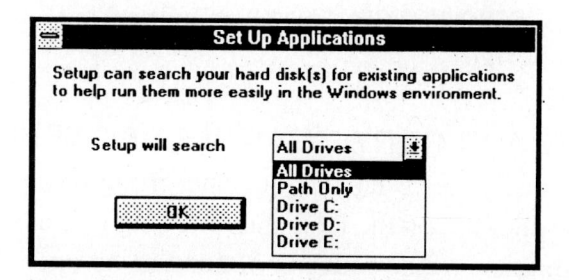

Depending on which search method you select, a screen similar to that shown in Figure 10-5 appears. The programs on the left are those found by SETUP. You can click on any of these to set them up for use with Windows. Note that you can select more than one item at a time. When you have selected all the items you want set up, click on the Add button. You can choose to add them all by clicking on the Add All button. To remove a program you added by mistake, highlight it and click the Remove button.

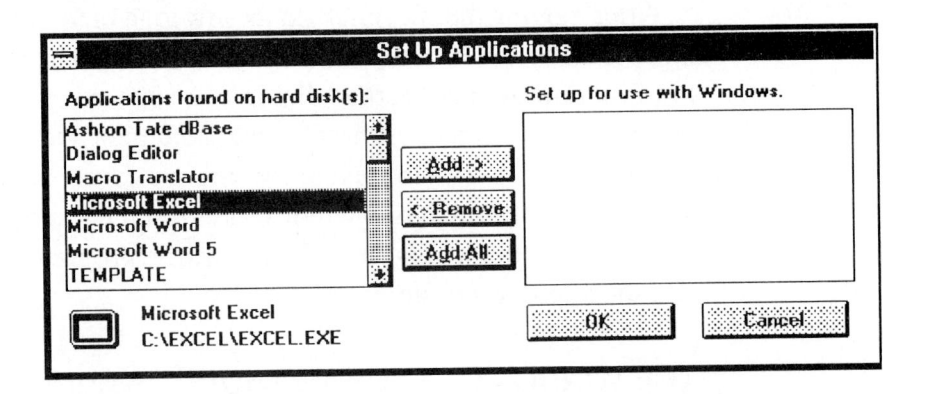

FIGURE 10-5. The SETUP program installs startup icons for any program it finds on your hard drive

When you are done, click on the OK button to have SETUP create the icons in the Program Manager. SETUP adds the icons to either the non-Windows Application group or the Windows Application group. You can then use the copy method described in the next section to copy these programs into group windows of your own design.

MOVING AND COPYING ITEMS BETWEEN GROUPS

You can easily move icons from one group to another with the mouse by clicking on the icon and dragging it to another window. The destination window does not need to be open, but you may want to open it so you can place the icon. By default, items are moved when you drag them to another window. If you want to copy an icon (make a duplicate of it) to another window, press the CTRL key as you drag the icon.

If you do not have a mouse, you can select an icon using the arrow keys, and then choose either Copy or Move from the Program Manager's File menu.

You can create a duplicate of an icon within the same group by pressing CTRL while you drag the icon to another location on the current window. When you let up on the CTRL key and mouse, a duplicate of the icon appears. Select Properties from the Program Manager File menu to give the copied icon new properties.

Running Applications

11

RUNNING APPLICATIONS UNDER WINDOWS

Ways to Start an Application
Types of Applications
Using Program Information Files

This chapter discusses how to start and use applications. By now, you are familiar with several ways to start an application. Still others are discussed here, including those used to start non-Windows applications.

Most non-Windows applications will run without a problem, but if problems occur, this chapter will help you resolve them. Part III of this book has additional information on each of Windows' operating modes.

WAYS TO START AN APPLICATION

The Program Manager and the File Manager both have methods for starting applications. Some of these methods were discussed in previous chapters but are reviewed here for your convenience. Applications can be started from the Program Manager by clicking on icons in group windows or by selecting the DOS prompt and working at the DOS level. Applications can be run in the File Manager by directly executing a program file, Program Information File, or .BAT file, or by using the Run option on the File Manager File menu. Each of these methods is discussed in the following sections.

Using the Program Manager

To start an application from a group window in the Program Manager, you need to add the program to a group as an icon. The procedure for doing this was covered in Chapter 10. To start a program, open its group window and double-click on its icon. If you use the keyboard, open the appropriate group window, select a program with the arrow keys, and then press (ENTER).

The Program Manager allows you to create icons for programs themselves or icons for documents that load at the same time an associated program is started. For more information, see Chapter 10.

Using the DOS Prompt

The DOS prompt is an icon in the Windows Main window that loads a copy of the DOS command interpreter while Windows stays resident in the background. At the DOS prompt, you can execute many DOS commands and programs as you normally do. You may need to use the DOS mode if you are attempting to run non-Windows applications which will be discussed later.

To start the DOS prompt, double-click on its icon in the Main window of the Program Manager. You should refer to your DOS manual for more information about working in this mode if you are not familiar with it.

To switch back to Windows, press **ALT-ESC** until the correct window appears. To exit the DOS prompt completely, type **EXIT** at the DOS command prompt.

You should use some caution when running the DOS prompt. For example, you might want to save all open documents before attempting to run unfamiliar programs from the DOS prompt. Some non-Windows applications may freeze your system so it may be best to close all Windows applications before using the DOS prompt.

You should never run the DOS CHKDSK /F (Check Disk) command while Windows is running. Any commands that modify DOS File Allocation Tables should be run only at the DOS level after you have completely exited from Windows.

Using the File Manager Direct Execution Method

The File Manager offers a unique and easy way to start applications. You must first open a directory window on the directory where the application resides, then double-click on its icon. Executable programs have the extensions .COM and .EXE. Other executable files are those with the .PIF and .BAT extensions, as discussed later in this chapter.

You can also click on document files that have been associated with programs, as discussed in Chapter 7.

In some cases, a document file may not be associated with a program. You can still start the program and load the file simultaneously by dragging the file icon on top of the program icon. Windows asks if you want to start the application with the selected file as the initial file.

> **Note:** The methods described here are not meant for everyday use. If you need to start an application often, create a startup icon for it using the Program Manager.

Using the File Manager Run Option

Applications can be started in the File Manager using the method just described, or by using the Run option of the File menu. The Run option displays the dialog box shown here:

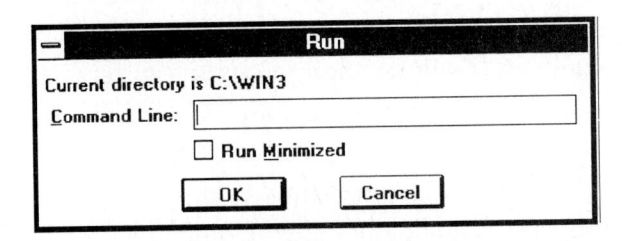

[Run dialog box: Current directory is C:\WIN3, Command Line field, Run Minimized checkbox, OK and Cancel buttons]

You can type the full path and name of a program you want to start in the Command Line field.

The Run option offers a convenient way to run an application outside of the current directory. You must type the path to the applications directory in the Command Line field. For example, to start dBASE in the DBASE directory of drive D, you would type **D:\DBASE\DBASE.EXE**. You can also specify the name of a file to open when the program starts. For example, to start a reporting program after dBASE is loaded, type **D:\DBASE\DBASE.EXE REPORTS.PRG**.

> **Note:** Use the Run option to start only those programs you run occasionally; programs you run often should be added to the Program Manager windows as an icon.

TYPES OF APPLICATIONS

While not every software program is designed to run with Microsoft Windows, you should attempt to run them in the Windows environment because it offers some benefits. For example, you can quickly load and switch to other applications and, in most cases, transfer information between applications.

Most applications written for DOS will run from the Windows environment, but a non-Windows program may have trouble running with Windows. If so, you can create or edit a *Program Information File* (PIF) for the program. This file supplies Windows with advanced information about the program, including its memory requirements, program parameters, and program directory location. Each non-Windows program can have its own PIF file, which is created or edited with the PIF editor included with Windows.

Applications designed to work with Windows use memory differently than do non-Windows applications. Windows applications are very generous with memory. Each application makes room for additional applications by giving up a portion of its own memory allocation. Non-Windows applications, on the other hand, are selfish with memory. They do not share it with other applications and, in the process, limit the total number of applications you can run at one time. These applications may also cause problems like system lock-ups, so it's a good idea to experiment with them before attempting to run them with your other Windows programs.

The sections that follow describe the four types of applications you can run under Windows, as outlined here:

- *Windows 3 applications*. Applications designed to run with Windows 3.

- *Pre-Windows 3 applications.* Applications designed to run with previous versions of Windows.

- *Non-Windows applications.* Applications that are not specifically designed to work with Windows, but will probably work with Windows using special considerations. Transferring information from non-Windows applications to other applications requires special procedures.

- *Memory-resident software.* Software that loads and stays in memory, such as Borland's Sidekick or software drivers used to handle special hardware or network support.

Each of these applications has its own special operating characteristics that you may need to consider when running the program, especially if you are running multiple applications under Windows. Refer to the appropriate section if you are having problems with an application.

Windows 3 Applications

Many applications are designed specifically to work with Windows 3, and many more are being introduced. In addition, many older Windows applications are being redesigned to take advantage of the new features of Windows 3. Windows' specific applications are designed to use the Windows graphic interface you have been introduced to in previous chapters. Features such as pull-down menus, resizable windows, and data transfer are taken advantage of and work the same as they do in other Windows applications like Windows Write and Windows Notepad.

Windows' specific applications are also aware of how memory is used in the Windows environment. They know how to share memory if you start applications in other windows. Alternatively, if you have plenty of extended memory, they know how to use that memory and share it with other applications.

You should encounter no problems running Windows 3 applications because they were written to work with all its features. You may need to refer to your application owner's manual to learn about any special loading instructions that may be required. In most cases, an icon will be created in the Program Manager for the application and it will be configured to work in the best possible way with your hardware. If an icon has not been created, you may need to use the SETUP program, as discussed in Chapter 10.

Pre-Windows 3 Applications

Windows 3 is a different product than previous versions of Windows because of its additional features and its ability to handle more memory. Many programs are being introduced to run in the Windows 3 environment, and many older Windows applications are being redesigned to work with it. If you have applications designed to work with older versions of Windows, first try to get an updated version of the application that works with Windows 3. If an update is not available, you can try the techniques discussed here to get it to work.

CHECKING THE VERSION You can tell if an application is designed for older versions of Windows by attempting to run it in Windows Standard mode or 386 Enhanced mode. To start Windows in Standard mode, type **WIN /S**. To start Windows in 386 Enhanced mode, type **WIN /3**.

Remember, you must have at least an 80286-based system with 1MB of memory to run the Standard mode and at least an 80386 system to run the 386 Enhanced mode. The 386 Enhanced mode requires 2MB of memory to run at its best. You can force the 386 Enhanced mode with less memory, but the system will run slower.

If your screen displays an Application Compatibility Warning dialog box, the application was not designed for use with Windows 3. Although you may be able to start the application and run it normally, it is more likely that the application will run abnormally and possibly crash your system. You then should try running the application in Real mode, as described next.

RUNNING PRE-WINDOWS 3 APPLICATIONS UNDER WINDOWS 3 As previously mentioned, you can attempt to run a pre-Windows 3 application in Standard or 386 Enhanced mode, but problems may occur. If you encounter problems, run the applications in Real mode on your system. To do this, you must first exit Windows if it is already started, and then start Windows in Real mode by typing **WIN /R**. You now can start the application as normal.

You may notice several problems with older Windows applications. For example, some menus and dialog boxes may not display fonts correctly, or an application may not display its colors correctly.

When Windows is running in Real mode, you may need to make alterations in the way your system uses memory. For example, the program may require expanded memory, which you may have disabled in preference for extended memory. For more information on running in Real mode, see Chapter 19.

HOW TO TRANSFER DATA If you had to resort to Real mode to run your older Windows application under Windows 3, you must follow the steps described here to transfer data from your Real mode programs to those that run under Standard or 386 Enhanced mode.

Start your Real mode application and cut or copy the information you want to transfer to the Clipboard. Then open the Clipboard and save the information to a file using the Save As option on the File menu of the Clipboard. Next, exit Windows and start it in the Standard or 386 Enhanced mode. You then can open the Clipboard and use the Open option on the File menu to retrieve the object you just saved. Finally, use the standard copy and paste techniques to get the object into your application.

Non-Windows Applications

Non-Windows applications were written by programmers who did not have Windows in mind. The application does not use the Windows interface or memory in the same way Windows-specific applications do. However, in most cases these applications also can run under Windows, with two minor differences:

- Standard applications may run in a window, or they may use the entire screen as they would if started from the DOS level.

- The commands for cutting and pasting between applications are different.

If you can run the 386 Enhanced mode, you probably can run a non-Windows application in a window of its own, as shown in Figure 11-1. While not all of the Windows pull-down menu features will be available in the window, you can still minimize, maximize, and size the window, as well as cut and paste between it and other windows. Figure 11-1 shows the Control menu for a non-Windows application running in a 386 Enhanced window. It has the normal menu options, as well as options for cutting and pasting, which are discussed later in this chapter. Notice that the Edit option opens a submenu that contains the Clipboard functions.

If you run a non-Windows application in Real mode or Standard mode, it takes up the entire screen rather than a single window. It does have a Control menu similar to that shown in Figure 11-1. This menu does not have the Settings option, which is only available in 386 Enhanced mode. To switch between applications, use the ALT-ESC key method.

values. However, if your application does not run properly, you must create a PIF or edit an existing PIF. PIFs may come with your non-Windows applications, in which case you should copy them from the application's disk set to your Windows directory.

PIFs also are created by the Windows SETUP program when you install Windows. As explained in Chapter 2, the SETUP program searches your hard drive for programs and then creates and stores PIFs for those programs in the Windows directory. You can also run SETUP at any time to do this, as explained in Chapter 10. The SETUP program creates PIFs only for those programs it recognizes, which are typically the most popular DOS-based programs. SETUP still allows you to install programs it does not recognize, but you may need to create your own PIFs.

Instructions for creating and editing PIFs are given in Part III of this book. Since the PIF editor options are similar for Real mode and Standard mode, they are both covered in Chapter 20. If you are operating in Real mode, read Chapter 19, and then refer to Chapter 20 for information on creating PIFs. If you are running in Standard mode, refer to Chapter 20 only. Those running in 386 Enhanced mode should refer to Chapter 21.

12

WINDOWS DESKTOP ACCESSORIES

Notepad
Calculator
Calendar
Cardfile
Recorder

This chapter shows you how to use the basic Windows accessories—Notepad, Calculator, Calendar, Cardfile, and Recorder. The accessories have many of the same menu options in common. Refer to Chapter 5 for a discussion of document loading, saving, editing, and printing techniques.

For your convenience, basic editing techniques are reviewed in the discussion of the Notepad accessory. You may want to review this section for descriptions of techniques used to jump through your document's text and to select text for editing or formatting.

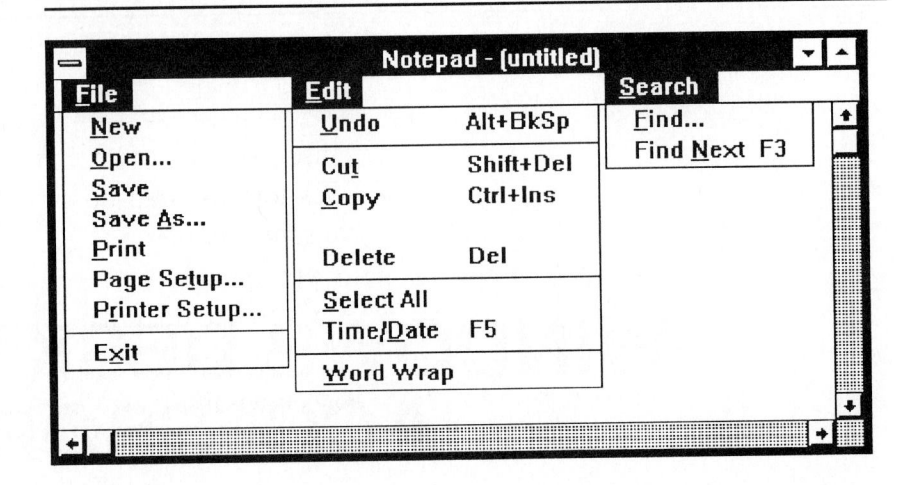

FIGURE 12-1. The Notepad window with its menus open

NOTEPAD

Notepad is a simple text editor designed for writing quick, non-formatted notes or messages. You can also use it to edit files used by DOS and Windows, such as batch files.

Startup and Overview

Start Notepad by clicking on its icon in the Program Manager, or by clicking on a document icon associated with it. The Notepad window opens with a basic workspace similar to that in Figure 12-1, which shows the following menus:

File	Used to open existing files, which have the extension .TXT. You can also save and print files using the techniques discussed in Chapter 5.
Edit	Has the standard Clipboard commands, including Select All, which allows you to

select all the text for copying or cutting to the Clipboard. The Time/Date option stamps the time and date at the location of the insertion point. The Word Wrap option causes text to wrap automatically at the right screen border.

Search   Lets you quickly locate and jump to text in the Notepad document.

The Help menu item is not shown in Figure 12-1; it is common to all menus and was discussed in Chapter 5.

Notepad creates standard ASCII text files that are saved without control codes or other formatting characters. You can usually merge Notepad files into any application, transfer them with a modem over telephone lines, or copy them to disk and give them to your associates who can read them with any DOS-based word processor.

Since Notepad takes up less space than a full-fledged word processor, you can leave it open all the time for quickly writing notes as you work with other applications. You can even open multiple copies of Notepad to help you juggle multiple blocks of text.

Notepad has a Time Log feature that lets you create a file for logging your activities. Every time you open the log file, it inserts a new date and time and then allows you to type an entry. The date, time, and text entries are saved for the next session. You can print the log at any time or clear it to start a new one.

Writing and Editing in Notepad

There is nothing hard about using Notepad; you simply start typing. You can use all of the keys on your keyboard, including (TAB), (BACKSPACE), and the direction keys. One thing to be aware of is that the (TAB) key indents the equivalent of five characters, but tabs are deleted as if they are one character. No characters appear on the screen to designate the placement of tabs as in some word processing packages, just blank space.

THE WORD WRAP OPTION The Notepad window can be resized as you see fit, but even with the window at its maximum width, the text may jump to the left when you type up against the right window wall. If this is inconvenient or distracting, you can choose to wrap text by selecting the Word Wrap option on the Edit menu. With Word Wrap on, the text you type will jump down to the next line when you hit the right window wall. If you are in the middle of typing a word that does not fit, Notepad moves the whole word to the next line.

If Word Wrap is off, you can type lines up to 160 characters in width. The horizontal scroll bar appears to let you scroll left and right in the text.

REVIEWING YOUR DOCUMENT Once you have typed the text of your document, you may want to review it by scrolling up and down or left and right in the document. You can use the following key combinations to move about in the document:

Arrow keys	Scroll in any direction, one character or line at a time
CTRL-RIGHT ARROW	Jumps to next word
CTRL-LEFT ARROW	Jumps to previous word
PGUP or PGDN	Scrolls up or down one window full of text or options
CTRL-PGUP	If the Word Wrap option is off and text extends past the left border, press this key combination to scroll left one window
CTRL-PGDN	If the Word Wrap option is off and text extends past the right border, press this

	key combination to scroll right one window
`HOME`	Jumps to the beginning of a line
`END`	Jumps to the end of a line
`CTRL-HOME`	Jumps to the beginning of a document
`CTRL-END`	Jumps to the end of a document

SEARCHING FOR TEXT If you want to search for a particular block of text, choose the Find option on the Search menu. The following dialog box appears:

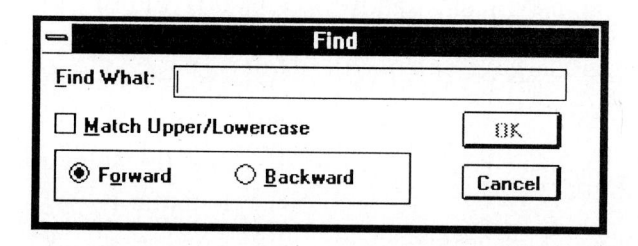

```
┌──────────────── Find ────────────────┐
│ Find What: [                        ] │
│                                       │
│ ☐ Match Upper/Lowercase    [  OK  ]   │
│                                       │
│ ⦿ Forward   ○ Backward    [ Cancel ]  │
└───────────────────────────────────────┘
```

Type the text you want to find in the Find What text box. You can narrow a search by specifying a search for only text exactly matching the upper- and lowercase characters you type. You can also click on either the Forward or Backward button to choose the search direction through the text.

EDITING YOUR DOCUMENT You can use the Clipboard options on the Edit menu to cut or copy parts of your text and paste them elsewhere in the document. To select a block of text, use the text selection techniques listed here. Each key combination in this list extends the selection from the position of the insertion point, so you may want to reposition it before pressing the selection keys. The insertion point acts as an anchor for the highlight.

`SHIFT-DOWN ARROW`	Extends the selection to the next line

`SHIFT-UP ARROW`	Extends the selection to the previous line
`SHIFT-END`	Extends the selection to the end of the line
`SHIFT-HOME`	Extends the selection to the beginning of the line
`SHIFT-PGDN`	Extends the selection down one window
`SHIFT-PGUP`	Extends the selection up one window
`CTRL-SHIFT-RIGHT ARROW`	Extends the selection to the next word
`CTRL-SHIFT-LEFT ARROW`	Extends the selection to the previous word
`CTRL-SHIFT-END`	Extends the selection to the end of the document
`CTRL-SHIFT-HOME`	Extends the selection to the beginning of the document

Once you have selected a text block, you can press `SHIFT-DEL` to cut it or `CTRL-INS` to copy it to the Clipboard. Reposition the cursor to the location you want to paste and press `SHIFT-INS`. You can also use the options on the Edit menu to cut, copy, and paste text.

Printing and Saving Your Document

To print a Notepad document, select the Print command from the File menu. You may want to set various page-printing features by selecting the Page Setup option on the File menu before you print. The Page Setup dialog box allows you to set new margins and create a header or footer for your document. Refer to Chapter 5 for more details. You can choose a different printer, different paper size, or other options by choosing the Printer Setup option on the

File menu. Follow the procedures outlined in Chapter 8 for changing the options on the printer dialog boxes.

The width of the printed text is determined by the margins you specify in the Page Setup dialog box and the width of the paper. The text will be the width of the paper, less the left and right margins. For example, if you select 14-inch paper and set left and right margins of 1 inch, the width of the text will be 12 inches.

> **Note:** If you select the Word Wrap option on the Edit menu, the text prints as wide as the Notepad window. If the Word Wrap option is not set, the text width is determined by the margins and paper width.

Notepad documents are saved as standard ASCII text files with the .TXT extension. Choose the Save or Save As option from the File menu to save the document, as discussed in Chapter 5. Remember, you can select another drive or directory when saving the file, and you can save the file with an extension other than .TXT by specifying your own extension. Be sure to separate the filename from the extension with a period.

The Notepad Time-Log Feature

Notepad allows you to create a special file called a Time-Log. When you open this file, it automatically adds the time and date to the last line of text, so you can make quick notes related to the current time and date.

The only requirement for creating such a file is to type **.LOG** on the first line of the document. Every time you open the file, the time and date currently set in your system is added to a line. You can then type text below it, such as a chargeable activity, and save the file for future use. You can have as many Time-Log files as you want as long as each log file is given a unique name.

CALCULATOR

The Windows Calculator comes in two versions, standard and scientific. The standard Calculator can be used for normal keypad-like calculations. It has a memory feature for storing and accumulating numbers. The scientific Calculator has advanced features such as number base conversions, statistical functions, and trigonometric functions.

Startup and Overview

You can select either calculator after you have loaded the calculator icon from the Program Manager Accessories window. When the calculator appears, you can choose either Scientific or Standard from its View menu. The standard calculator is shown in Figure 12-2 and the scientific calculator is shown in Figure 12-3.

The menu bars of both calculators provide copy and paste functions under the Edit menu and the Calculator selection options under the View menu. The remaining features of the calculator are its buttons.

With the mouse, you can point to any Calculator button and click. If you are using the keyboard, you can use corresponding keys on the numeric keypad or one of the function keys described later in this chapter. For example, all numbers and basic operators (+,− ,*,/,=) are available on the keyboard. The asterisk (*) is used for multiplication and the slash (/) is used for division. Be sure to press the NUMLOCK key before using the numeric keypad.

Calculations are performed in the normal way. For example, to add two numbers, click or type the first number, press the operator, type the second number, and then type the equal sign. The result appears in the calculator's display.

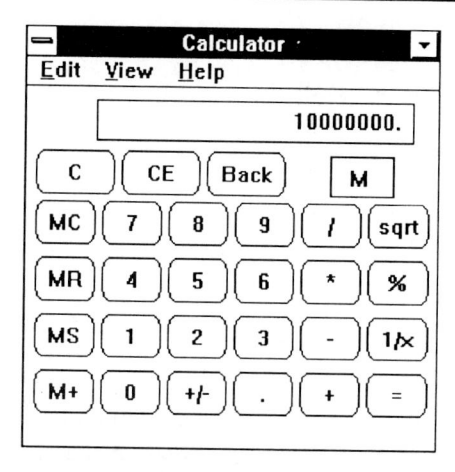

FIGURE 12-2. The standard Calculator

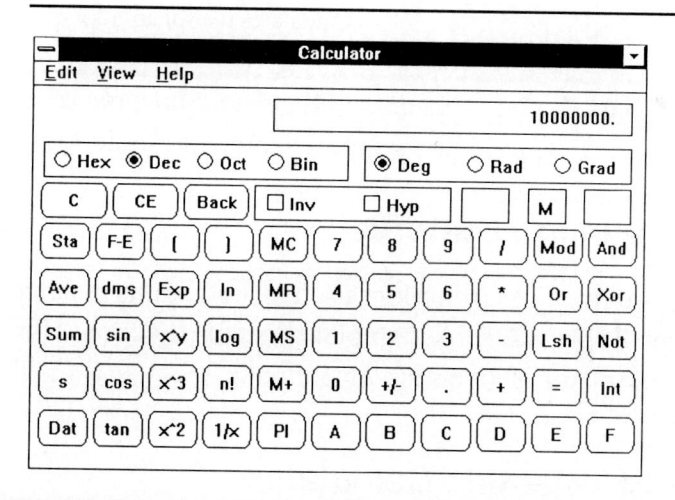

FIGURE 12-3. The scientific Calculator

Button	Key	Function
+	+	Adds
–	–	Subtracts
*	*	Multiplies
/	/	Divides
+/–	F9	Changes the sign of the displayed number
.	.	Inserts a decimal point in the displayed number
%	%	Calculates percentages
=	=	Executes an operation (or press Enter)
1/x	r	Calculates the reciprocal of the displayed number
Back	BACKSPACE	Deletes the rightmost digit
C	ESC	Clears the current calculation
CE	DELETE	Clears the displayed number
M+	CTRL-P	Adds the display value to any value already in memory
MC	CTRL-C	Clears any value stored in memory
MR	CTRL-R	Recalls the value stored in memory. The value remains in memory
MS	CTRL-M	Stores the displayed value in memory
Sqrt	@	Calculates the square root of the displayed value

TABLE 12-1. Standard Calculator Functions. (See Appendix D for scientific calculator functions.)

Calculator Function Buttons

The calculator functions used by both kinds of calculator are listed in Table 12-1. A complete list of functions for the scientific calculator is given in Appendix D.

Standard and Scientific Calculator Shared Keys

The memory keys and clear keys are common on both kinds of calculators. In addition, the Clipboard copy and paste functions available from the Edit menu can be used.

CLEAR KEYS The C (Clear) button clears all numbers from the display, whereas the CE (Clear Entry) button clears the number you are currently entering but retains the previously entered number. The Back button is used to back up one number and is the same as the (BACKSPACE) key on the keyboard.

MEMORY KEYS The calculator's memory keys are used to store a number in memory for later use or to accumulate numbers. The MS (Memory Store) button places the current value in the calculator display in memory, replacing its contents. The M+ button adds the current value in the calculator's display to the current value in memory. The MR (Memory Recall) button displays the contents of memory in the calculator's display and can be used during calculations to recall constants. The MC (Memory Clear) button clears memory.

CLIPBOARD KEYS The Calculator Edit menu has keys for copying and pasting from the Clipboard. The Copy option is used to copy a calculated result in the calculator's display and paste it to another application. You can use the Paste option to paste a number from another application. The Paste option also has some interesting features. You can create small scripts by using the paste characters shown in Table 12-2 that automate or repeat various keystrokes or calculations.

In Figure 12-4, the Notepad accessory is placed on the desktop next to the Calculator to create scripts. The scripts are copied to the Clipboard from Notepad and pasted to the Calculator. In this example, the script multiplies the contents of memory by 10 and displays the results each time it is pasted. The script shown on the Notepad uses :R to recall memory and multiplies it by 10. Then :M is used to store the new value back in memory, and the result remains in the calculator's display. Note that 100 was initially stored in the memory. By repeatedly pasting the script, an increasing value is displayed and placed in memory.

Character	Function
:	If placed before a number from 1 to 12, a function key is simulated; for example, :1 simulates F1.
:C	Equivalent to the MC (Memory Clear) button.
:E	If in decimal mode, allows entry of numbers in scientific notation. Can be followed by + or − to indicate the sign of the exponent. If in hexidecimal mode, the number "E" is specified.
:M	Equivalent to the MS (Memory Store) button.
:P	Equivalent to the M+ button. Adds the currently displayed value to memory.
:Q	Clears the display. Equivalent to the C button.
:R	Equivalent to the MR (Memory Recall) button.
\	Same as the Data button on the scientific calculator.

TABLE 12-2. Calculator Paste Characters

Of course, you can create more complicated scripts. You can even create a whole Notepad file full of scripts you use on a regular

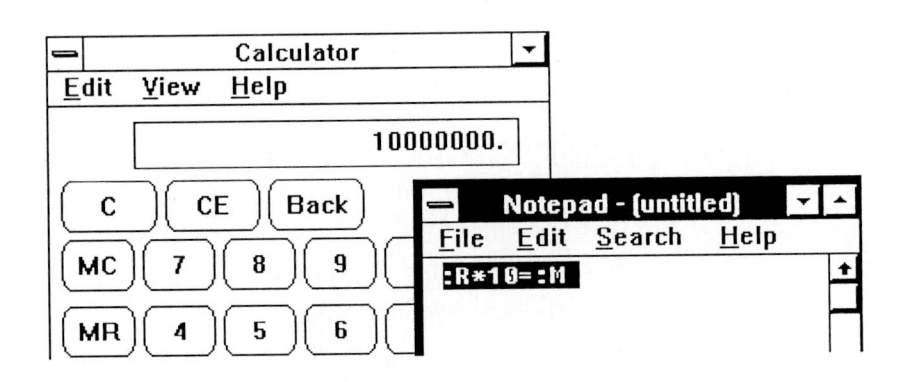

FIGURE 12-4. Notepad can be used to create Calculator scripts

basis, each of which can be preceded by a descriptive name on the same line. You can then easily highlight the script portion, copy it to the Clipboard, and paste it into the Calculator to automate many of your calculator routines.

Converting Numbers with the Scientific Calculator

The scientific calculator is normally set to operate in the base 10 number system. You can also work in binary, octal, and hexidecimal and easily convert between number systems. Notice that the scientific calculator has the characters A through F used in the hexidecimal number system.

To convert a number to another number system, first select the number system you want to convert from by clicking one of the buttons in the upper-left portion of the calculator. Enter the value, and then click the button of the number system you want to convert to. After switching to the new number system, you can choose one of the measurement settings on the upper-right portion of the calculator.

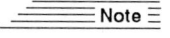

> **Note** Numbers with decimal places are changed to integers when converted to another number system.

Statistical Functions with the Scientific Calculator

The scientific calculator can perform statistical calculations such as averages and standard deviation. The Statistics Box dialog box appears when you press the Sta button on the calculator. You should move this box to the side so you can use the Calculator buttons at the same time. The box is shown here with values entered:

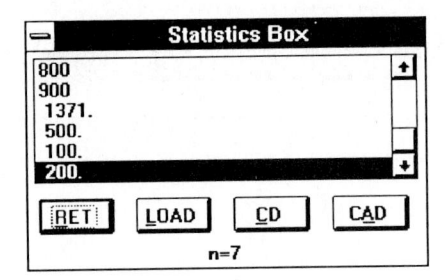

Points or values are entered into the Statistics Box by clicking on the calculator keys and pressing the Dat key after each one. The numbers appear in the box one by one. If you are using the keyboard, type **R** to press the RET (Return) key to get to the calculator, then use the numeric keypad to enter the numbers. Once the values are entered, click the Ave (average), Sum, or s (standard deviation) button.

The buttons on the Statistics Box are used as follows:

RET	Jumps to the main calculator for typing numbers
LOAD	Copy the selected Statistics Box number to theCalculator's display
CD	Delete the currently selected number
CAD	Delete all numbers

CALENDAR

The Windows Calendar provides a month-at-a-glance view of appointments and schedules and allows you to zoom in on a single day. The daily schedules allow you to add messages and set alarms on the hour, half hour, quarter hour, or any special time.

Startup and Overview

To start the Calendar, double-click on the Calendar icon in the Program Manager Accessories window. The Calendar window

```
┌─────────────────────────────────────────────────┐
│ ─        Calendar - [untitled]            ▼ ▲  │
│ File  Edit  View   Show   Alarm   Options  Help│
│  8:51 AM    ← →   Friday, January 19, 1990     │
│     9:00 AM                                  ↑ │
│    10:00                                       │
│    11:00                                       │
│    12:00 PM                                    │
│     1:00                                       │
│     2:00                                       │
│                                              ↓ │
└─────────────────────────────────────────────────┘
```

FIGURE 12-5. The Calendar window

appears similar to Figure 12-5, and can be resized to fit your desktop. Just below the menu bar are the current time and date you are viewing in the Calendar. Below that are the hourly time slots where messages and alarms can be placed. The right- and left-arrow keys are used to move horizontally on the message line. Note that you can change the hourly increment to half-hourly or quarter-hourly.

The menus of the Calendar, shown in Figure 12-6, are briefly described here:

File	Has options for creating a new Calendar, saving changes to an existing Calendar, and printing a range of dates.
Edit	Has the normal Clipboard options, as well as a Remove option that lets you remove a range of dates from the Calendar.
View	Switches between day and month view.
Show	Has options for moving up or down through the days of the Calendar. The Date option lets you enter a specific date.

ADDING SPECIAL TIMES Special times can be inserted between the time increments you have chosen. You must specify each special time individually by choosing the Special Time option from the Options menu. The following dialog box appears:

```
┌─────────────────────────────────────────┐
│ ═                Special Time            │
│ Special Time:  [9:20]    ⦿ AM   ○ PM    │
│   [Insert]   [Delete]   [Cancel]         │
└─────────────────────────────────────────┘
```

Type in the special time and click on the AM or PM button. Click on Insert to insert the new time. To remove a special time, type the time to remove in the Special Time field and then click on the Delete button.

Entering Appointments

Since Calendar displays the appointment schedule for the current day (the day set in your computer's clock), you may want to change to another day before entering appointments. When you get to the day you want, you can scroll to any time and type the text of the appointment.

CHANGING THE DAY You can change the day displayed in the appointment area in several ways. One of the easiest ways to jump to a different day in the same month is to choose Month from the View menu. You can double-click on the date you want to view.

Another method for changing days is to select one of the following options on the Show menu:

Today	Jumps to the appointment view for the current date. Use this option if you have been working on another day.

Previous	Jumps back one day. Press `CTRL-PGUP` continuously to move back one day at a time.
Next	Jumps ahead one day. Press `CTRL-PGDN` continuously to move ahead one day at a time.
Date	Displays a dialog box that lets you enter the exact date you want to jump to. Use the date format previously described when typing a date in the Show Date dialog box.

TYPING APPOINTMENTS To enter appointments, use the up- or down-arrow key, or the scroll bar to move to any time increment. You can type up to 80 characters in the message area of each appointment time. The message scrolls to the left as you type. Use the arrows at the top of the screen to move the message left or right for viewing.

The `PGUP` and `PGDN` keys can be used to move up or down one screen. You can use the `CTRL-HOME` key combination to move to the starting time, which is the time that initially appears at the top of your screen and is set using the Day Settings option on the Options menu. Press the `CTRL-END` key combination to move 12 hours past the starting time.

To edit appointments, use the arrow keys to move the insertion point to the message to be edited. You can then move to a position in a message where you want to insert new text or delete text.

NOTES AND REMINDERS Each daily appointment window has a note area at the bottom of the screen where you can type a message or note of up to three lines. The notes you type in this area are stored with the day, and each day can have its own note.

REMOVING APPOINTMENTS You can remove the appointments for an entire day or a range of days by choosing the Remove option from the Edit menu. When the Remove dialog box appears, type the beginning date in the From box and the ending date in the To box. Then choose OK to remove the days.

Setting Calendar Alarms

You can set an alarm on any time in the daily appointment window. When the alarm goes off, Calendar can alert you in several ways. If the Calendar window is active, a dialog box appears on top of it to display your message. If the alarm sound is on, you also hear a beep for a few seconds. If the Calendar window is inactive, the alarm sounds and the title bar flashes. The message is displayed when you select the window. If Calendar is reduced to an icon, the icon flashes. When you select the icon, the message is displayed but the Calendar window is not opened.

To set an alarm, move the insertion point to the appropriate time and choose the Set option on the Alarm menu. To change any of the Alarm options, choose the Controls option from the Alarm menu. The following Alarm Controls dialog box appears:

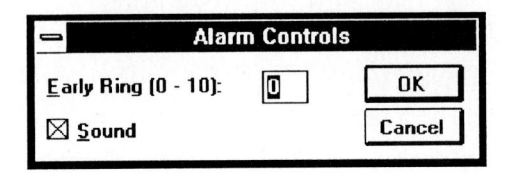

```
┌─────────────────────────────────────┐
│ ▬        Alarm Controls             │
├─────────────────────────────────────┤
│ Early Ring (0 - 10):  [0]    [ OK ] │
│ ☒ Sound                    [Cancel] │
└─────────────────────────────────────┘
```

The Alarm Controls box lets you set an early alarm. Type the amount of time, from 0 to 10 minutes, for the early warning. You can also click the Sound box to turn the alarm sound off or on.

To remove an alarm, move to the time that has an alarm you want to remove, and then select Set from the Alarm menu, which toggles the alarm off.

Marking Dates

Calendar provides a set of five marks you can use to call attention to certain dates. The marks, as shown in the following illustration, appear in the day box on the monthly overview. The Day Markings dialog box shown here can be opened by choosing Mark on the Options menu:

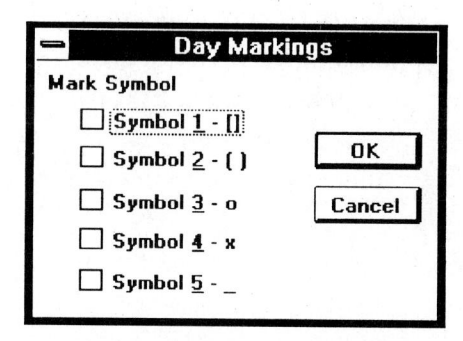

```
┌─────────────────────────────────────┐
│─            Day Markings            │
│ Mark Symbol                         │
│   ☐ Symbol 1 - []                   │
│                         ┌────────┐  │
│   ☐ Symbol 2 - ( )      │   OK   │  │
│                         └────────┘  │
│   ☐ Symbol 3 - o        ┌────────┐  │
│                         │ Cancel │  │
│   ☐ Symbol 4 - x        └────────┘  │
│   ☐ Symbol 5 - _                    │
└─────────────────────────────────────┘
```

You might want to designate immediately how you will use the marks. For example, the box (symbol 1) could be used to designate birthdays, whereas the "x" (symbol 4) could be used to designate deadlines.

To mark a day, first display the month view by selecting Month from the View menu. Click on the day you want to mark, and then choose Mark from the Options menu. Click on the mark you want to add and click on OK. To cancel a mark, use the same procedure, but click on the box that has an "X" when the Day Markings dialog box appears.

Saving and Printing Appointments

Calendar is saved like any other document, by choosing the Save option on the File menu. All Calendar files are saved with the .CAL extension, unless you specify another extension. When opening a Calendar file that has already been saved, you can click on a box called Read Only, which lets you view the Calendar but not make changes. This option can be used to prevent you from accidentally making changes to the Calendar of another user.

To print your appointment, select the Print option from the File menu. The Print dialog box allows you to specify a range of days to print. When the Print dialog box appears, type the beginning date in the From box and the ending date in the To box, and then choose OK to print the appointments. You can set margins and other printing features by choosing the Page Setup or Printer Setup option from the File menu, as discussed in Chapter 5.

CARDFILE

Cardfile is an information storage and retrieval system that resembles an index card filing system. You can place an index title at the top of every card and fill the rest of the card with text. Searches

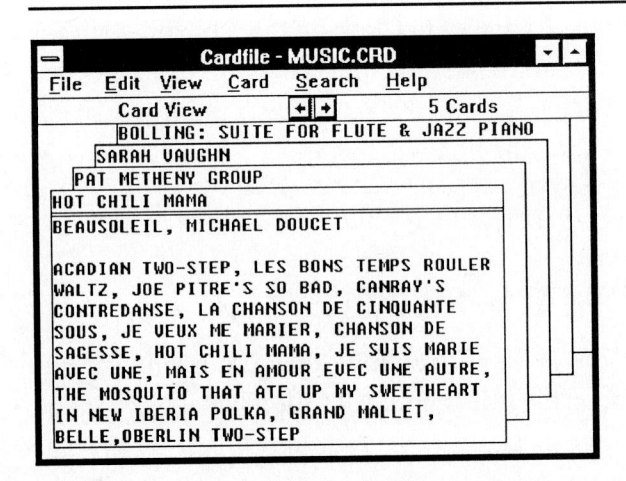

FIGURE 12-7. The Cardfile window

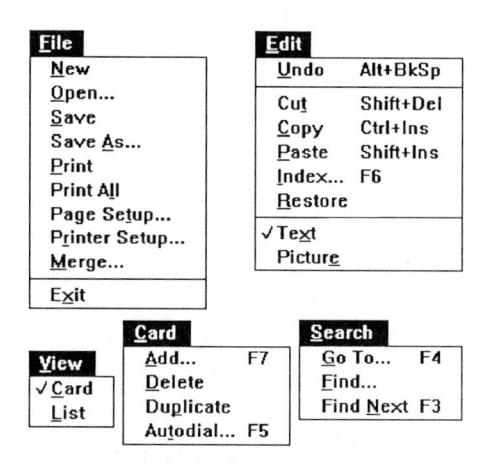

```
File                    Edit
New                     Undo     Alt+BkSp
Open...                 Cut      Shift+Del
Save                    Copy     Ctrl+Ins
Save As...              Paste    Shift+Ins
Print                   Index... F6
Print All               Restore
Page Setup...
Printer Setup...        √ Text
Merge...                Picture
Exit

          Card              Search
View      Add...    F7      Go To...    F4
√ Card    Delete            Find...
List      Duplicate         Find Next F3
          Autodial... F5
```

FIGURE 12-8. The Cardfile menus

can be done on the index title or any of the text in the text area. You can keep several different sets of index card files on your system. For example, you can keep a name and address list, a music list, or a household inventory list.

Startup and Overview

To start Cardfile, double-click on its icon in the Program Manager Accessories window. The Cardfile window appears, similar to Figure 12-7, which shows several index cards in the work area. The Cardfile menus and options, shown in Figure 12-8, are briefly described here:

File	Has most of the same options as other Windows applications, as discussed in Chapter 5. Cardfile has an additional option called Merge that allows you to merge two Cardfile indexes.

Edit	Has the standard Clipboard options. In addition, an Index option lets you edit the index field of the cards. The Text and Picture options let you specify the type of information to be placed on a card.
View	Used to view individual cards or a list of their index headings.
Card	Lets you add new cards, delete them, or duplicate them. Use the Autodial option with a name and phone number index to dial phone numbers.
Search	Lets you go to cards with the index heading you specify or to search the text area of cards for specific text.

The Cardfile window, as shown in Figure 12-7, has the standard menu bar. Under this is a status bar that shows the view type, which can be a view of the card or of just the index headers. The status bar also shows how many cards are in the stack. The left- and right-arrow keys can be used to scroll through the cards in a circular fashion, from front to back or from back to front.

The actual index cards are located in the Cardfile work area. They automatically form a stack as you add new cards. At the top of each index card is an *index header,* which can be seen in the cards further back in the stack of Figure 12-7. The index header is used to sort the cards in the stack, so the information you type in the header should reflect the way you want the cards sorted and organized. For example, in a business card index, you might want to type the profession or business activity of each person in the list, such as doctor, attorney, or broker, followed by their name. In this way, the cards are sorted into groups so you can easily locate people by their businesses or professions.

Note You might want to come up with a coding scheme to make Cardfile information easier to type and search. For example, the following codes would be useful in a business file: "D" for doctor, "A" for attorney, and "B" for broker.

Cardfile Setup and Editing

Select the New or Open option from the Cardfile File menu to start a new index or work with an existing index. Initially, new index card files have a single blank card. You must add new cards as you go along. Each card is then automatically arranged in the stack in alphabetical order according to the characters in the Index line of each card.

ADDING NEW INDEX CARDS To create new index cards for the current index file, choose the Add option on the Card menu. When the Add dialog box appears, enter the text to appear in the index header for the card and click on OK or press (ENTER). The new card appears at the top of the stack. You then can type information in its text area.

CHANGING AN INDEX HEADER If you want to change the text in an index header, choose the Index option on the Edit menu. You may want to do this to change the order of a card in the stack or to change the header of a card that has been duplicated by the Duplicate option on the Card menu.

TYPING INDEX CARD TEXT To type information in the text area of a card, make sure the card is at the top of the stack and type the text as normal. Cardfile wraps the text at the end of each line to a new line. You cannot type any more text than will fit in the text area. Remember that words in the text area can be used in a search, so you may want to include important keywords used to locate the index card and leave out any unnecessary words.

AUTOMATIC DIALING If your system is connected to a Hayes-compatible modem, you can enter a telephone number on the index header or text area of a card. Cardfile automatically prepares to dial the first number it finds in the card when you choose the Autodial option on the Card menu. When the Autodial dialog box appears on the screen, as shown here, the number is in the Number field. You can click on OK or press (ENTER) to dial the number.

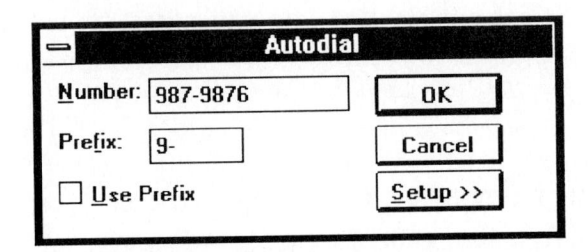

```
┌─────────────── Autodial ───────────────┐
│ Number: [987-9876]        [   OK    ]  │
│ Prefix: [9-      ]        [ Cancel  ]  │
│ □ Use Prefix              [ Setup >>]  │
└────────────────────────────────────────┘
```

> **Note** The phone number must always be the first number to appear on a card. Other numbers may be typed after it.

If you click the Setup button, you can select a Tone or Pulse dial, the communications port of the modem, and the baud rate. Refer to Chapter 9 or Chapter 15.

Viewing and Searching for Cards

Once you have a stack of index cards, you can start browsing or searching through them. Cards can be viewed as a list that only displays the index card header, or you can view cards in a stack.

CHANGING THE VIEW To view the list of cards, select the List option on the View menu. This produces a compact listing of the card headers. You can then scroll through the list to highlight a particular card. Choose the Card option on the View menu to return to the stack view with the selected card on top of the stack.

BRINGING A CARD TO THE FRONT OF THE STACK The right or left arrow at the top of the Cardfile workspace can be used to browse through the card list. Think of the cards as forming a circular file; as you browse you eventually come back around to the beginning card.

Another way to bring a card to the front of the card stack is to click on the index heading of those cards lower in the stack. If you are using the keyboard, press (CTRL) while you type the first letter in the index heading of the card you want to see.

You can use the typing method in a more specific way. Select the Go To option on the Search menu to display the Go To dialog box. You can type as much of the index header text as you feel will narrow the search down to exactly the card you want to see.

SEARCHING FOR TEXT The text area of index cards can contain freeform text you can search to locate a specific topic beyond what has been typed in the index header. For example, assume you have a card file of your music collection in which the index header information is used to classify the music by type, such as jazz, classical, or rock. The text area might then contain information about musicians or song titles. By using the Cardfile text search option, you can search the text area for a particular musician or the name of a song.

To search the cards, choose the Find option on the Search menu. When the dialog box appears, enter the keyword you want to search for and click on OK or press (ENTER). The first card that matches is displayed on the screen. If further matches are possible, you can choose the Find Next option on the Search menu or press (F3).

Manipulating Cards and Card Information

Using standard Clipboard procedures, you can copy or move information from one card to another in an index card stack, as outlined in this section.

PASTING GRAPHICS INTO CARDS You can easily paste graphics information on a card using the Clipboard commands, but first you must bring the card that is to receive the picture to the top of the stack and then choose the Picture option on the Edit menu. Next, choose the Paste option on the Edit menu to paste the picture, assuming you have already placed the picture on the Clipboard.

When the picture appears, you can drag it to any position on the card. Finally, choose Text from the Edit menu to return to text mode and permanently position the picture.

Note: You can create a scrapbook of graphics images by pasting the pictures you use often onto individual cards in a card file. When you need an image while working in another application, you can start Cardfile, locate the card containing the image, and copy it to the Clipboard.

DUPLICATING A CARD You may have a card that contains information needed to create a new card. You can duplicate the card and then make changes to its duplicate if necessary. One use for duplications is when creating name and address cards that have the same city and ZIP code. Simply make as many copies as you need, and then use the Index option on the Edit menu to change the index header for each card.

RESTORING A CARD You can restore cards to their original condition after an edit if you change your mind or make a mistake. Choose the Restore option on the Edit menu. You cannot restore a card if you move it from the front of the stack.

DELETING CARDS You can delete cards by bringing them to the front of the stack and then choosing Delete from the Card menu. You are asked to confirm the card's deletion. Remember that before deleting a card you can copy useful information from it to other cards by using the Clipboard functions.

MERGING CARD FILES You can merge the cards in one file to the cards in another file by using the Merge option on the File menu. The File Merge dialog box is similar to the Open dialog box in that it displays a list of card files in the current directory, but File Merge lets you specify another directory or the exact path and name of the file you want to merge.

When two card files are merged, their contents are sorted in alphabetical order on the index header as normal. You may want to save the merged file under a new name using the Save As option on the File menu.

Printing and Saving Card Files

Cards can be printed in three ways. Select Card on the View menu, and then choose Print from the File menu to print only the top card. Choose Print All to print all the cards. If you just want to print the index headers as a single listing, choose List from the Edit menu and then select Print All.

Card files are saved with the .CRD extension, unless you specify another extension. You can create and save as many card files as you want.

RECORDER

The Recorder allows you to record a series of keystrokes you use often and then play them back at any time by pressing a `CTRL` key or `SHIFT` key sequence. The key sequence you record is called a *macro*. Several macros can be stored in a file, and you can store several different files. Each file might contain macros to work with specific applications like Write and Paintbrush.

For example, you might use a macro to record a selection from a pull-down menu in an application such as Windows Write. Write has a Character menu you can pull down to change the font of the currently highlighted text. You can choose Fonts on the Character menu to open a Fonts dialog box, on which you can select the font type and font size. This process becomes tedious if you need to change the fonts often. Using Recorder, you can automate the whole menu selection process and assign it to a single key sequence.

Recorder does have some peculiarities. Mouse movements do not record well because window sizes and click points made during a recording session may not be the same when you play the macro back at a later time. It is best to use the `ALT` key sequences to make selections from menus. Keep in mind that the conditions under which you record a macro will not always be the same when you play the macro back. For best results, limit your macros to menu selection in specific applications. Switching windows while recording poses logistics problems that may not be worth trying to overcome. If you do need to switch applications, record a separate macro for use in each application.

Startup and Overview

The Recorder is started by double-clicking on the Recorder icon in the Program Manager Accessories window. A window similar

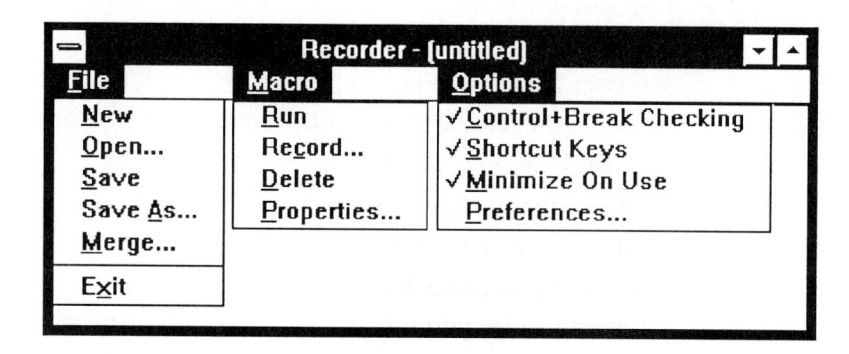

```
┌─────────────────────────────────────────────────────────┐
│ ▬                   Recorder - (untitled)          ▼ ▲ │
│ File        Macro           Options                    │
│  New         Run             √ Control+Break Checking  │
│  Open...     Record...       √ Shortcut Keys           │
│  Save        Delete          √ Minimize On Use         │
│  Save As...  Properties...     Preferences...          │
│  Merge...                                              │
│  Exit                                                  │
└─────────────────────────────────────────────────────────┘
```

FIGURE 12-9. The Recorder and its pull-down menus

to that shown in Figure 12-9 appears. For your convenience this figure shows each Recorder pull-down menu. They are outlined here.

File	Has the standard options for opening and saving macro files. You can also merge macros from other files into your current file.
Macro	Used to run, delete, or change the properties of an existing macro. The Record option is used to record a new macro.
Options	Has options for settings and preferences of Recorder and the macro recording process.

The following section presents an example of recording a macro to select fonts in Windows Write and explains the macro features and menus.

Recording a Macro

In the example that follows, you will create a macro for easily selecting the 24-point Roman font on the Windows Write Fonts dialog box. If your system does not have a Roman font, choose a suitable substitute from the dialog box.

SETUP TO RECORD Before you begin recording a macro, make sure everything is set up the way it will be later when you play the macro back. Recorder begins recording all keystrokes and mouse movements immediately, so you do not want to include things like moving or closing windows that will not necessarily be on the desktop during playback.

For this example, double-click on the Windows Write icon in the Main group window and the Recorder icon in the Accessories group window. Minimize all windows except the Write window, but make sure the Recorder icon can be seen at the bottom of the desktop so you can select it in a minute.

Make the Write window active. This is important because Recorder will switch you to the most recently active window when you start recording. Do not include the keystrokes to switch among windows in your macro, because these would then be replayed when you use the macro and would switch you out of the window you are trying to play the macro in. As previously mentioned, Recorder can be tricky to use because you need to consider what the desktop will be like when you play back macros.

OPENING THE RECORDER DIALOG BOX Next, double-click on the Recorder icon to open the Recorder window. Choose the Record option on the Macro menu to display the Record Macro dialog box shown in Figure 12-10. This dialog box contains several fields you can fill out to make the macro run in various ways. For this simple macro example, you need to fill in only two fields. In the Récord Macro Name box, type **Roman 24 Font/Write**, and in

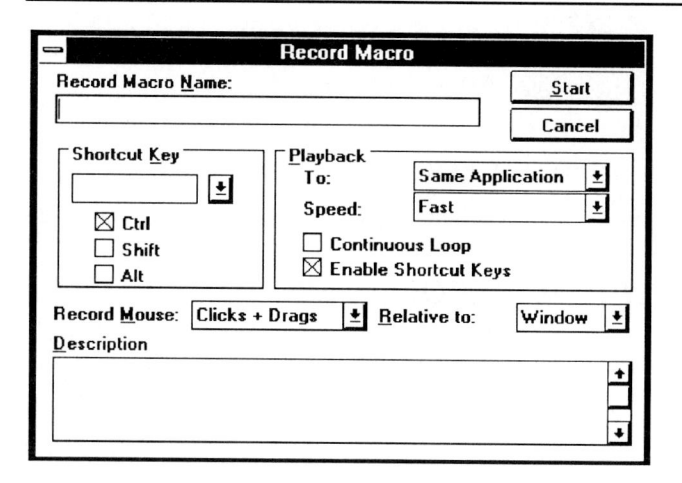

FIGURE 12-10. The Record Macro dialog box

the Shortcut Key box, press (F1). Make sure the Ctrl box is checked in the Shortcut Key box. This gives a descriptive title to the action of the macro and assigns it to (CTRL-F1).

RECORDING To start recording, click on the Start button or press (ENTER). Recorder immediately displays the Write window (assuming it was the most recently active) and minimizes itself to a flashing icon, indicating that it is in record mode. From this point on, all keystrokes are recorded and will be replayed in your macro. You must press the following key sequence to record the key sequence for the macro. Do not use the mouse to make the selections.

1. Press (ALT-C) to select the Character menu.

2. Type **F** to select the Fonts option.

3. Type **ROMAN** in the Font Name field.

4. Tab 3 times to the Point Size field and type **24**.

5. Press (ENTER) to accept the changes.

STOP AND SAVE THE MACRO RECORDING   To end recording, press (CTRL-BREAK). The following dialog box appears:

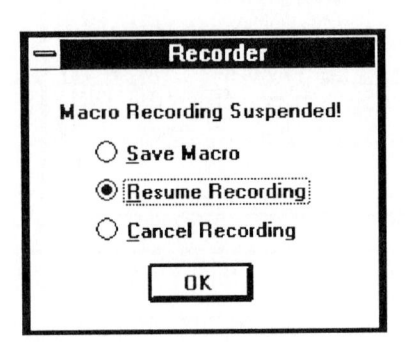

```
┌─ Recorder ──────────────┐
│                         │
│ Macro Recording Suspended! │
│   ○ Save Macro          │
│   ⦿ Resume Recording    │
│   ○ Cancel Recording    │
│     ┌────┐              │
│     │ OK │              │
│     └────┘              │
└─────────────────────────┘
```

You should click on the Save Macro and OK buttons to save the macro. If you click on the Recorder window, you will see the (CTRL-F1) macro listed in the window. The macro is available for use in your current Windows session. To save it for future sessions, you must save the macro to a file by using the Save As option on the File menu. Since the macro is for Windows Write, you may want to name the file Write. Recorder adds the extension .REC to all saved macro files. Keep in mind that you can add a number of other macros to this file at any time.

PLAYING BACK THE MACRO   You can try out the macro by switching to the Write window. Type a couple lines of text, but first switch to another font so you can test the macro. Select Font from the Character menu, and then choose Courier or some other type style from the Fonts box and click on OK. Next, highlight a portion of the text and press (CTRL-F1). The highlighted text should convert immediately to 24-point Roman.

You can also open the Recorder window and use the Run option on the Macro menu to play back the macro. Recorder immediately switches to the most recently active window and plays the macro.

> **Note** If you need to stop a macro, press `CTRL-BREAK`.

More About Recorder

The Record Macro dialog box offers the following options and boxes that will affect how your macro runs:

- *Record Macro Name.* Type a descriptive name for the macro that will differentiate it from other macros in the same file.

- *Shortcut Key box.* Click on the Ctrl, Shift, or Alt button for the key combination you want. Then click on the down-arrow button to see a list of possible key combinations. The Alt button is not recommended since it is used to access Windows menus.

- *Playback box.* The following options can be set in the Playback box to specify how the macro should be played back:

    To   You can play the macro back to the same application it was recorded in or to any application.

    Speed   You can play back the macro at fast speed or at the speed it was recorded. In some cases, you may want to play back a series of keystrokes at the same speed they were recorded for use as a demonstration.

    Continuous Loop   If you check this box, the macro continuously repeats until you press `CTRL-BREAK`.

| Enable Shortcut Keys | If you check this box, you can include the shortcut keys of other macros in the macro you are recording. |

- *Record Mouse box.* Used to set how mouse movements and clicks are recorded, as described here:

Ignore Mouse	If you select this option, all mouse movements you make are ignored. You can set this option if you want to record macros for other machines that do not have the same video graphics resolution.
Clicks+Drags	All keystrokes and mouse movements are recorded if a button is pressed.
Everything	Set this option if you want to record all mouse movements and clicks, even if a mouse button is not pressed.

- *Relative To box.* Used to select whether the macro will be recorded relative to the entire screen or a window. Choose Screen when running full-screen applications.

- *Description box.* Used to enter a brief description of the macro for future reference or to explain its use to other users.

If you need to change any of these options on a previously recorded macro, select the Properties option on the Macro menu. If you want any of the settings to be the default settings, choose the Preferences option on the Options menu and make the same settings.

13

WINDOWS WRITE

Startup and Overview
Write Concepts
Typing and Editing in Write
Other Editing Features
Formatting in Write
Saving and Printing Your Document

Write is a word processing program for writing letters, reports, and other documents. Unlike Notepad, which is a simple text editor designed for writing quick, non-formatted notes or messages, Write allows you to format text, change the indentation of paragraphs, insert and manipulate graphics, and perform many other advanced tasks. But you can use your Notepad skills when you use Write, because their basic operations are the same when it comes to typing, editing, selecting, and moving through text.

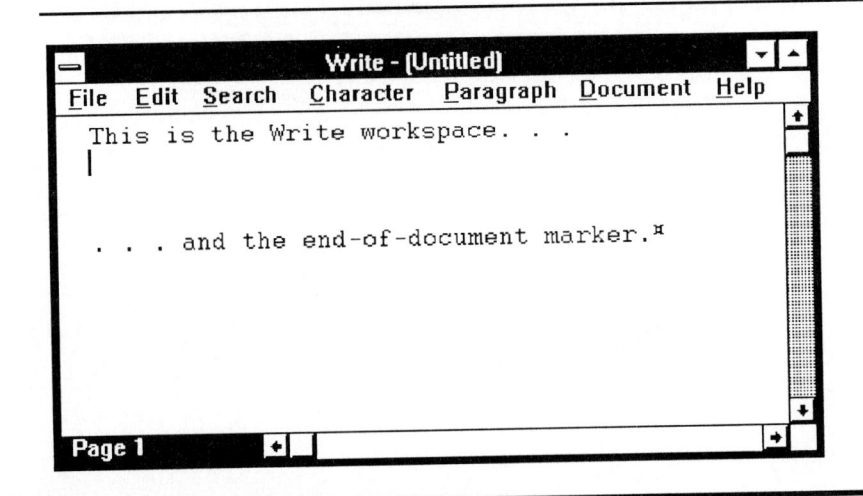

FIGURE 13-1. The Write window

STARTUP AND OVERVIEW

Start Write by clicking on its icon in the Accessories window of the Program Manager, or by clicking on a document icon associated with it. The Write window opens with a basic workspace similar to that shown in Figure 13-1.

The complete set of Windows pull-down menus (except the Help menu) can be seen in Figure 13-2. Each menu is described here:

File	Used to open existing files, which have the extension .WRI. You can also save and print files using the techniques discussed in Chapter 5. The Repaginate option is used to place page breaks in a document.

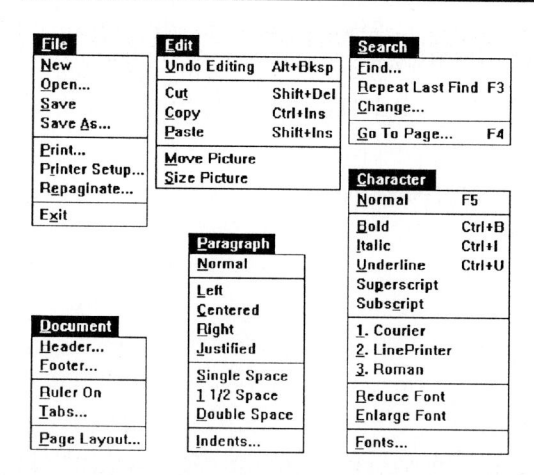

```
File              Edit                        Search
New               Undo Editing   Alt+Bksp     Find...
Open...           Cut            Shift+Del    Repeat Last Find  F3
Save              Copy           Ctrl+Ins     Change...
Save As...        Paste          Shift+Ins    Go To Page...     F4
Print...          Move Picture
Printer Setup...  Size Picture                Character
Repaginate...                                 Normal            F5
Exit                                          Bold              Ctrl+B
                  Paragraph                   Italic            Ctrl+I
                  Normal                      Underline         Ctrl+U
                                              Superscript
                  Left                        Subscript
Document          Centered
Header...         Right                       1. Courier
Footer...         Justified                   2. LinePrinter
                                              3. Roman
Ruler On          Single Space
Tabs...           1 1/2 Space                 Reduce Font
                  Double Space                Enlarge Font
Page Layout...    Indents...                  Fonts...
```

FIGURE 13-2. Write pull-down menus

Edit	Has the standard Clipboard commands. You can also use it to move and size pictures placed in a document.
Search	Lets you quickly locate and jump to text in the Write document. You can also change found text and go to any page, assuming the document is paginated.
Character	Used to apply fonts and styles to the text of your document. Any highlighted text is affected by the options selected on this menu.
Paragraph	Used to specify the alignment of paragraphs and the spacing of a selected portion of text.
Document	Used to create headers and footers and to set tabs. You can also turn on a ruler that appears at the top of the document to indicate tab

settings and paragraph alignments. The Page Layout dialog box is used to specify margins and starting page numbers.

Elements of the Write Window

Before going further, you should choose the Ruler On option on the Document menu if the ruler is not already on. This feature helps you see the position of tabs and other document elements. You can remove the ruler if you want to see more text, but normally it should be left on.

With the ruler on, you can see the measure bar, the tabs, and line spacing and paragraph alignment buttons, as shown in the following illustration:

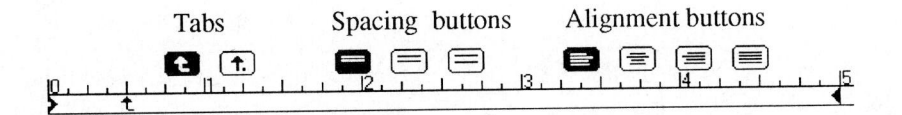

Clicking on any of these boxes causes its feature to be applied to the current paragraph. Moving from left to right, the first two boxes are pressed to set a normal tab or a decimal tab in the current paragraph. The middle three boxes are clicked to set single, one and a half, or double spacing. The four boxes on the right are used to set left, center, right, or proportional paragraph spacing.

A dialog box showing the current page number is at the bottom of the Write window. Scroll bars are also available at the bottom and on the right for moving through text, or you can also use the standard direction keys to move through text.

WRITE CONCEPTS

You should become familiar with the concepts covered in the following sections before working with Write. If you've worked with other word processors, you may already be somewhat familiar with them. They are especially characteristic of Microsoft Word and Word for Windows.

Character and Paragraph Elements

Write documents are composed of *characters* and *paragraphs*. At first that may seem elementary, but Write treats each as a unit that is selected and formatted in its own way. For example, characters are first highlighted and then altered by applying character formats such as boldface and underline. You can also change the font and character size of the highlighted text.

Paragraphs are a separate element composed of words, sentences, and a invisible *paragraph end marker*. To apply some paragraph formats, you can simply click anywhere on the paragraph with the mouse. Once the paragraph is selected, you can set its alignments, indents, and line spacings. The paragraph concept becomes obvious when you consider that paragraphs are composed of one or more sentences that automatically wrap at the end of each line and end with a paragraph end marker, which is applied when you press (ENTER). A new paragraph then begins. Each paragraph is formatted separately, thus giving you complete control over the look of your document. For example, you can indent and center one paragraph, left align another, and create numbered or bulleted lists in another.

If you change the alignment, indents, or other features of a paragraph and then press (ENTER), those changes are retained in the next paragraph. It is recommended that you create a few blank, unformatted paragraphs ahead of your current paragraph so you can easily return to a "normal" paragraph mode. Press (ENTER) five or six times when you start a new document, and then press (CTRL-HOME) to return to the top of the document. Another procedure is to end a paragraph by pressing (ENTER) and then jump back up to it to apply formats. This leaves an unformatted paragraph just below so you can resume typing in the normal way after formatting the previous paragraph.

The Invisible Paragraph Marker

A new paragraph is formed when you press the (ENTER) key. Do not press (ENTER) at the end of each line, since Write automatically word wraps text to the next line.

Pressing (ENTER) creates a new paragraph and inserts an *invisible paragraph marker* at the end of the paragraph. If you apply special formats to a paragraph, like indents, they are held in the invisible paragraph marker. If you delete the paragraph marker, the paragraph joins the paragraph below it and inherits its special formats. In some cases you may want to delete a paragraph marker to combine two separate blocks of text. Keep in mind that removing a paragraph marker may cause special formats to be replaced by those in the next paragraph.

Layout

The layout of your document is determined by how the text fits on the printed page. Select the Page Layout option on the Document menu to set margins so you can control the placement of all paragraphs within their borders. Margins affect the entire document and are not used to change the width of a single paragraph. Paragraph width is set separately for each paragraph by applying left or right indents. The indents are measured by their distance from the page margin settings.

The Ruler

The ruler has three moveable markers you can use to adjust the left and right indents, as well as the indent or outdent on the first line

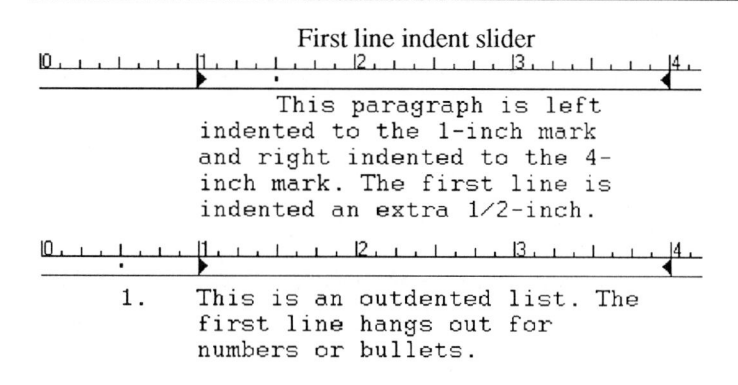

```
                        First line indent slider
|0. . . . . . . |1. . . . . . |2. . . . . . |3. . . . . . |4.
              ▶                                          ◀
              This paragraph is left
              indented to the 1-inch mark
              and right indented to the 4-
              inch mark. The first line is
              indented an extra 1/2-inch.
|0. . . . . . . |1. . . . . . |2. . . . . . |3. . . . . . |4.
      •       
              ▶                                          ◀
         1.   This is an outdented list. The
              first line hangs out for
              numbers or bullets.
```

FIGURE 13-3. The ruler settings and resulting paragraphs for indents (top) and outdents (bottom)

of the paragraph. You can move these markers left or right with the mouse or by typing their position in the Indents dialog box.

Figure 13-3 shows how the ruler looks for two different paragraphs. Both paragraphs are indented to the one-inch mark on the left and the four-inch mark on the right. The first line in the top paragraph is indented an extra half-inch. The triangles in the ruler represent the left and right indents, and the *tick* represents the indent of the first line. In the second paragraph, the first line is outdented to form a numbered list. Note the *tick* at the 1/2 inch mark.

Selecting Text and Paragraphs

You must select text before you can format it. For character formatting, you can drag the mouse over the exact text you want to select, whether that is a single character, word, sentence, paragraph, or a whole document. You can click and drag over any contiguous block of text to select it, or you can use the text selection techniques discussed in Chapter 5.

If you have a mouse, you can click in the selection area of the Write window. The *selection area* is a small vertical strip just to

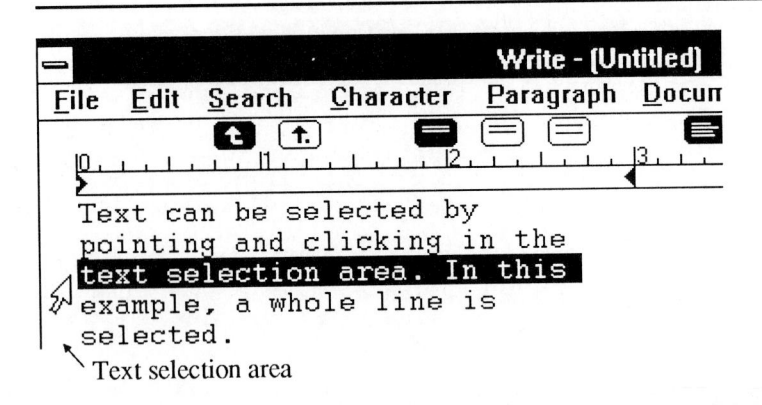

```
┌─────────────────────────────────────────────────┐
│ ▬                              Write - [Untitled]│
│ File  Edit  Search  Character  Paragraph  Docum │
│         ⬆  ⬆              ▬  ▬  ▬           ▤  │
│ |0....|....|1....|....|2....|....|3....        │
│ ▶                                                │
│   Text can be selected by                       │
│   pointing and clicking in the                  │
│   ▰text selection area. In this▰                │
│  ⬈ example, a whole line is                     │
│   selected.                                     │
│   ↖ Text selection area                         │
└─────────────────────────────────────────────────┘
```

FIGURE 13-4. The text selection area, located between the left window edge and the text, is used to select lines and paragraphs

the right of the left window border, where the mouse pointer is shown in Figure 13-4. The mouse points right when you land in the selection area. By clicking, you can select a single line, a whole paragraph, several paragraphs, or the whole document, as outlined here:

Single click	Selects the line to which the arrow is pointing.
Double click	Selects the entire paragraph.
Click and drag	Selects each line you drag through. If you double-click initially, paragraphs are selected as you drag.
CTRL-CLICK	Selects the entire document.

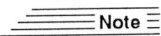

Note You can apply tab settings, alignments, and most other paragraph formats to several paragraphs at once by selecting them in advance.

How Write Saves Files

Write saves files using its own format, but you can choose to save files as standard ASCII text files, which are saved without control codes or other formatting characters. Write files saved in this way usually can be merged into any application, transferred by modem over telephone lines, or copied to disk and given to other users. See *Saving and Printing Your Document* later in this chapter.

TYPING AND EDITING IN WRITE

All you have to do to start using Write is begin typing. You can create any document without knowing much more than how to print and save. However, Write has many features worth learning, which are covered in the rest of this chapter.

As you work with your documents, remember to keep track of how your paragraphs are formatted. If you apply formats to a paragraph as you type it, the invisible paragraph marker retains the formats for the next paragraph. You can either change the formatting in the next paragraph or create a number of extra paragraphs before starting your document, as mentioned earlier.

Also remember that Write automatically wraps text at the end of each line. Do not press ENTER unless you want to start a new paragraph.

Reviewing Your Document

Once you have typed the text of your document, you may want to review it by scrolling up and down or left and right in the document. Write has a set of jump keys not available with other Windows accessories. These keys and their actions are listed here.

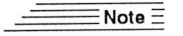

> **Note** Press **5** on the numeric keypad for the GOTO key referred to in the following list.

Key	Action
Arrow keys	Scroll in any direction, one character or line at a time
`CTRL-RIGHT ARROW`	Jumps to the next word
`CTRL-LEFT ARROW`	Jumps to the previous word
`HOME`	Jumps to the beginning of a line
`END`	Jumps to the end of a line
`GOTO-RIGHT ARROW`	Jumps to the next sentence
`GOTO-LEFT ARROW`	Jumps to the previous sentence
`GOTO-DOWN ARROW`	Jumps to the next paragraph
`GOTO-UP ARROW`	Jumps to the previous paragraph
`GOTO-PGDN`	Jumps to the next page (the document must be paginated)
`GOTO-PGUP`	Jumps to the previous page (the document must be paginated)
`CTRL-PGUP`	Jumps to the top of the window
`CTRL-PGDN`	Jumps to the bottom of the window
`CTRL-HOME`	Jumps to the beginning of a document
`CTRL-END`	Jumps to the end of a document

Moving to a Specific Page

You can jump to any page of your document if it has been paginated by using the Go To Page option on the Search menu. Pagination divides your document into numbered pages. When the Go To dialog box appears, simply type the number of the destination page and click on the OK button.

> **Note** You may need to paginate occasionally as you add text to the inner parts of your documents; otherwise the page numbers are not accurate.

Finding and Changing Text

Instead of jumping from page to page to look for a particular block of text to edit, you can use the Find option on the Search menu to jump quickly to a specific place in your document. For example, you can jump quickly from subtitle to subtitle or to each occurrence of a person's name.

You can also use the Change option to search for a block of text and change it. For example, you could change all occurrences of "Jim" in a document to "John." You can also use it to expand abbreviations or acronyms you didn't completely type when you wrote the document. For example, you could change all or specific occurrences of "NASA" with "National Aeronautics and Space Administration."

You can use special wildcard characters in the fields of the Find or Change dialog boxes. The following wildcard characters are extremely convenient when you need to locate or change occurrences of spaces, tabs, paragraph marks, or page breaks:

?	A replacement for any character in a search string you are not sure of. For example, you could type **m?n** to find occurrences of "man" and "men."
^w	Searches for spaces.
^t	Searches for tabs. You can also place this character in the Change To field of the Change dialog box to include or change any character to a tab.
^p	Searches for paragraph markers. It can also be used in the Change To field of the Change dialog box to include or change any character to a paragraph marker.
^d	Searches for manual page breaks or changes found text to manual page breaks.

The wildcard characters can be used with the Change dialog box in a variety of ways. For example, you may have typed spaces instead of using tabs to indent paragraphs. The Change option can be used to search for and convert spaces to tabs. In this case, you would want to selectively make changes since not every space should be converted. You also might need to create page breaks at the end of various paragraphs in your document. Using the Change option, you could search for existing paragraph markers and replace only the ones you want with page breaks. In this second example, you would type **^p** in the Find What field and **^p^d** in the Change To field. This keeps the paragraph marker and adds a page break to it.

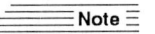

> **Note** You can limit the Find and Change options to a specific part of your document by highlighting the section to search before choosing the commands.

SEARCHING FOR TEXT The Find option on the Search menu can be used to move around in a document. You may want to search for text to edit, or simply move to passages of your document. You can even mark parts of your document you want to return to later for further editing. For example, you could type **@@@** as a mark and then search for it later.

The Find dialog box is shown here:

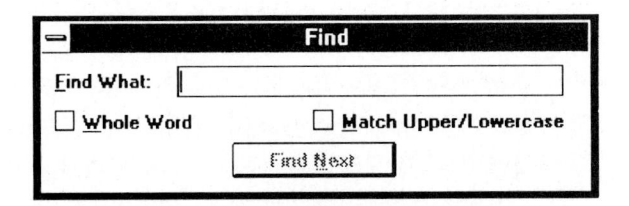

```
┌─────────────────────────────────────────┐
│ ─              Find                     │
├─────────────────────────────────────────┤
│  Find What: │                         │ │
│                                         │
│  ☐ Whole Word      ☐ Match Upper/Lowercase │
│           │  Find Next  │                │
└─────────────────────────────────────────┘
```

Type the text to search for in the Find What field. By specifying upper/lowercase and whole words only, you can narrow a search using Find.

The Find window stays open after finding the first occurrence of the string so you can click on Find Next to search for the next occurrence. When the final occurrence has been found, a dialog box appears to indicate the search is complete.

CHANGING TEXT To change one string of text to another, choose the Change option on the Search menu. The following Change dialog box appears:

```
┌─────────────────────────────────────────────────┐
│ ═                      Change                    │
│ Find What:  [                              ]     │
│ Change To:  [                              ]     │
│  □ Whole Word      □ Match Upper/Lowercase       │
│  [ Find Next ] [ Change, then Find ] [ Change ] [ Change All ] │
└─────────────────────────────────────────────────┘
```

Type the text you want to search for in the Find What field and the text you want to change it to in the Change To field. You can then specify whether the string in the Find What field is a whole word or can be used to find part of a word by checking the Whole Word box. With the Match Upper/Lowercase box, you can specify an exact upper- or lowercase match between the searched and found text.

The buttons at the bottom of the menu let you control how text is searched and replaced. You can press the Find Next button to locate the next occurrence of a string. If you want to change it, click on Change. If you want to change it and move to the next occurrence, click on the Change, Then Find button. If you want to change all occurrences without monitoring the process, click on Change All.

Selecting Text to Edit or Format

To select a block of text, use the click and drag mouse method or the techniques listed in this section. All the key combinations shown in this section extend the selection from the position of the insertion point, so you may want to reposition it before pressing the selection keys. Recall from Chapter 5 that the insertion point acts as an anchor for the highlight.

Once you have selected a block of text, you can format it using the formatting techniques discussed later in this chapter, or you can cut, copy, or paste it using the standard Clipboard options on the Edit menu. Remember, you can press SHIFT-DEL to cut text or CTRL-INS to copy it to the Clipboard. Reposition the cursor to the location you want to paste and press SHIFT-INS.

SHIFT-DOWN ARROW	Extends the selection to the next line
SHIFT-UP ARROW	Extends the selection to the previous line
SHIFT-END	Extends the selection to the end of the line
SHIFT-HOME	Extends the selection to the beginning of the line
SHIFT-PGDN	Extends the selection down one window
SHIFT-PGUP	Extends the selection up one window
CTRL-SHIFT-RIGHT ARROW	Extends the selection to the next word
CTRL-SHIFT-LEFT ARROW	Extends the selection to the previous word
CTRL-SHIFT-END	Extends the selection to the end of the document
CTRL-SHIFT-HOME	Extends the selection to the beginning of the document

OTHER EDITING FEATURES

Use the following features to further enhance your document. You can create optional hyphens to break lines in the middle of words, paginate your document, and paste graphics.

Inserting Hyphens

Depending on how your text is aligned or justified, you may want to insert hyphens to square the edges a little better or remove gaps in a line. Write's *optional hyphens* let you specify the position in a word where a line break is allowed. The best time to add optional hyphens to words is when you scan through your final draft before you paginate a document. To add an optional hyphen, press `CTRL-SHIFT-HYPHEN` at each desired hyphenation point. You can specify multiple points in each word.

Optional hyphens are useful because the lines of your text may not always break in the same place from one editing session to the next. For example, you may have specified an optional hyphen to line-break a word and later added additional text to the line so that it no longer breaks on that word. Write hides the hyphen you originally specified.

Paginating and Breaking Pages

Page breaks can be added at any time, or you can use Write's pagination feature to automatically add page breaks and assign page numbers to your document.

CREATING MANUAL PAGE BREAKS

Manual page breaks are added as you type the text of your documents or as you review and edit the document when you need to start a new page. To add a page break, press `CTRL-ENTER`. A dotted line appears across the page to indicate a page break.

Note Page breaks can be highlighted and deleted.

PAGINATING DOCUMENTS Your document can be paginated at any time to break it into pages and assign page numbers. You may want to paginate so you can use the Go To Page option on the Search menu. You may also want to paginate just to see how long a document is. If a document has already been paginated and you add additional text to it, the text probably will expand past the current page breaks. You may need to repaginate to establish new page breaks. This is especially true if you use the Go To Page option.

Use the Repaginate option on the File menu to paginate a document. The Repaginate Document dialog box is shown here:

You can click on the Confirm Page Breaks box if you want to confirm each recommended page break. This gives you a chance to move the page break up or down before confirming. A dialog box like this will appear at each recommended page break:

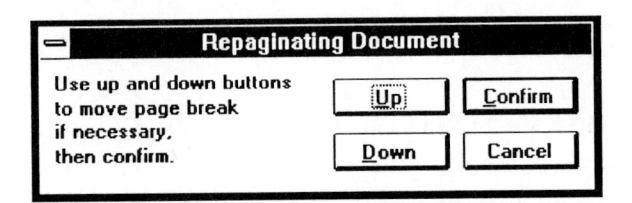

You can press Up to move the page break up. In most cases you cannot extend a page break down because Write recommends the maximum number of lines that can fit on the page. Down can be used to adjust a manually set page break.

Adding and Editing Graphics

Using the Clipboard, you can cut and paste graphic images created in Windows Paintbrush or other compatible applications to your Write documents. The procedure for cutting and pasting between applications using the Clipboard has been covered in previous chapters. In most cases, you have two windows open, one for the source graphic and one for Write. The window with the graphics image is made active for copying or cutting, and then the Write window is made active for pasting.

When a picture is pasted into a Write document, it appears against the left margin at the location of the insertion point. The picture is then selected and resized or moved left or right using options on the Edit menu.

Note Color pictures are converted to black and white.

When a picture is placed in Write, it is displayed at the resolution of your currently selected printer. Some pictures appear distorted on the screen, but print properly.

PASTING, MOVING, AND SIZING A PICTURE Before pasting a picture into a Write document, move the insertion point to the position where the picture should go, and then select the Paste option on the Edit menu.

You can resize the picture by choosing the Size Picture option on the Edit menu. A square cursor appears. When this cursor is moved, a dotted frame shrinks and grows to indicate the size of the picture. When the picture is the size you want, click the mouse button.

> **Note:** To keep a picture correctly proportioned, watch the sizing information that appears in the lower-left corner of the Write window and try to maintain whole numbers rather than fractional amounts.

A picture can be positioned horizontally by selecting the Move Picture option on the Edit menu. A square cursor appears, and a dotted frame moves back and forth as you move the mouse. When the frame is where you want to place the picture, click the mouse button.

FORMATTING IN WRITE

As mentioned earlier, you can format individual characters of a Write document with fonts and type styles and you can change the alignment of paragraph elements and page layout. Each of these formatting routines is covered in separate sections here.

Character Formatting

Character formatting in Write is accomplished through the Character menu. Selected characters are formatted or the text you are about to type assumes the new format. Characters can be formatted with bold, italic, and underline styles, with superscript and subscript line placements, or with different fonts and font sizes. Any of these character formats can be combined to form just the look you may need in your documents.

Write's graphics screen usually displays the text in the same format and size in which the text is printed. The number of characters across and the height of the characters will be true to form when printed, assuming you have a matching screen font for the text you want to print. If you are unsure about your screen fonts, refer to Fonts in Chapter 9.

APPLYING CHARACTER FORMATS To apply a character format, first select the text to be formatted. To apply a new font to the whole document, press (CTRL) while clicking in the selection bar. Pull down the Character menu to view a list of selections. Figure 13-2 illustrates a typical Character menu, although yours may be different, depending on the fonts your printer supports.

The Normal option lets you remove any styles applied to characters, such as bold, italic, underline, superscript, and subscript. The menu also lists the most-used fonts, but you can choose the Fonts option to view other fonts or to select special sizes. The Reduce Font and Enlarge Font options are used to reduce or enlarge the current font to the next size up or down.

Note Remember, you can change fonts and styles as you type. You can also go back and select any text to change its font or style. When a font or style is active, a checkmark appears in front of its option on the Character menu.

CHANGING FONTS AND SIZES You can change fonts and sizes quickly if they appear on the Character menu. Some fonts may not appear on this menu, so you may need to open the Fonts dialog box, shown in Figure 13-5, by choosing the Fonts option.

The Fonts dialog box gives you more control over the fonts and sizes you want to use in your document. If you use a font from this box frequently, Write will add it to your normal Character menu.

To choose a different font or size, you can type the font name in the Font Name box, or you can scroll through the list in the Fonts text box. To choose a different size, you can scroll in the Sizes box or you can type the size you want in the Point Size box. When you are done, click on the OK button to assign the new options to the selected text.

CREATING A TYPE STYLE TEST SHEET You might find it valuable to print a test sheet of all the fonts, font sizes, and styles

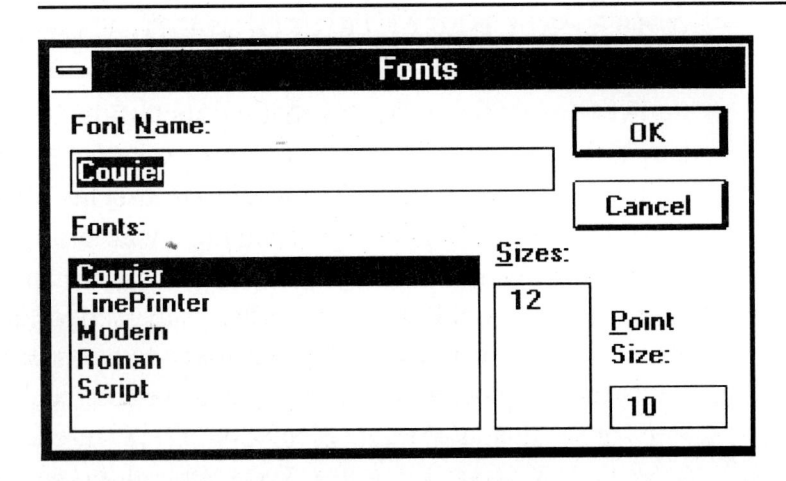

FIGURE 13-5. The Fonts dialog box has more options for changing fonts than the Character menu

available for your printer. You can start by typing some sample lines, as shown in Figure 13-6. The top five lines are examples of the Courier style. You can create a similar block of styles for each

FIGURE 13-6. A type style test sheet

font available on your system. The second block of lines in Figure 13-6 is in the Modern font.

Rather than typing and formatting each style for each font, you can use the following shortcut to create the test sheet. Type and format just the lines for the Courier font, as shown in Figure 13-6. Be sure to apply the appropriate italic, underline, and other styles to each line. Then highlight the lines and duplicate them using the Clipboard commands once for each available font. Use the Change option on the Search menu to change the font names on each line. For example, you would change Courier to Modern in the second block of lines. Finally, go back to each block and change its font format to the name you gave it. You should now have a representative sample of each type font and style.

Next, highlight the whole thing and select a starting font size, then print it. Repeat this process for each font size you want to try or think you will use. Eventually you will build up a catalog of fonts, sizes, and styles for your particular printer which you can use when trying to develop the look of your documents. This procedure also gives you an idea of the fonts and styles that do not work on your printer. For example, referring to Figure 13-6 again, you can see that Courier italics is not available.

Paragraph Formatting

Recall that a paragraph is a continuous set of characters that ends with an invisible paragraph marker. The paragraph marker holds the formatting information for the entire paragraph, such as indents and alignments. If you remove the paragraph marker, you will remove its formats; the paragraph will join the paragraph below and will take on its formats.

This section explains how to align paragraphs from the ruler bar or from the Paragraph menu. It is best to make the ruler bar visible when formatting a paragraph unless you really need the extra room on the screen for viewing your document. Only the ruler bar methods of formatting paragraphs are discussed in this section. The Paragraph menu can be used to set the options by typing numbers in their dialog boxes. You can set the options manually and then view the dialog boxes to see their settings.

ALIGNING PARAGRAPHS You begin paragraph alignment by first clicking with the mouse in the paragraph to be aligned and then clicking one of the alignment icons, as shown here:

The leftmost icon is the left-align button, followed by the center-align button, right-align button, and justification button. The justification button produces both left and right alignments but may cause unsightly spacing gaps between words.

SPACING PARAGRAPHS You can click on a spacing icon to select a different line spacing for the current paragraph. If you want to print the entire document with a particular line spacing, select it by pressing the CTRL key while clicking in the selection bar. In the following illustration, the left button selects normal spacing, the middle button selects one and a half spacing, and the right button selects double spacing.

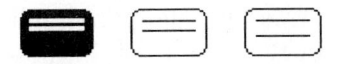

FIRST LINE INDENTING Indents are applied to individual paragraphs by sliding the indent marks on the ruler bar. Point to either the left or right indent, click the mouse, and drag in either direction to adjust the indent. To adjust the first line indent or outdent, click on the *tick mark* and drag left or right. In the following illustration, the first line has been indented one half inch.

```
 0         1         2         3
 ▶    ▪                        ◀
         This is an example of
      first line indenting with a
      right indent of 3 inches.
```

FIRST LINE OUTDENTING   Outdents are used to create numbered or bulleted lists. In this example the left indent is set at the one-inch mark and the first line indent is set at the one-half-inch mark.

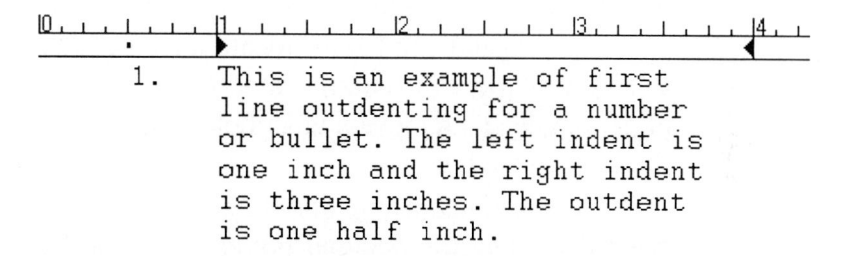

```
 0         1         2         3         4
           ▶                             ◀
      1.    This is an example of first
            line outdenting for a number
            or bullet. The left indent is
            one inch and the right indent
            is three inches. The outdent
            is one half inch.
```

Note that a tab was pressed after the number.

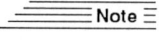

> **Note** If you choose the Indents option on the Paragraph menu, you can view the indent settings. Outdents appear as negative numbers since they are measured from the normal indent settings.

INDENTING LEFT AND RIGHT   You can set indents on both the left and right by sliding the indent triangles to the correct position on the ruler. Each paragraph can have its own indent settings.

Altering the Page Layout

Page layout settings are those that affect the entire page or document. For instance, tabs can be set only for the whole document, not individual paragraphs. Margins are set to adjust how the entire document fits on the printed page.

SETTING TABS The tab icons are shown in this illustration:

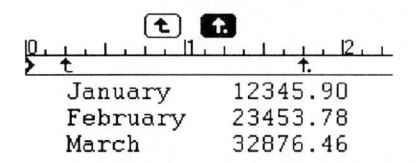

```
         ┌─┐ ┌─┐
         │t│ │↑│
     0   └─┘ └─┘  |1         |2
     |...t...|.........|...t...|
     January       12345.90
     February      23453.78
     March         32876.46
```

The up arrow on the left is used to set a normal tab. Simply click its icon and then point to the location on the ruler bar where you want to place a tab. The up arrow on the right is a decimal tab, which you use to align the decimal points of numbers in tables. Click its icon and point to the location on the ruler to place it. You can slide tabs from left to right after text has been typed to visually align a table. To remove a tab, click on its marker and drag it off the ruler to the left.

In the previous example, notice how the months align to the normal tab and the decimal points in the numbers align to the decimal tab.

≡Note≡ Tab settings apply to the whole document only.

You can set tabs manually by opening the Tabs dialog box. Choose Tabs from the Document menu to display the box shown in Figure 13-7. The Tabs dialog box is split in two, with the top settings for leftmost tabs and the bottom settings for those further to the right. Type a ruler number in the Positions box for each tab you want to set from left to right. The boxes correspond to left and right tabs. Click on the corresponding Decimal box to set a decimal tab. Click on OK when you are done. To clear all tabs, press the Clear All button.

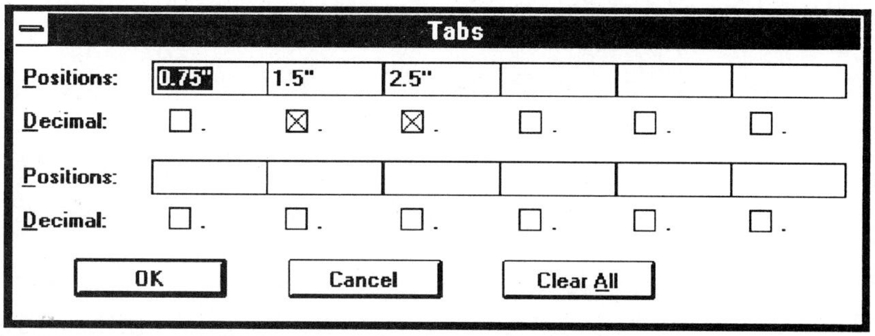

FIGURE 13-7. The Tabs dialog box

Headers and Footers

A *header* is text that appears at the top of every page, and a *footer* is text that appears at the bottom of every page. Headers and footers usually contain page numbers, document titles, or dates, and you can have both a header and a footer on each page. You can also control whether a header and a footer appear on the first page.

To create a header or footer, select either option on the Document menu. Two windows appear similar to those shown in Figure 13-8. The upper HEADER (or FOOTER) window is where you type the header or footer text. Below it is the Page Header (or Page Footer) dialog box, where you can specify how and where the header or footer should appear.

Notice in Figure 13-8 that a title and page number appear in the header. A tab was set at the three-and-one-half-inch mark for the page number. With the insertion point at that tab marker, the Insert Page # button on the Page Header dialog box was clicked to insert "(page)," which causes a page number to be printed in the final document.

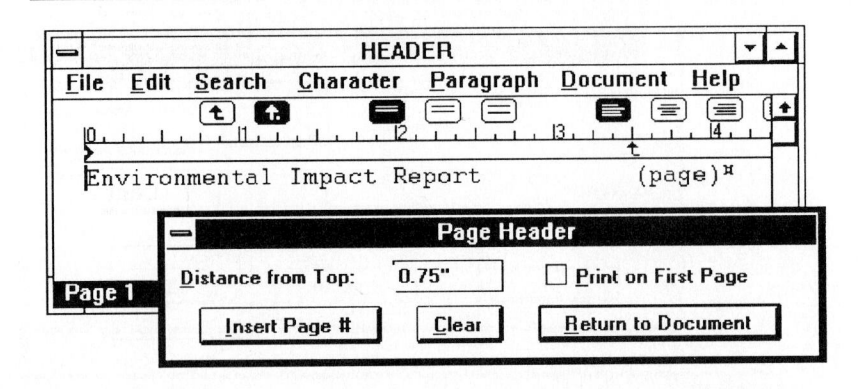

FIGURE 13-8. Two windows appear when setting headers and footers, one for text and one for selecting options

If you want to print the header (or footer) on the first page of the document, click the Print on First Page box. Use the Distance from Top (or Distance from Bottom) box to specify how far the header (or footer) is printed from the edge of the paper. When you are done, click on the Return to Document button.

Setting Margins and the Starting Page Number

Margins and the initial starting page number are set by choosing the Page Layout option on the Document window and opening the Page Layout dialog box shown in Figure 13-9. Margins are set from the edge of the paper by entering the appropriate numbers in the Margins boxes. All paragraph indents are then set according to the margin settings, as discussed previously.

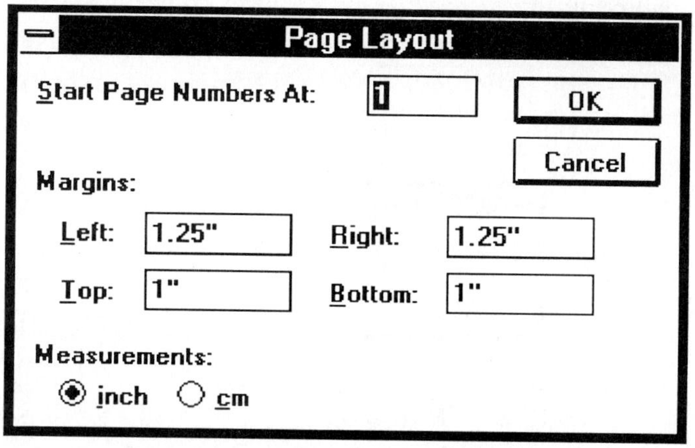

FIGURE 13-9. The Page Layout dialog box

SAVING AND PRINTING YOUR DOCUMENT

You should save your documents as often as possible so valuable work is not lost if there is a power failure or something goes wrong with your system. Don't forget to make backups on diskette to protect yourself from hard disk failure. In addition, you may want to save your documents before attempting to print them, just in case the system locks while printing.

Saving Your Documents

To save a Write document, choose the Save As or Save option on the File menu. Previously saved and named documents can be saved with the Save As command. When the File Save As dialog box appears, you can type a filename. Write gives all its files the extension .WRI unless you type another extension.

The File Save As box allows you to save your documents using any of the following options:

- *Make Backup*. If this box is checked, Write saves the last version of the file before the most recent changes as a backup file. The file is given the same filename and a .BAK extension. This file is overwritten the next time you save using the Make Backup option. You can use it to recover from editing sessions or as a separate file to be renamed.

- *Text Only*. Files saved with the Text Only format are simple ASCII text files without any formatting codes. Use care when selecting this option. Formats such as boldfacing, font changes, and paragraph alignments will be lost. Text-only files can be used on other systems and other word processors with no problems, however.

- *Microsoft Word*. Select Microsoft Word format if you plan to use and edit the file on this advanced word processing package, or if you are transferring the file to a person who uses Word. All character and paragraph formats will be saved and converted for use with Word.

Printing Your Documents

To print a Write document, select the Print command from the File menu. The following Print dialog box appears:

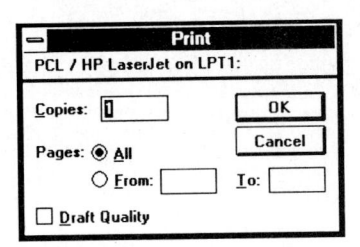

This dialog box allows you to specify the number of copies to print and the page range. You can print all pages or a specific range of pages by typing the first page in the From box and the last page in the To box. Check the Draft Quality box to print the document in low-quality, high-speed mode, if your printer supports it.

Remember, you can choose a different printer, different paper size, or other options by choosing the Printer Setup option on the File menu. Follow the procedures outlined in Chapter 8 to change the options on the printer dialog boxes.

14

WINDOWS PAINTBRUSH

Startup and Overview
Paintbrush Concepts
Drawing Techniques
Text and Graphic Editing Techniques
Special Techniques
Retrieving, Saving, and Printing

Windows Paintbrush is a drawing program that gives you a full box of drawing tools and a palette of colors. You can create simple or complex images that can be transferred to other documents. This chapter explains Paintbrush's features, gives you some ideas on how you can use them, and offers useful tips and techniques.

Paintbrush is a mouse-oriented program and is not recommended for use with the keyboard, unless you have a high frustration level. The mouse makes it much easier to point and select the many options on the window and to draw in the freestyle manner associated with this type of drawing program.

For those who still want to tackle Paintbrush with the keyboard, the following keys are used as substitutes for the left and right mouse buttons:

(INS)	Single click of the left button
(DEL)	Single click of the right button
(F9-INS)	Double click of the left button
(F9-DEL)	Double click of the right button

STARTUP AND OVERVIEW

To start Paintbrush, double-click on the Paintbrush icon in the Accessories group window of the Program Manager. The Paintbrush window, shown in Figure 14-1, consists of a drawing area where graphic images are drawn. On the left is the toolbox, which contains a set of tools used to draw or paint with the color selected

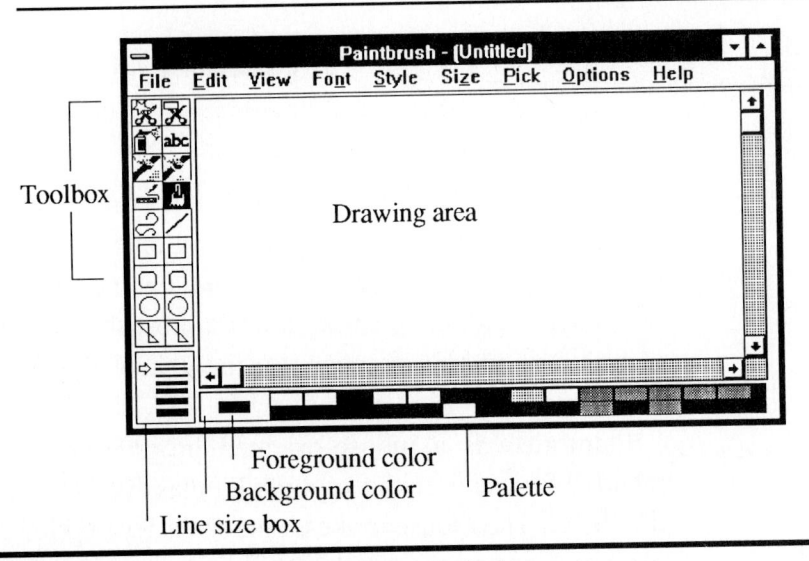

FIGURE 14-1. The Paintbrush window

in the color palette area at the bottom of the screen. If you are drawing lines or boxes, the line width is selected by moving the arrow in the line size box. To select a drawing color, click on any color in the palette.

Each of the elements of the Paintbrush window is briefly discussed in the following sections, along with a description of the Paintbrush tools in the toolbox area.

The Color Palette

The color palette is the strip of colored boxes at the bottom of the Paintbrush window. The leftmost box is the foreground/background color indicator that displays the current color selections. Foreground and background colors are used with fill tools to create distinct fill and border colors. Eraser tools change or erase colors depending on the current foreground and background colors. For example, if you drag the color eraser tool over the currently selected foreground color in the drawing area, that color changes to the selected background color. No other colors in the eraser's trail are affected.

To select a foreground color, click on a color with the left mouse button. To select a background color, click on another color with the right mouse button. Both then appear in the foreground/background box located to the left of the color palette.

The Toolbox

The toolbox, shown in Figure 14-2, is on the left side of the Paintbrush window. Clicking on one of the tools selects it for use in the drawing area. Each tool is briefly described here, moving from left to right at the top. Techniques for using each tool are covered later in this chapter; you should try each one as you read along. Notice that the mouse pointer changes shape depending on the type of tool you are using.

Scissors	Pick
Airbrush	Text tool
Color eraser	Eraser
Paint roller	Brush
Curve tool	Line
Box tool	Fill box tool
Round tool	Fill round tool
Circle ellipse	Fill circle ellipse
Polygon	Fill polygon

FIGURE 14-2. The Paintbrush toolbox

Scissors	A freeform cutout tool used to surround an object in the drawing area for cutting or copying to the Clipboard, or for dragging to other parts of the drawing.
Pick	Defines a rectangular cutout and is used in the same way as the scissors.
Airbrush	Used to spray the currently selected palette color.
Text tool	Adds captions to your drawings. Fonts, font sizes, and font styles are selected on the Paintbrush pull down menus.
Color eraser	Changes the selected foreground color to the selected background color.
Eraser	Changes all foreground colors to the selected background color. If the background color is white, the colors are effectively erased.
Paint roller	Fills in any closed shape or area with the selected foreground color.

Brush — Used for freehand drawing. You can choose from a selection of brush shapes in the Brush Shapes dialog box (which appears when you choose Brush Shapes from the Options menu). Select a line in the line size box to set the width of the brush.

Curve — Draws curved shapes using the line width set in the line size box and the foreground color set in the palette.

Line — Draws straight lines using the line width set in the line size box and the foreground color set in the palette.

HOLLOW AND FILL TOOLS The remaining tools on the toolbox are grouped in pairs. The left tool in the pair is used to draw the shape in a hollow form, and the right tool is used to draw and fill the shape with the current foreground color.

Box — Draws a box or rectangle of any size or shape with square corners.

Rounded box — Draws a box or rectangle of any size with rounded corners.

Circle/ellipse — Draws circles and ellipses.

Polygon — Draws odd-shaped triangles, boxes, or other multisided objects.

The Line Size Box

The line size box is shown here:

You use it to change the width of the current drawing line by sliding the arrow to the desired width. Select the top line to draw invisible lines, which are used to create filled boxes or circles that do not have border lines.

The Paintbrush Menus

Figure 14-3 shows the following Paintbrush menus:

File   Has the standard options for opening, saving, and printing, as discussed in Chapter 5.

Edit   Has the standard Clipboard Cut, Copy, and Paste options. In addition, the Copy To option saves a cutout portion of a drawing

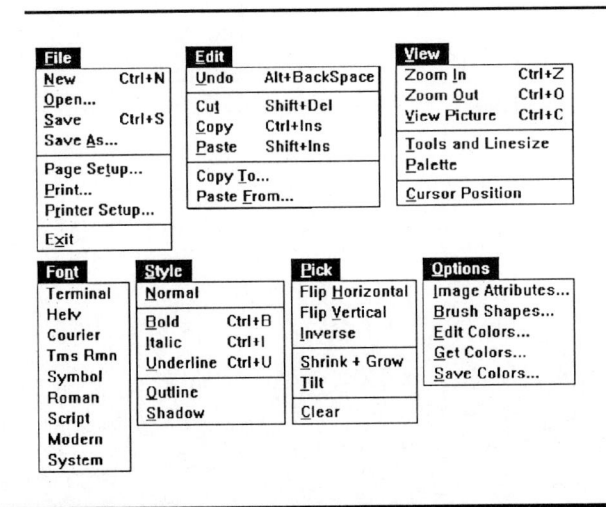

FIGURE 14-3. The Paintbrush pull-down menus

	to a disk file. The Paste From option recovers a cutout file.
View	Has a Zoom In option that lets you expand a portion of your drawing so you can manipulate its individual dots. The Zoom Out option is used to see the drawing on the whole page, or if you previously had zoomed in, to go back to normal size. To make the drawing area larger, you can remove the tools, line size box, and palette. The Cursor Position option displays the cursor position in a small box for detail work.
Font	Used to select a specific font for the text typed with the text tool.
Style	Used to select a specific style for the text typed with the text tool.
Pick	Available only when an object has been selected with the scissors or pick tool. It provides options for flipping, inverting, sizing, and tilting a cutout object.
Options	Contains five options that open dialog boxes. The options are used to set the Paintbrush operating parameters and brush shapes. In addition, you can edit, select, and save custom colors.

The Size and Help menus are not shown in Figure 14-3. The Size menu simply lists a series of numbers you can select to change the point size of a font.

PAINTBRUSH CONCEPTS

While the basic operation of the program is straightforward, there are some important Paintbrush concepts and a few techniques you should learn to improve the quality of your drawings and the efficiency of your drawing methods.

The Cursor

The cursor is the same as the mouse pointer and is used in the familiar way when selecting tools, colors, or menu items. In the drawing area, however, the cursor changes shape depending on the tool you have selected. When working with the cutout tools, the line drawing tools, and the box, circle, and polygon tools, the cursor changes to a crosshatch. When working with the text tools, the cursor is the familiar insertion bar or I-beam.

When working with the eraser tools, the cursor is a box that matches the size of the current line width. You should take care when erasing since it is possible to erase a larger area than you want. If this happens, select the Undo option from the Edit menu, and then select a smaller line size.

The Paintbrush cursor matches the current line width and the shape you select in the Brush Shapes dialog box shown here:

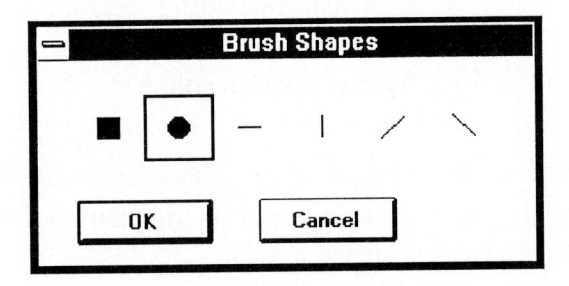

To change brush shapes, choose Brush Shapes from the Options menu and click on the shape you want to use. In the previous example, a round brush shape is selected, as indicated by the box that surrounds it. You should experiment with the other shapes available on this dialog box by selecting each in turn. Try different line widths as you draw.

The Drawing Area

The drawing area is where images are drawn with the tools, line sizes, and colors you have selected. This section shows you how to clear the drawing area, change some of its features, and expand its size.

CLEARING THE DRAWING AREA When you first start Paintbrush, the drawing area is blank. Many times you may start doodling and then decide you want to clear the screen for a new drawing. Also, if you have just finished one picture and want to start a new one, you must clear the screen using one of the following methods:

- Select one of the cutout tools and surround the graphics you want to clear. Then choose Cut from the Edit menu.

- Double-click on the eraser. Note that this method retains the filename if you want to redo the graphics in the workspace.

- Choose the New option on the File menu.

ESTABLISHING PAINTBRUSH FEATURES You may want to set a few features before you start drawing. Paintbrush establishes a default drawing area size based on the amount of memory your system has. The drawing area may be smaller than the Paintbrush window due to memory limitations. You should close other windows and remove memory-resident software if you have this problem.

To increase the size of the drawing space and set other features, choose Image Attributes from the Options menu. The window in Figure 14-4 appears. Enter the drawing size measurements in the

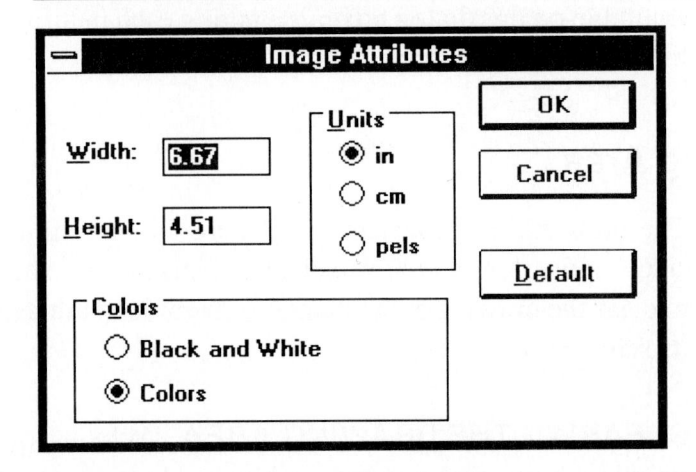

FIGURE 14-4. The Image Attributes dialog box

Width and Height fields. Keep in mind that this size affects how large the disk file will be. In addition, any extra space not used by the actual drawing, such as around its borders, is retained in the file and may be hard to crop in some applications if you are transferring the disk file to them.

You can adjust the measurement used by Paintbrush in the Units field of the Image Attributes dialog box. The units can be inches, centimeters, or pels. Pels are picture elements, sometimes referred to as pixels, and are the dots that make up a picture.

The Colors box in the Image Attributes dialog box offers you the choice of Black and White or Color drawing. If you change the color selection, you must exit Paintbrush and start it again to initialize the new colors. When Paintbrush is restarted, the palette has a black and white gray scale or colors, depending on your choice.

Note To return to the default settings, click on the Default button on the Image Attributes dialog box.

WHEN YOU NEED MORE ROOM If you do not have enough room on the screen itself to work with your drawings, you can take a few steps to increase it. This is often the case when you paste an object that does not fit. The first thing you can do is maximize the Paintbrush window. If this still does not give you enough room, you can remove the toolbox and line size box to increase horizontal space, or you can remove the color palette to increase vertical space. Choose Tools and Linesize or Palette on the View menu to remove them. You can choose both if you wish.

Tip: If you paste an object that does not fit on the screen, part of it is cropped. You can temporarily turn off the tools and palettes while you paste, and then turn them back on when the image is secure in the drawing area. See "Securing an Object" later in this chapter for more information.

VIEWING YOUR DRAWING Once you have drawn on the screen, the best way to view it is to choose the View Picture option from the View menu. This removes all tools, palettes, and windows from the screen so you can view your drawing by itself. You cannot make changes to the drawing in the View Picture mode. To return to the Paintbrush window, click the mouse button or press (ESC).

ZOOMING IN CLOSE Another way to view a drawing is to zoom into it. A zoomed view shows a close-up view, or bit view, of a selected portion of the drawing. Zoom in mode allows you to click on any bit to change it to the current foreground color. Working at the bit level allows you to control the accuracy and detail of your drawings.

Choose Zoom In on the View menu. A rectangle appears that moves with the mouse. Place it over the part of the drawing you want to zoom and press the mouse button. In the zoom in mode, the original size of the drawing can still be seen in a small rectangle

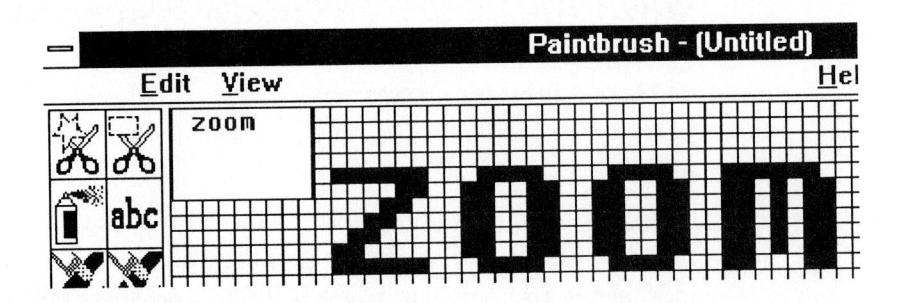

FIGURE 14-5. An example of zoom in mode

at the top left. To zoom out, choose Zoom Out from the View menu.

Figure 14-5 illustrates the zoom in mode. The word "zoom" has been typed and then selected for the zoom. Note that each bit falls in a grid. If you click on a square, it converts to the current foreground color. Notice that the original view appears in the upper-left corner of the drawing area.

ZOOMING OUT The Zoom Out option on the View menu is used to get an overview of a large drawing that does not fit on the normal screen. In the zoom out mode, you can use the scissors or the pick to cut pieces from a drawing and place them elsewhere. You might want to use this mode to adjust the entire drawing on the drawing area. To return to regular mode, choose Zoom In from the View menu or press (ESC).

Securing an Object

Objects you draw or objects you paste are not "secured" or "pasted down" on the drawing area until you click another Paintbrush tool.

Until then you can remove them by pressing the (BACKSPACE) key. In some cases, changes to a drawing may be accidentally removed when you scroll or select a zoom mode. Always click another tool when you finish drawing an object.

EFFECTS OF UNDOING The Undo option on the Edit menu can be used to undo your last drawing action or editing change. It is important to understand that the Undo command removes all changes made with the current tool. For example, if you draw four separate lines with the line tool, Undo removes all four lines, not just the last one drawn.

You can use the (BACKSPACE) key to make quick edits while a drawing tool is still selected. This method can be used in place of the Eraser tool. Press the (BACKSPACE) key to convert the current tool to a temporary eraser, and then erase any portion you want by clicking and dragging over it. When you release the mouse, the drawing tool immediately returns.

Zooming in or out may undo some changes you have made to a drawing. For example, if you change a foreground color to a background color and then go into a zoom mode, the colors may revert to their original state when you return from zoom. To avoid this, select another tool before zooming.

Line Width and Color Effects

The size of the line selected in the line size box affects the widths of lines drawn with the line tool, curve tool, brush, airbrush, and the box, curve, and polygon tools. The line size also affects how large the eraser tip is, so be careful when erasing.

The brush tip can be altered in two ways. You can select the tip shape by opening the Brush Shapes dialog box on the Options menu, and you can change its size by selecting a line in the line size box.

Foreground and Background Colors

Foreground and background colors are important when you draw objects with fill areas. For example, if you select red as the foreground color and black as the background color, then draw a box with the filled box tool, it will have a black border and red fill. Foreground and background colors are also important when using the color eraser tool. It replaces the foreground color with the background color as you drag over your drawing with the eraser tip.

The foreground color is selected by clicking on a color in the color palette with the left mouse button. The background color is selected by clicking on a color with the right mouse button. The foreground/background box then displays the current colors.

DRAWING TECHNIQUES

To draw with any of the drawing tools, simply click on the tool in the toolbox, and begin drawing in the drawing area by holding down the mouse button as you drag. The position of the cursor when you click the mouse is the *anchor point* for the object you are drawing. If you are using a freehand tool, the anchor point is not too important, but if you are drawing boxes, circles, or polygons, the anchor point is the object's starting corner or edge. As you drag the mouse, the object expands from its anchor point.

Detailed Drawing

Sometimes you need more detail in your drawings. For example, you may want to position two objects exactly parallel to each other, or you may want to draw perfectly straight lines or square boxes. The techniques described here explain how to do this.

VIEWING CURSOR POSITIONS Paintbrush can display the current x and y coordinates of the cursor in a window to help you align objects more accurately. Choose the Cursor Position option on the View menu to display the Cursor Position window. If the window appears in an inconvenient location, you can move it elsewhere.

The x and y coordinates are useful when you create boxes, circles, and polygons, and when you move them to other locations on the screen or try to align them with other objects.

USING THE (SHIFT) KEY To create straight lines, perfect circles, and perfect squares, hold down the (SHIFT) key while drawing. When you draw a line while pressing the (SHIFT) key, the line is restricted to straight vertical, horizontal, or 45 degrees. When you draw boxes and circles while pressing the (SHIFT) key, rectangles and ellipses are restricted. When you draw polygons, only vertical, horizontal, and 45-degree lines are allowed if you are pressing the (SHIFT) key.

ZOOMING FOR DETAIL As mentioned previously, the best detail work you can perform in Paintbrush is at the bit level using the zoom in mode. You can draw objects one bit at a time or you can add colors one bit at a time in this mode. Shades you would normally add with the airbrush are often easier to control in zoom in mode.

One way to use Zoom In is to draw a rough draft in normal view and then choose Zoom In to touch up the details.

Using the Painting Tools

The painting tools include the airbrush, the paintbrush, the roller, and to some extent, the color eraser. All of these are considered freehand tools because they allow different shapes and motions.

AIRBRUSH TECHNIQUES Select the airbrush to spray the current foreground color on your drawing. Move to the drawing area and click the mouse to start spraying. Drag the mouse to spray paint on your drawing and release the mouse to stop spraying.

Here are some tips to help you use the airbrush:

- Press (SHIFT) to spray along a horizontal or vertical line.
- Select a line width in the line size box to change the size of the spray.
- The speed of the cursor across the screen determines the density of the spray. For a dispersed effect, drag quickly over an area many times.
- You can try switching colors as you spray to get an interesting effect. If a color becomes too concentrated, try spraying over it with white or another color.
- Zoom in for touch-ups.

BRUSH TECHNIQUES The brush is used to paint in a freehand style using different brush shapes and sizes. To select a different brush shape, choose Brush Shape from the Options menu and then click on the shape you want. To select a different brush size, make a selection in the line size box.

Here are some tips to help you use the brush:

- Be sure to select a color in the palette before you begin drawing.
- The brush can be square, round, or a variety of chisel shapes. Select a chisel shape to produce a calligraphy effect, in which lines are drawn both thick and thin, depending on the angle of the chisel.
- Press (SHIFT) to restrict the brush to a vertical or horizontal movement.

- Brush colors completely overlap existing colors, even if they are lighter, unlike airbrush colors.

The shapes drawn by each of the brush chisel points are shown here:

The top stroke is from the horizontal point, the second stroke is from the vertical point, and the third and fourth strokes are from the 45-degree points.

ROLLER TECHNIQUES The roller tool is used to fill an enclosed area formed by a circle, square, or other object. These objects normally can be filled using the fill tools. The primary purpose of the roller is to fill areas that may form when objects overlap. For example, in the following illustration, the diamond formed by the intersection of two triangles can be filled with the roller:

To use the roller, click on its icon and point to the target area with its tip. Keep the following guidelines in mind.

- Be sure to select a color before filling.

- If the area to be filled has any breaks, the color will leak out onto other parts of the drawing. These small openings may not be immediately visible. Use the Zoom In option on the View menu to look at the edges of an object. Note the opening in the following triangle as seem from the zoom in mode:

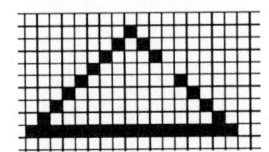

If a color leaks, immediately select the Undo option on the Edit menu, then close the opening, as described next.

- To close an object, click on the bit squares with the same color as the object being filled.

Using the Text Tool

The text tool is used to add captions and other text to your drawings. It is somewhat limited in its editing features compared to other Windows applications. For example, once text has been typed and you have selected other tools, the text becomes a graphics object, not text you can edit. You cannot insert additional text, change the font, the style, or place the I-beam in the text for further editing.

To begin typing text, first select a text font from the Font menu, a text style from the Style menu, and a font size from the Size menu. Then click on the text tool. The cursor changes to an I-beam shape. Move to the drawing area and click the mouse where you want to begin typing. Note the following as you create text objects.

- You can use the (BACKSPACE) key to edit text you have just typed, but once you reposition the mouse or click another tool, text can no longer be edited in this way.

- The currently selected foreground color will be the color of the text.

- Text can only be drawn in solid colors, not color combinations (colors with patterns). Paintbrush selects the next solid color if you choose a combination color.

- When you select a size for the font from the Size menu, be sure it has an asterisk. Asterisk-labeled fonts provide the most precision because they match your printer.

Using the Line and Curve Tools

The line and curve tools are used to draw lines that assume the width selected in the line size box.

THE LINE TOOL The Line tool draws straight lines at any angle with the currently selected foreground color. Alternatively, you can hold down the (SHIFT) key to restrict the lines to horizontal, vertical, or 45-degree angles.

To draw a line, select the line tool in the toolbox. Move the cursor to the drawing area, where it becomes a crosshatch. Click in the area where you want to start the line and drag the mouse. Release the mouse when the line is the correct length.

THE CURVE TOOL The curve tool is one of the most interesting tools in Paintbrush. It uses a simple "anchor and pull" technique to draw perfect curves. It takes some getting used to, so you need to experiment with the curve tool on a clear drawing area before you can expect to draw curves the way you like.

To draw a curve, select a foreground color and then select the line width in the line size box. Move the cursor to the drawing area, and then click and hold the mouse button as you drag it to the approximate length you want the curve to be. Release the mouse button, click in the approximate area you want the line to curve to, and drag the cursor to enhance the stretch in the curve. When you are done, release the mouse button.

This process is shown in the following illustration:

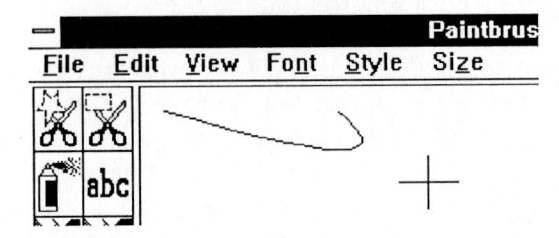

The ends of the curves are anchored at the top, and the cross bar pulls the line out. Think of the curve line as a rubber band stretched by the cursor between two posts, which are the anchor points.

Using the Box, Circle and Polygon Tools

The box, circle, and polygon tools come in two varieties, those that remain hollow and those that fill with the selected foreground color. The filled tools are on the right side of the toolbox.

If you draw a hollow box, circle, or polygon, its borders are drawn with the current foreground color. If you draw a filled box, circle, or polygon, it is filled with the current foreground color, and its borders are drawn with the current background color.

To begin drawing with one of the tools, click on its icon in the toolbox. Move to the drawing area and click the mouse where you want its corner to rest. Hold the mouse button and drag until the object is the size you want. When you let up on the mouse, the box is formed with the current line widths, border colors, and fills.

When you use the polygon tools, click and drag the first line, and then click at each subsequent connecting point.

Here are some tips for using these tools:

- The box tools draw hollow or filled boxes and rectangles with either square or curved corners, depending on which tool you select.

- To create filled boxes, circles, or polygons with no border, make the foreground and background colors the same.

- Remember to press (SHIFT) while drawing if you want to create squares and circles; otherwise, rectangles and ellipses are created, unless you draw with great precision.

TEXT AND GRAPHIC EDITING TECHNIQUES

Editing techniques are used on objects that have been pasted to a drawing. Unpasted items, which are still in the process of being drawn, can be removed by pressing the (BACKSPACE) key. Use the tools and techniques described in this section to select whole objects or parts of objects and move or remove them from the drawing. You can also change colors and erase objects.

Using the Cutout Tools

The cutout tools are the scissors and the pick. Recall that the scissors tool is used to cut out odd-shaped objects, and the pick is used to make square or rectangular cuts. Click on either tool and move the mouse to the drawing area. Figure 14-6 illustrates the two clipping methods. The scissors surround the irregularly shaped object. On the right, the pick grabs the whole object.

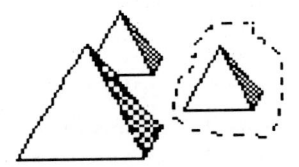

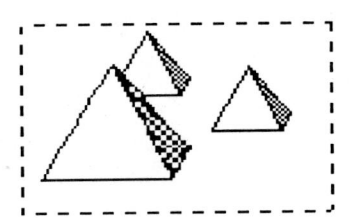

FIGURE 14-6. Scissors and pick clipping methods

Once you have selected objects, click on them, drag to another location on the drawing, and then release the mouse button. Cutouts can also be copied to the Clipboard for later use, or they can be pasted in other Windows applications.

Note the following regarding the cutout tools:

- You can duplicate a clipped item by pressing (SHIFT) as you drag. The original object stays intact.

- If you press the right mouse button when dragging an object, the entire cutout area, including any background color such as white, becomes part of the cut area and overlaps any object beneath it when placed.

Using the Eraser Tools

The eraser and color eraser remove or replace colors in your drawings.

THE ERASER TOOL The eraser changes all foreground colors to the currently selected background color. This can be confusing unless you think of the eraser as you would the brush: It leaves a trail of the currently selected foreground color in its path. If that color happens to be white and the normal background of your drawing area is white, the trail will be effectively erased. If you select a foreground color that is different than the current drawing area background color, the eraser leaves a trail of the color you have selected, which is more akin to the action of the brush.

Keep in mind that the size of the eraser point can be set by selecting a line width in the line size box. If you need to erase small details, select the smallest line size, carefully place the eraser, and click to remove colors from the area below it. To erase larger areas, click on a larger line size and drag the eraser around the screen as required.

Note When you need to erase only part of an image with the eraser, complete the process by selecting Zoom In to remove individual bits that might remain or to correct areas you accidentally erased.

THE COLOR ERASER TOOL The color eraser works in two ways. You can use it like the eraser but only to remove one selected color rather than all colors. The second way to use the color eraser is to automatically replace all occurrences of a color with another color, rather than dragging the mouse over the whole screen.

To replace a color with another color, first use the left mouse button to click on the color in the palette you want to change, making it the foreground color. Then use the right mouse button to click on the color in the color palette you want to change it to, making it the background color. Next, drag over the colors you want to change and they will be converted to the new color. In the following example, yellow has been replaced with black along the trail of the color eraser tool.

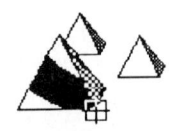

To change all occurrences of one color to another, select the color to change by clicking on it in the color palette with the left mouse button, and then select the color to change it to by clicking on the color in the color palette with the right mouse button. Next, double-click on the color eraser icon in the toolbox. All of the foreground colors convert to the background color on the current window.

Note You may need to move other parts of the drawing into the window and then repeat the color-change process.

Tip Be sure to select another tool before zooming or saving the graphics, because the colors might revert back to their original shades.

SPECIAL TECHNIQUES

The following techniques can enhance the images you have drawn in Paintbrush. They also can make the drawing process easier by duplicating and repeating objects you have already drawn or by providing special effects.

Sweeping a Cutout

You can "sweep" an object across the screen, thus leaving a trail of the object behind it, as shown in this illustration.

To sweep an object, use one of the cutout tools to select it and then press (CTRL) while dragging. The speed you drag the mouse makes a difference in how the trail of the sweep looks, so you may have to select Undo from the Edit menu and try the technique several times before you get it the way you want.

≡ Note ≡ Pressing the left mouse button while you sweep causes only the object itself and not the background to sweep. Pressing the right mouse button sweeps the entire cutout area, including any excess background colors in the cutout. The object will overlay other parts of the drawing.

Shrinking and Enlarging a Cutout

When you select an object, the options on the Pick menu become available. The Shrink + Grow option is used to resize the cutout. You can also replace the cutout with the resized object by selecting the Clear option on the Pick menu.

To resize an object, first select it with a cutout tool, and then choose Shrink + Grow from the Pick menu. If you want to clear the original version of an object after it has been resized, choose the Clear option at the same time. Move the cursor to the new anchor point for the object to be sized, and then hold down the mouse button as you drag. A frame indicates the new size of the object. When the frame is the correct size, release the mouse button. The cutout shrinks or grows to the new size.

≡ Tip ≡ To retain the proportions of the original object, press (SHIFT) as you resize.

> **Note** Some distortion may occur in the resized object. You can use the Zoom In option on the View menu to remove extra bits from enlarged objects or add extra bits to reduced objects.

Flipping, Inverting, and Tilting Techniques

A cutout can be flipped, inverted, and tilted in a combination of ways using the Flip Horizontal, Flip Vertical, Inverse, and Tilt options on the Pick menu. First select an object with the cutout tools, and then select one of these options from the Pick menu. Here are some tips to using these options:

- You can flip an object four ways by combining the horizontal and vertical flip options.

- To tilt an object, choose Tilt from the Pick menu, position the mouse at the new anchor point, and move the mouse back and forth until the tilt angle is achieved.

- The Inverse option inverts the colors of the objects in a cutout. Any portion of the drawing area included in the cutout is also inverted, so if it is white, the object will be surrounded by black after the operation. You can use the eraser and the Zoom In option to remove any excess colors.

Creating Custom Colors

The Options menu has options for creating, saving, and retrieving special colors. This section explains how to use the options.

EDITING COLORS When you select Edit Colors from the Options menu, the dialog box shown in Figure 14-7 appears. You can adjust the Red, Green, and Blue slider bars with the mouse to change the color in the sample box on the right. You can also type

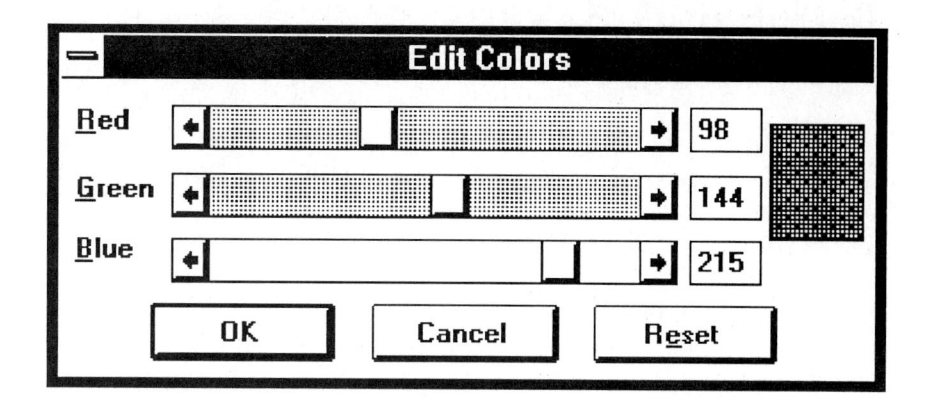

[FIGURE 14-7. The Edit Colors dialog box]

a number between 0 and 255 in the number boxes to the right of the slider bars if you need to set an exact color intensity.

Before adjusting colors, pick the color you want to adjust from the color palette. In the Edit Colors dialog box, slide the Red, Green, and Blue buttons to the right to increase the brightness of each color or the left to decrease the brightness. When the new color is the way you want, click on OK. The new color now appears in the color palette.

Tip: Double-click on any color in the color palette to quickly display the Edit Colors dialog box and change its colors.

SAVING AND RETRIEVING COLORS   Once you have made changes to the color bars, you can save them for later use by choosing the Save Colors option on the Options menu. A dialog box appears, which allows you to type the name of the color palette file. Paintbrush recommends the .PAL extension for the file. If you want to use the customized palette at a later date, choose the Get Colors option on the Options menu.

RETRIEVING, SAVING, AND PRINTING

The following sections explain how to save your drawings or cutouts from your drawings, how to print drawings, and how to retrieve saved drawings or cutouts.

Saving Your Work

You should save your drawing regularly as you work with Paintbrush. You can save the entire drawing, or you can save a portion of it for use in other drawings or as a way to temporarily remove an object from a drawing.

You can save your drawing in several formats by pressing the Options button on the Save dialog box. The methods are listed here:

- PCX Paintbrush file
- Monochrome bitmap
- 16-color bitmap
- 256-color bitmap
- 24-bit bitmap

SAVING A CUTOUT To save a cutout of your drawing, use the scissors or pick tool to highlight only the portion of the drawing you want to save. Choose the Copy To option from the Edit menu. In the Copy To dialog box, type the name you want to give to the cutout and click on the OK button to save it.

You can click the Options button on the Copy To dialog box to select a Save As parameter. The cutout can be saved in one of the formats listed in the previous section.

To retrieve a cutout, select the Paste From option on the Edit menu.

SAVING THE COMPLETE DRAWING To save your entire drawing, click on the Save As option in the File menu. When the File Save As dialog box appears, you can press the Options button to choose a format for saving the file.

Printing a Drawing

To print your drawings, use the Print option on the File menu. The Print dialog box is shown in Figure 14-8. You can print the entire drawing or selected parts of it using the options in the Window box. If you want to print a selected portion, click on the Partial box. When you click on the OK button on the Print dialog box, the entire image becomes visible for a moment. The cursor then becomes a box that you can click and drag over the portion of the

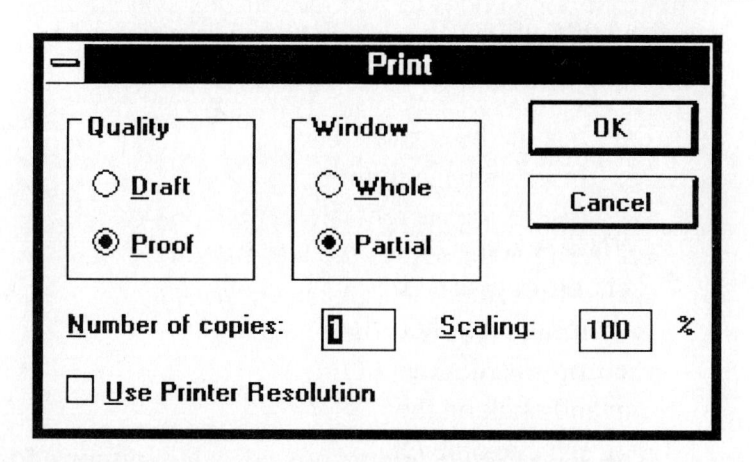

FIGURE 14-8. The Print dialog box

drawing you want to print. When you release the mouse button, that portion of the drawing is printed.

You can also select Draft or Proof quality in the Quality box. Draft mode is available on some printers and is a low-quality, high-speed print mode. You can also specify the size of the drawing by entering a percentage in the Scaling box. For example, if you wanted to print a drawing at half the size, you would type 50 in the Scaling box to represent 50%. The Print dialog box also lets you control the number of copies printed.

Click on the Use Printer Resolution box if you want your drawing to print at the resolution of your printer rather than at screen resolution. This sets up a one-to-one relationship between the pixel on the screen and the dot resolution of your printer. In most cases the actual printed object will be much smaller in size. Normally, Paintbrush stretches objects to make them appear more like the screen.

HEADERS AND FOOTERS You can include headers and footers in your drawing by choosing the Page Setup option on the File menu. Type the header or footer in the appropriate box. Use the following codes to include various system parameters or text alignment options:

&d Inserts the current date
&p Inserts a page number
&f Inserts the current filename
&l Aligns the text to the left margin
&r Aligns the text to the right margin
&c Centers the text (default)
&t Inserts the current time

The Page Setup dialog box also has options for setting the margins on the printed page. The measure in the margins should be from the edges of the paper.

15

WINDOWS TERMINAL

Establishing a Communications Session
Dialing and Connection
On-Line Activities

Windows Terminal is a communications program you can use to connect to other systems and transfer files. The systems you can connect to can be local systems connected with special cable, or remote systems connected with phone lines and modems. If you are using a modem, you should become familiar with the communications protocols of the systems to which you are connecting. Usually these protocols are published by the services themselves. If you are not sure, you should contact the other party before making connections.

When connecting two local computers together, you need a special null modem cable, which can be purchased at most computer stores. For best results, both machines should run Windows Terminal and have the same protocol settings.

Terminal is easy to use once you have established the correct communications settings. This chapter will present the steps you should go through to establish an initial communications session and give you a brief explanation of the features you must set. In the first section you learn how to start an initial session. The next section covers the tasks you can perform like transferring files while connected to another system. The last section then covers topics of special interest.

ESTABLISHING A COMMUNICATIONS SESSION

To start Terminal, double-click on its icon in the Accessories window of the Program Manager. A window appears similar to Figure 15-1, which also shows the Settings pull-down menu. This

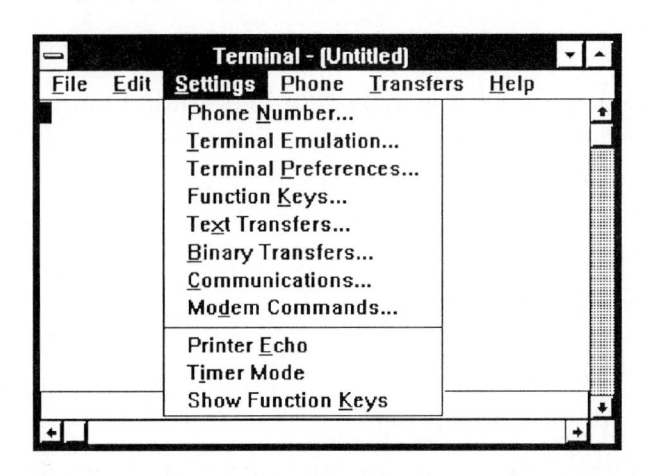

FIGURE 15-1. The Terminal window with the Settings pull-down menu open

menu has many of the options you need when setting up the initial communications session.

To prepare for a communications session, you must know the settings of the computer you will connect with so you can set the options on your computer to match. You may want to call a user at the remote location, or if you are connecting with on-line services like Compuserve, refer to the manual that comes with the Compuserve package.

Saving and Retrieving Communications Settings

Most of the settings you specify for a communications session can be saved in a file for use at another time. This *settings file* is saved with the Save option on the File menu and given the .TRM extension by Terminal. The settings saved in a .TRM file include the phone number of the remote location or on-line service, the communications settings such as transmission speed, and other parameters. You should save the settings of any communications session you may need to use again in the future.

If you need to call a remote system or on-line service at a later time, you can retrieve the settings by opening the .TRM file using the Open option on the File menu.

Terminal's ability to save the settings of a communications session for a later time is a powerful feature you will no doubt use on a regular basis.

Basic Settings

The following sections describe the required and optional settings you need to start a communications session. Each section describes the options on the Settings menu.

SESSION TIMER Before you begin a session, you may want to set the session timer on. This helps you keep track of the amount of time you have been logged on to the remote system.

To see the Timer, you must first set the function key display on. Choose Show Function Keys from the Settings menu. A set of ten boxes appears at the bottom of the screen. The lower-right box contains the system timer. Initially, it shows the normal time. To begin timing a session, choose the Timer Mode option on the Settings menu. To turn the timer off, select the Timer Mode option again. The timer itself will toggle from clock to timer if you click on it.

PHONE NUMBER OPTION The first option to set when you are establishing a communications session is the telephone number. Choose the Phone Number option from the Settings menu to see the following dialog box:

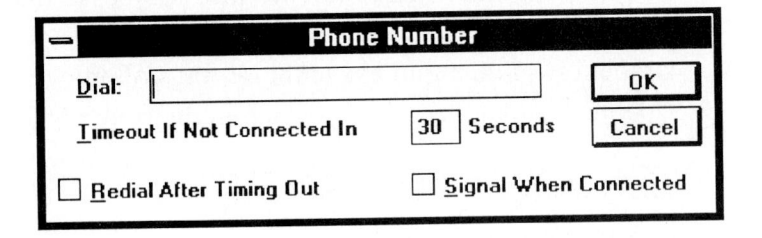

```
┌─────────────────── Phone Number ───────────────────┐
│                                                     │
│  Dial: [                              ]    ┌─────┐  │
│                                            │ OK  │  │
│  Timeout If Not Connected In  [30] Seconds └─────┘  │
│                                            ┌───────┐│
│                                            │Cancel ││
│  ☐ Redial After Timing Out  ☐ Signal When Connected │
└─────────────────────────────────────────────────────┘
```

Type the number to be dialed in the dialog box. Parentheses and dashes are optional, but you may need to type commas to provide delays for your phone system. For example, if you need to dial 9 to get an outside line, you must often pause a few seconds before dialing the outside number. Each comma placed in the number introduces a two-second pause. In the following example, a four-second pause is introduced after the 9 is dialed:

9,,1-234-567-8910

The remainder of the options on the Phone Number dialog box are discussed here:

Timeout If Not Connected In — Sets the number of seconds you want Terminal to wait for a response from the remote system. If the remote system does not respond in the amount of time set, it may be busy or disconnected.

Redial After Timing Out — Terminal continues to redial the number after it fails to connect when you check this option.

Signal When Connected — Click this option if you want the computer to beep when a connection is finally made.

TERMINAL EMULATION OPTION When you connect with some remote computers, you may need to emulate a specific terminal (screen and keyboard). When your system is set to emulate a terminal, its keyboard functions will be like those used on the remote system, not like those of your own system. In most cases, only a few keys will be different.

The Terminal Emulation dialog box is shown in the following illustration:

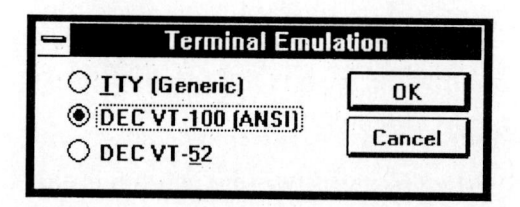

```
┌─────────────────────────────────────┐
│         Terminal Emulation          │
│  ○ ITY (Generic)        ┌────────┐  │
│  ● DEC VT-100 (ANSI)    │   OK   │  │
│  ○ DEC VT-52            ├────────┤  │
│                         │ Cancel │  │
│                         └────────┘  │
└─────────────────────────────────────┘
```

You can select between two DEC (Digital Equipment Corporation) terminal emulation modes or a more standardized TTY mode. If you are not sure, select the TTY mode.

TERMINAL PREFERENCES OPTION The Terminal Preferences option specifies how you want your system to perform

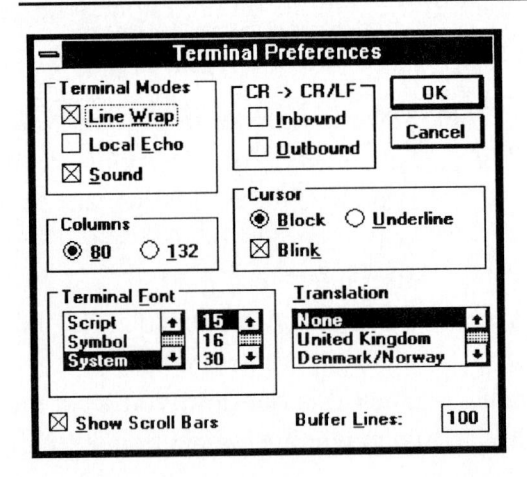

FIGURE 15-2. The Terminal Preferences dialog box

during a communications session. The settings control sound, line wrap, and other features. Choose Terminal Preferences from the Settings menu to display a dialog box similar to the one in Figure 15-2. Each of its options, from left to right, are described here:

- *Line Wrap.* Specify line wrap in most cases. It causes characters to wrap at column 80. This is important if the remote system is sending larger width columns.

- *Local Echo.* Most systems operate in what is called a *full-duplex mode,* which means the remote system sends the characters back to you so you can verify that they have been transmitted properly. This is known as a *remote echo.* Leave Local Echo off if operating in full-duplex mode.

- *Sound.* Click this option to turn sound on or off.

- *CR to CR/LF.* When characters reach the right border, they usually wrap to the next line because of a combination carriage return and line feed. The carriage return moves the cursor to the left border and the line feed advances one line. If text received from a remote system is typed over previously received text, the remote system is sending you inbound data that does not have a line feed. Click on the Inbound box to correct this problem. If the remote system receives text from you that types over itself on the same line, you can click on Outbound to include a line feed with your transmissions.

- *Columns.* If you have a 132-column monitor, select 132; otherwise select 80.

- *Cursor.* Specifies whether the cursor is a block or an underline and whether it blinks.

- *Terminal Font.* Allows you to select one of the Windows fonts for displaying the characters you type and those received from the remote system.

- *Translation.* Specifies the country setting to use when sending and receiving data.

- *Show Scroll Bars.* Use this option to set the scroll bars on or off.

- *Buffer Lines.* The buffer is used to store incoming lines if your system is temporarily paused or running slowly. You can specify from 25 to 400 lines of buffer storage, depending on the amount of memory your system has.

COMMUNICATIONS OPTIONS To communicate with another system, you must share various protocols and parameters. For example, both systems need to communicate at the same data transfer rate. This rate is often determined by the type of modem being used and is referred to as the *baud rate*. The structure used to transmit each character must also be the same between both systems. For example, most systems transfer standard ASCII text characters using 8 bits (zeros and ones) as a code to define the character.

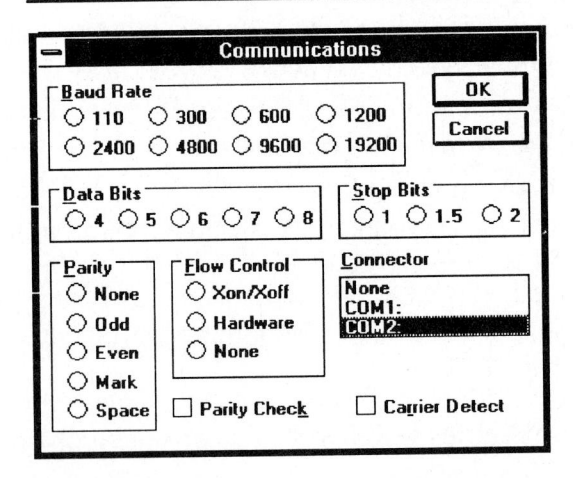

FIGURE 15-3. The Communications dialog box

To determine the settings you need to communicate with another system, you may need to call a user at that system. If connecting to an on-line service, refer to the owner's manual that comes with the subscription.

To display the Communications dialog box shown in Figure 15-3, choose the Communications option on the Settings menu. Each option on the menu is discussed here:

- *Baud Rate*. Select the speed at which data is to be transmitted over the phone lines. The speed usually is determined by the modems being used in remote connections, but it can be high when two computers are directly connected with a null-modem cable.

- *Data Bits*. Specify the number of data bits in each packet sent between two computers. This is usually 7 or 8. If Parity is set to None, use 8 data bits.

- *Stop Bits*. Specifies the timing units between characters.

- *Parity*. Set Parity to None, Odd, Even, Mark, or Space depending on the settings of the remote system.

- *Flow Control*. Flow control is a method of temporarily halting transmission if the buffers become full on either side of the session. Xon/Xoff is a software "handshaking" method. If handshaking is done through the hardware, select Hardware. If None is selected, Terminal uses no flow controls and you may need to set a slow transmission (baud) rate.

- *Connector*. Select the serial port to be used, either COM1 or COM2. Select None if a null modem is being used.

- *Parity Check*. If you check this box, Terminal displays a question mark for every character that was transmitted improperly.

- *Carrier Detect*. Sets the use of the modem's carrier detect. If off, Terminal's carrier detection method is used.

DIALING AND CONNECTION

When the communication parameters for a session have been specified, you are ready to dial the remote system. Choose Dial from the Phone menu. Terminal dials the number you typed in the Phone Number dialog box and attempts to connect with the remote system.

If the connection is made and works properly, you can use the Save option on the File menu to save the settings for future use.

When You Have Connection Problems

If you have problems making a connection, first check to make sure your modem is getting the dial signals from Terminal. Turn the volume up and listen for the dial tones. If the modem is not dialing, you may have it connected to the wrong communications port. Try switching the cable to another port, or specify the port it is currently connected to in the Connector field of the Communications dialog box.

If the modem is dialing, check the cables from the modem to the wall jack. It may be connected improperly or simply busy. Call the remote site and request assistance. If you know the system is ready for your call and you still cannot get through, the remote site is probably not connected properly, or you may need to match the settings on the Communications dialog box with the settings being used at the remote site. You usually can connect with a remote system even if the settings are not matched, but the system will not work properly and transferred data will be garbled.

When you connect to an on-line service, various log-on or welcome messages are sent to your system immediately. If they appear normal and readable, the connection is good. When you connect to a remote system that is being operated by another user, try typing a few characters such as **are you there** to make sure the session is operating properly. The remote user should then respond by typing a message. If the connection seems to be good, you can get on with the session by reading the next section on line activities. If the messages are garbled, compare the communications parameters between the systems.

A session may appear good until you start to transmit data. Problems can occur if the transmission speed is too fast or not matched properly. You should also check to make sure both systems are using the same flow control protocols, which make sure that the sending system suspends while the receiving system catches up. If data files are not being sent or captured properly, you may want to use the Xon/Xoff method or the binary file transfer method discussed in the next section.

ON-LINE ACTIVITIES

Once you connect properly to another system, you can perform file transfers or chat with other users. This section covers methods for transferring files and the options visible on the Transfer menu.

Types of Files and Transfer Methods

You can send and receive two types of files with Terminal. The first is the standard *text file,* which contains ASCII characters. Notepad and many other programs are capable of creating these files. ASCII is an industry-wide standard used to code alpha-numeric characters. Every DOS-based PC and most other computer systems are aware of the coding scheme and are capable of reading such files. Text files do not contain special formatting codes or control characters and may be transmitted using simple text transfer methods.

Binary files are typically program files or files with special formatting and control codes that use the extended ASCII character set. Binary files must be transmitted without any type of alteration. If you are sending program files with the extension .COM or .EXE, you must use binary transfer methods.

In most cases you can transmit all your files, including text files, using the binary transfer method. It provides several advantages over text transfer methods. For example, errors are more thoroughly tested and corrected in a binary transfer. In fact, you should only use text transfer methods when connected to a system that does not have its own binary transfer capabilities, which is rare in today's world of sophisticated communications software.

Both types of file transfers are covered in the following sections.

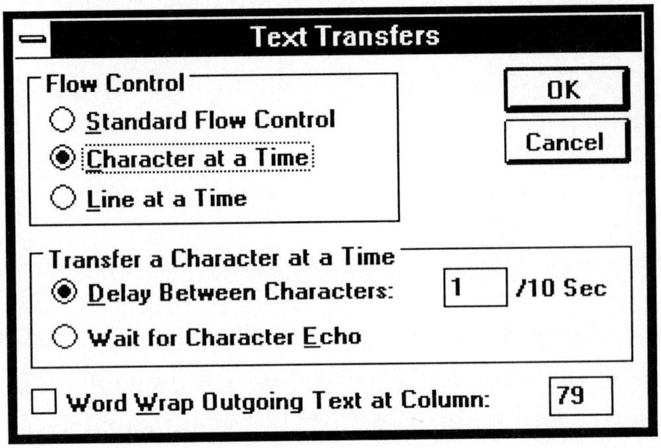

FIGURE 15-4. The Text Transfers dialog box

Transmitting Text Files

To begin transferring a text file, first choose the Text Transfers option on the Settings menu. From the resulting dialog box, shown in Figure 15-4, select the options as described in the following list to set the initial parameters for the file transfer. When done, click on the OK button.

- *Standard Flow Control.* Click this option to use the flow control selected on the Communications dialog box.

- *Character at a Time.* Click this option to send text files one character at a time. When this option is selected, these two options appear in the lower part of the menu:

    Delay Between Characters. You can set this option to transmit at a slow, even rate without verification. The slow rate may ensure accuracy in transmission. Use the default delay rate or, if you have problems, increase the delay time.

Wait for Character Echo. Set this option to have Terminal send a character, then receive it back from the remote site for verification.

- *Line at a Time.* Click on this option to send text one line at a time. When the option is selected, the following additional options appear:

    Delay Between Lines. Set this option to transmit lines at a slow, even rate without verification. The slow rate may ensure accuracy in transmission. Use the default delay rate, or if you have problems, increase the delay time.
    Wait for Prompt String. Sends one line and then waits for a response from the remote system before sending another line.

- *Word Wrap Outgoing Text at Column.* Use this option to specify the column where lines will break.

SENDING TEXT FILES After specifying the text transfer settings in the Text Transfers dialog box, choose the Send Text File option on the Transfers menu. When the dialog box appears, enter the name of the file you want to send in the Filename field.

You can click on Append LF to add a line feed to the end of each line of text, or you can click on Strip LF if you need to remove extra line feeds from the text you send. Click on OK to begin sending the file. As the file is sent, it scrolls in the Terminal window.

> **Note:** Control buttons appear at the bottom of the screen for pausing, resuming, and stopping a transmission.

RECEIVING TEXT FILES After specifying the text transfer settings on the Text Transfers dialog box, you can choose the Receive Text File option from the Transfers menu. Type the name you want to assign to the received file in the Filename field. The

Receive Text File dialog box contains the following options for specifying how the received file should be handled:

Append File — Appends the incoming text to an existing file. You must specify the existing file name in the Filename box.

Save Controls — Saves the codes if formatting codes are being transmitted with the file, such as those used to change fonts or styles. Not all codes can be transmitted.

Table Format — Replaces two or more consecutive spaces with a tab.

Click on the OK button when the settings are the way you like. The file will scroll on the Terminal window as it is received.

> **Note** You can print incoming data by choosing Printer Echo from the Settings menu.

VIEWING A TEXT FILE The View Text File option on the Transfers menu can be used to look at a text file before sending it or after one has been received. Choose View Text File from the Transfers menu, and then type the name of the file you want to view. You can specify whether line feeds should be added or removed by checking the Append LF or Strip LF boxes, respectively. Click on OK to view the file.

Transmitting Binary Files

Setting up a communications session to transmit binary files is easy. All you have to do is choose one of the following standardized protocols. Both systems must be using the same protocol.

- *XModem/CRC*. Uses all 8 bits as data bits and requires that the Parity option be set to None on the Communications dialog box. An error-checking method called Cyclic Redundancy Check (CRC) ensures data is transferred properly. If the remote system does not use CRC, a checksum scheme is used.

- *Kermit*. Uses either 7 or 8 bits with parity specified as Even, Odd, or None. If you are sending files with extended ASCII characters or program files, use the 8 bits setting and None for parity.

Click on OK after setting the appropriate option.

SENDING BINARY FILES To send a binary file, choose the Send Binary File command on the Transfers menu. Type the name of the file in the Filename box and click on OK to send the file.

RECEIVING BINARY FILES To receive a binary file, choose the Receive Binary File command on the Transfers menu. Type the name of the file in the Filename box, and click on OK to start receiving the file.

> Note: You can print incoming data by choosing Printer Echo from the Settings menu.

Working in the Terminal Window

You can type messages or paste information from the Clipboard in the Terminal window to send to the remote location. To send the contents of the Clipboard, choose Paste from the Edit menu. The pasted information is then sent to the remote site. You can also type text in the window, highlight it, and then choose Send from the Edit menu to send it to the remote site.

Ending a Communications Session

To end a communications session with a remote system, you may need to log out of the remote system first. After doing so, choose the Hang-up option on the Phone menu to hang up the modem.

16

PLAYING GAMES

Reversi
Solitaire

This chapter gives you brief instructions for playing the two games supplied with Windows, Reversi and Solitaire.

REVERSI

The object of Reversi is to finish the game with more of your red pieces on the board than the computer has blue pieces. If you have a monochrome monitor, your pieces are white and the computer's pieces are black.

To begin the game, open the Games group window and double-click on the Reversi icon. The Reversi game board shown in Figure 16-1 appears. You might want to select a skill level by choosing one of the options on the Skill menu. If you are familiar with the game, you can choose one of the more advanced options. The

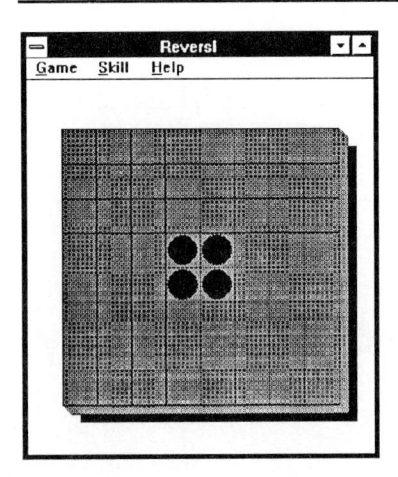

FIGURE 16-1. The Reversi game board

computer takes longer to calculate its own moves in the more advanced skill modes.

You can start the game, or click Pass on the Game menu to let the computer start first. You can also choose Pass when you cannot make a legal move. Moves are legal when the pointer in a square changes to a cross and at least one of the computer's pieces lies in a horizontal, vertical, or diagonal line between one of your pieces and the place where you want to move.

Click on the square where you want to move. The computer's pieces in between yours then turn to your color and the computer makes its move. The computer moves quickly so it may at first be hard to determine what has happened.

Depending on the skill level you have selected, the computer gives you a hint as to where it would move if playing your pieces. Choose Hint from the Game menu and the cross appears over the square on the board suggested by the computer.

The game ends when the squares are filled. The player with the most pieces wins.

SOLITAIRE

Windows Solitaire is a computerized version of the popular single-player card game. The object of the game is to build up the four suits by stacking cards in order starting with the ace. The cards are automatically shuffled, stacked, and dealt for you.

To play the game, double-click the Solitaire icon in the Games group window. When the Solitaire window appears, the cards are arranged, ready for play. You can pull down the Game menu to change some of the game's features. For example, choose the Deck option to select a different pattern for the card backing.

> **Note** You can choose the Undo option on the Game menu to undo the last card movement.

Solitaire has three game areas:

- The deck in the upper-left corner of the playing area.

- Four suit stacks in the upper-right corner of the playing area, which start out empty.

- Seven row stacks below the deck and suit stacks. The number of cards in each row stack increases from one to seven from left to right. The top card of each row stack is face up; the rest are face down.

Cards are drawn from the deck and used to build stacks. Solitaire shows either the first or third card in the deck, depending on which Draw option you select. When you get to the end of the deck, you can turn the deck over and start drawing cards again.

You can move a card from the deck to a suit stack or to a row stack. You build up row stacks in descending order, alternating between red and black cards (light and dark if you have a monochrome monitor). You can move a card in a row stack to another row stack or to a suit stack. If you uncover a face-down card in a row stack, you can turn the card face up.

Kings can be moved to empty row stacks. You build up suit stacks in ascending order, starting with the ace.

You win the game when you have used all the cards in the deck to build up all four suit stacks from ace to king. To play a new game, choose Deal from the Game menu.

The Solitaire Options Menu

The Solitaire Options menu sets the game's characteristics and play modes, as described here:

Draw One	One card on the deck is turned over during each draw
Draw Three	Every third card is turned over during a draw
Scoring	Select Standard, Vegas, or None
Timed Game	Solitaire tracks the time of your game
Status Bar	Displays the command status bar at the bottom of the Solitaire window
Keep Score	When using Vegas scoring, Solitaire keeps a running total of your score from game to game
Outline Dragging	Solitaire shows an outline of the card being moved and changes the color of the space or card you are moving to if the move is valid

17

A TYPICAL DAY WITH WINDOWS

Opening the Calendar
Writing Notes
Organizing the Desktop
Tips and Techniques for Writing
Writing a Letter
File Manager Techniques
Playing a Game
Creating Scrapbooks
Archiving Files

This chapter gives you ideas on how to use Windows for your own activities and in your daily work schedule. It presents several examples of how Windows might be used on a regular basis. Many of the programs and accessories you have used on an individual basis are used together in an integrated approach.

OPENING THE CALENDAR

One of the first things you might want to do with Windows is create personal and business calendars. Then, when you start your system each day, you can load those calendars for review. To start a business calendar, open Calendar and create a new file called BUSINESS or some other descriptive name. You can leave Calendar on the desktop as a window, or you can reduce the window to an icon on the desktop to save memory. Remember, loaded icons provide quick access to your files but do not clutter the desktop or use too much memory.

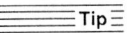

> **Tip** Chapter 18 discusses how Windows can automatically place your Calendar file on the desktop, ready for use, every time you start your system.

Since it's a good idea to have a printout of your daily activities, one of the first things to do is print the daily schedule. If you also want to print the schedule for the previous day as a log and the schedule for the next day as a reference, specify the date range from yesterday to tomorrow in the Print dialog box.

Assume that you notice a 3:00 appointment with an associate down the hall. Since you know you'll be working at your computer just before the appointment, you can set an alarm for 3:00. Choose the Control option on the Alarm menu to set a 10-minute advance ring, just enough time to save your work and turn off your computer before going to the appointment.

Keeping a Personal Calendar

You can use the Calendar file just discussed for your business activities, but you also might want to keep a calendar of your personal activities and important dates, such as your children's birthdays. Create a second Calendar file called PERSONAL or some similar descriptive name and keep it open on the desktop. As a matter of fact, you can create as many calendars as you need.

WRITING NOTES

The Notepad is another useful accessory to keep on your desktop. Once the program is loaded, you can reduce it to an icon, thus saving memory but keeping Notepad always available for quick notes and memos. Consider saving the notes and messages that accumulate in Notepad to a file called DAILY or a similar descriptive name. Then, at the end of each day or whenever necessary, you can print the notes, review them, or consolidate them into other documents, as discussed later in this chapter. After the notes have been printed or copied elsewhere, you can delete the DAILY file and start a new one the next day.

Along with the DAILY file, you can keep a second Notepad file to track your daily chargeable or expense-related activities. This file can be called TIMELOG. When you start an accountable activity, simply click on the Notepad TIMELOG desktop icon to make a new date and time entry in the file. These entries are made one after the other and can be time and date stamped using the Time/Date option on the Notepad Edit window. This option inserts the current time and date at the beginning of each entry. In this way, the file becomes an accumulation of time- and date-stamped activities in chronological order that you can use to bill your clients, create expense reports, or document your activities for tax purposes. Once the activities have been documented as necessary, you can clear the file to start a new week or month.

ORGANIZING THE DESKTOP

At this point, your desktop may look something like that shown in Figure 17-1. Each open application is reduced to an icon for quick

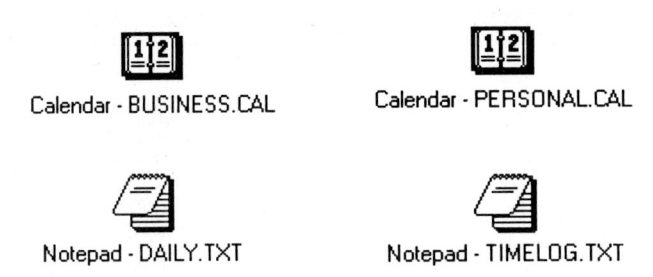

FIGURE 17-1. A desktop for daily use

access during the day. Since you might be creating many daily files, you should consider where those files will be stored. The idea is to keep them separate from program files and other types of data files. The methods of organizing your system using directories, which were covered in Chapters 6 and 7, are used here to organize your daily files. Keep in mind that you can use the techniques described here to organize any set of files on your hard drive.

First you must copy the daily files to a new directory of their own. You then use the Program Manager to create startup icons for each of the files and a group window called DAILY where the icons can be kept. Assume for this discussion that the Notepad and Calendar daily files discussed in the last section were created in a directory called WIN3 and will be copied to a new directory called DAILY.

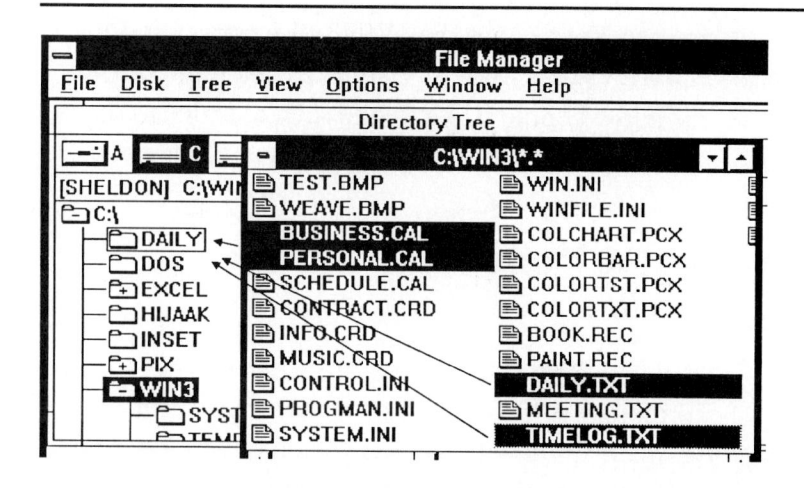

FIGURE 17-2. Copying the daily files to a new directory

Moving the Files to Their Own Directory

To copy the files, open the File Manager by double-clicking its icon. When the Directory Tree window appears, create a new directory by choosing the Create Directory option on the File menu. In the Name field, type **\DAILY**. The backslash ensures that the directory will be a subdirectory of the root directory if you are currently logged into another directory.

The next step is to open the WIN3 directory (remember, this is just an example directory) by double-clicking its icon in the File Manager window. Select each daily file to be reorganized into the new directory by clicking on each as you press (CTRL). The (CTRL) key is the bridge key for selecting multiple items. Figure 17-2 shows how the File Manager windows are arranged for this operation. Notice that the WIN3 directory window is open, and the DAILY directory is visible as an icon on the Directory Tree window behind it. Move the selected files to the DAILY directory by dragging with the mouse.

Creating Startup Icons for the Daily Files

Now that the daily files are in their own directory, the WIN3 directory is closed and the DAILY directory is opened. It is then resized along with the File Manager window to fit on the right side of the desktop, as shown in Figure 17-3.

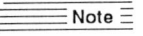

Note Keep in mind that, for this discussion, the DAILY group window in the Program Manager is not the same as the DAILY directory window in the File Manager.

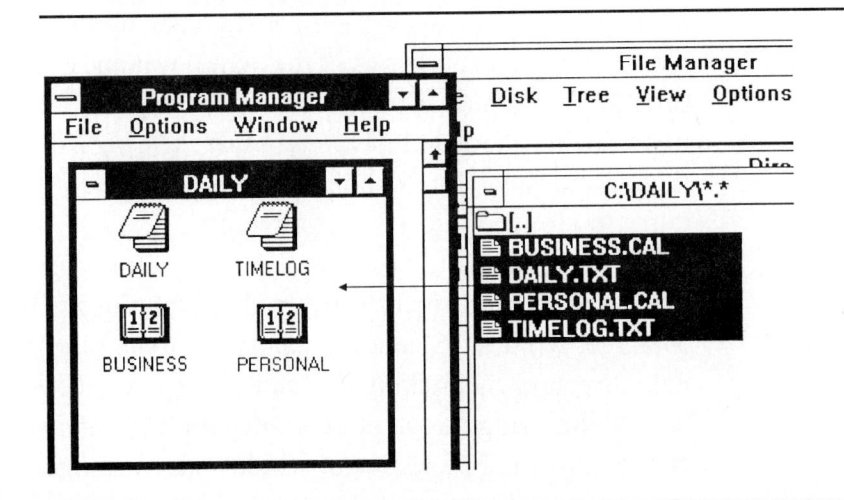

FIGURE 17-3. Creating startup icons for the daily files by dragging between the File Manager and the Program Manager

Next, the Program Manager is opened and resized to fit on the left side of the desktop, as shown in Figure 17-3. A new program group called DAILY is created using the New option on the Program Manager File menu. Finally, the four files in the DAILY directory window are dragged to the DAILY group window and the four new icons appear as shown in the DAILY group window of Figure 17-3.

The method of dragging document files from the File Manager to the Program Manager may not work on some versions of Windows. To create a similar DAILY window, drag two copies each of CALENDAR.EXE and NOTEPAD.EXE to the DAILY window from the Windows Accessories group window. Next, associate the appropriate file in the DAILY directory to each icon using the Properties option on the Program Manager File menu, selecting each icon in the DAILY window in turn, and then opening the Properties dialog box. In the dialog box, type a name for the icon in the Description field and add the path and filename to the Command Line field. An example for the TIMELOG icon is shown in Figure 17-4.

The daily files are now associated with their programs, and startup icons are available so you can easily load them at any time. You may want to leave the DAILY group window open in the Program Manager. To do so, place the open window where you want and, as you exit Windows, click on the Save Changes box.

TIPS AND TECHNIQUES FOR WRITING

Once you have written a lot of notes with Notepad, you may want to use them in other applications or consolidate them in various ways, as described in the following sections.

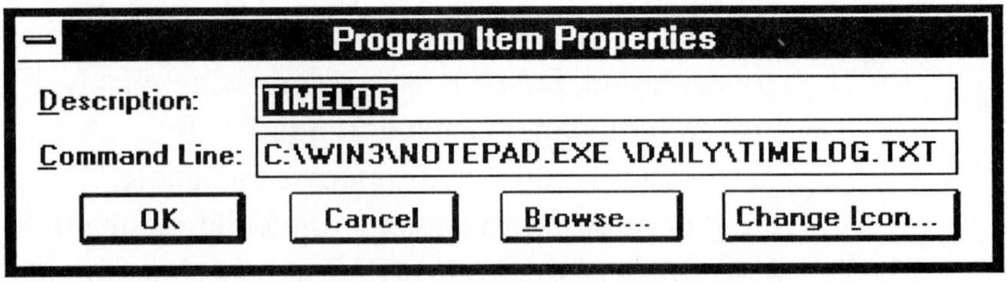

FIGURE 17-4. The startup command for the TIMELOG file is shown in the Program Item Properties dialog box

Writing and Consolidating Notes

Assume you have accumulated a series of notes in your DAILY Notepad file and you now want to sort through them. Some of the notes throughout the file are related to each other, while others might be text to include in a drawing, a card file, or your appointment schedule.

Consolidating notes is easy since Windows lets you run two versions of an application at once. You can open your DAILY file in one Notepad window and a new file in another Notepad window. Then, as you scan through the DAILY file, you can use the Clipboard commands to move selected notes from it to the new file. You might want to use the Clipboard Cut command so that notes are removed from the DAILY file as you proceed. In this way, you reduce the DAILY file as you scan it. Eventually, each note in the DAILY file may be discarded or consolidated into a new file. You can then start a new DAILY file for the next day.

Comparing and Copying Between Files

Another way to use multiple running copies of applications is to compare two files or extract text from one file into another. For example, assume an associate has given you a large document written in Windows Write. You want to keep the file intact but extract certain passages from it for a new file. This is easy to do using the method described here.

First, open two Write windows by double-clicking on the Write icon twice. In the first window, load the document file you received from your associate. Scroll through the document to find the blocks of text you want to extract and use the Clipboard Copy command to place them on the Clipboard. With the text on the Clipboard, switch to the other Write window and paste.

Tip It helps to place one window on the top half of the screen and the other on the lower half.

You can also use the dual window method to compare two files. Open each application in a separate window, and then page through each simultaneously, switching from one window to another. Scan through the text to find their differences.

WRITING A LETTER

Windows Write is a powerful word processing program for writing letters and other documents; however, it lacks features like mail merge and style sheets. You can use the Windows accessories to make up for these deficiencies.

Boilerplates

Boilerplates are blocks of text used over and over from one document to the next. Legal documents are often composed of a whole series of prewritten blocks of boilerplate text. You can create your own boilerplates by using Notepad or Cardfile. Use Notepad if the boilerplate text is extensive and will not fit on a

Cardfile index card. Cardfile is preferred if you have a lot of text blocks that would benefit from its indexing and search features.

To create a boilerplate with Notepad, simply type the text in the Notepad workspace, and then save it with an appropriate filename. Alternatively, you can copy long blocks of text you have already typed in an existing document to Notepad to save it for later. When you need boilerplate text, simply start Notepad and open the appropriate document, then copy the text to the Clipboard, and paste it in the target document.

Clipboard provides a way to index and quickly search for blocks of boilerplate text. Figure 17-5 shows a Cardfile stack used by a real estate agent to create contracts. Notice that each index card holds individual sections of a contract that can be pieced together to form a new contract. In the figure, the text on the top card has been pasted to the Write window in the background.

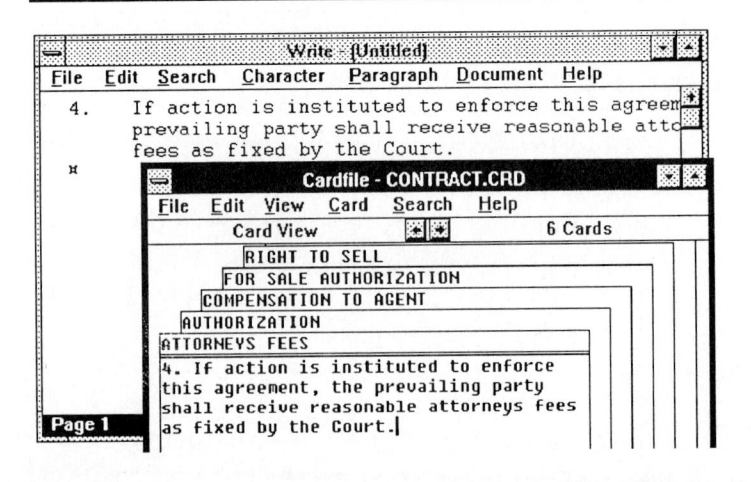

FIGURE 17-5. A Cardfile stack used as a scrapbook for often used text

Retrieving an Address

You can also use Cardfile to store and index names and addresses. You then can use the information on the cards in copy and paste operations, quickly pasting the name and address from a card into a document you are writing. For example, to quickly insert an address in a letter, open the Cardfile index, search for the name of the recipient, copy the address information on the card to the Clipboard, and then switch back to your document and paste it in. If you are writing a number of letters, you may want to keep the Cardfile index open on the desktop to quickly retrieve addresses.

Adding a Letterhead

At times you may want to insert graphics images in your documents on a regular basis. If you have a lot of graphic images, you can create a *scrapbook* of images using Cardfile. In this way, you can index and search through the graphics images. A Cardfile scrapbook is described in a later section, "Creating Scrapbooks".

If you have only one or two images, you can save them as Clipboard images using the Save option on the Clipboard menu. For example, assume you belong to a chess club and want to create a logo for the club's newsletter and stationery. Windows comes with a file called CHESS.BMP that is stored in your Windows directory. You can open this file with Paintbrush and clip any of the chess pieces that appear on it for use in your own documents. You might want to look at other Paintbrush files supplied with Windows for additional art.

Figure 17-6 shows a letterhead with a knight chess piece that was clipped from the CHESS.BMP file and altered to a black and white image for use in Write. Color Paintbrush images convert to black and white when pasted in most applications, so you may want to alter the colors of the objects in Paintbrush before copying them. The club name was added to the right of the image, and the whole

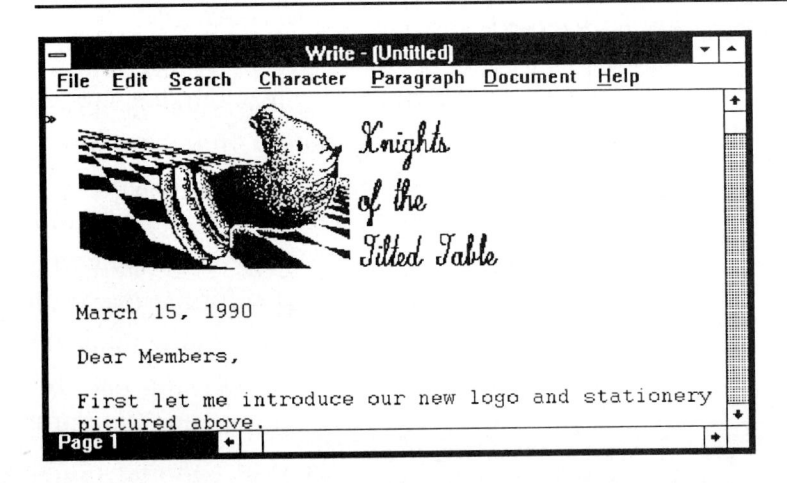

FIGURE 17-6. A graphics image is pasted to the top of a Write document to serve as a logo

thing was saved as a Clipboard file. Switching to Write, the image was then pasted at the top of the document. Since the Clipboard image was saved as a disk file, it can be recalled and pasted at any time.

FILE MANAGER TECHNIQUES

The File Manager provides file-handling routines that are superior to working at the DOS command prompt. One of the advantages of the File Manager is its ability to run in a separate window, which means you can quickly switch to it to execute file operations whenever necessary.

Switching to the File Manager

The File Manager is such a useful utility that you should start it at the beginning of each day and keep it available as a reduced icon on your desktop until needed. Assume you are working in a program like Write or Paintbrush and decide you want to store your current file in a directory that does not exist yet. You can quickly create the directory if you switch to the File Manager. Then you can switch back to your program and save the file in the new directory.

The File Manager also is useful for quick file operations. For example, assume you are working in a Write window and an associate who needs a copy of a file stops by your office. You don't need to exit your current applications and go to DOS to copy the file. Instead, you can simply switch to the File Manager, open a window on the directory where the file exists, and copy it to a diskette. You can even format a diskette if necessary. When you are done, simply switch back to Write and resume writing.

Sending Disk Files

The documents you create in Windows can by used without modification by other Windows users. Since Windows provides a common user interface, documents created in one application can, in some cases, even be used in other types of applications. If you transfer files to other Windows users, always try to retain the filename extension Windows gives to its files. For example, Write files have the extension .WRI, and Notepad files have the extension .TXT.

If you need to send files to users who do not have Windows, be sure to save the files in an appropriate format. This is often a basic text-only format without control codes. For example, you can save a Write document as an ASCII text file by clicking on the Text Only box on the File Save As dialog box. If the recipient of the file uses Microsoft Word, you can save Write files in the Word format by choosing the Microsoft Word Format option on the File Save As dialog box.

III

ADVANCED TOPICS

18

MODIFYING WINDOWS STARTUP

Altering the Windows Startup Files
Working with Your System's Startup Files

You can alter how Windows starts and runs in two ways. First you can change the startup files used by your system when it first boots. The information in these files governs the amount of memory available for Windows and its applications, and the parameters of the disk-caching program, SMARTDrive. The parameters in the startup files are usually set during Windows setup, so not all users need to make changes to them. If you do, refer to the section, "Working with Your System's Startup Files" later in this chapter.

The second way to alter how Windows starts is concerned with changing the look and feel of the program itself. Windows keeps track of the settings you made in previous sessions, like the color scheme of windows or the layout of windows in the Program

Manager, by placing the settings in information files. You can make alterations to these files for various reasons, the most important of which is to specify the programs you want Windows to automatically load when it starts.

ALTERING THE WINDOWS STARTUP FILES

Your Windows program directory contains several files with the .INI extension that Windows uses to store its operating information. The files hold startup parameters from one session to the next and are updated every time you make a change to the Windows operating modes using the Control Panel, the File Manager, or the Program Manager. The .INI files are also changed when you add new programs with the SETUP utility.

Of interest in this chapter is the WIN.INI file, which contains several blank command lines on which you can specify custom changes. For example, you can specify programs you want to load or start when Windows starts. You can also specify how file extensions are used in file listings and program associations.

To view or alter the WIN.INI file, start the File Manager and open a directory window on your Windows directory. Scroll to the WIN.INI file icon and double-click on it. Since it is associated with Notepad, it loads into the Notepad workspace.

As you scroll through WIN.INI you will notice several sections that begin with a title in square brackets. The first section should be titled [windows]. Scanning through the file, you will notice other sections that contain settings normally made from Windows' Control Panel. For example, the current setting for mouse speed is on a line that reads MouseSpeed. Most of these lines are not of interest here since you can more easily change their settings from the Control Panel. Four options in the [windows] section and the entire [Extensions] section are discussed in the following sections.

Loading Programs

You can use the load option in the WIN.INI file to load an application as an icon on the Windows desktop when you start Windows. You can specify one or more programs that you want to have available for immediate access during your Windows session. Locate the following line under the [windows] heading in the WIN.INI file:

load=

Type the name of any program file you want to load as an icon. You can also specify documents that are associated with programs. For example, in Chapter 17 you created several Notepad and Calendar daily files. If you want to load these as icons every time you start Windows, you can include their path and full filename on the load= line. In the following example, Calculator and the DAILY Notepad file are loaded as icons on the Windows desktop.

load= CALC.EXE \DAILY\DAILY.TXT

Notice that the file CALC.EXE is located in the Windows program directory, so a path is not necessary. A path is required for the DAILY.TXT file in the DAILY directory. Keep in mind that it is associated with Notepad, so loading the file also loads Notepad.

Note: The exact name of a program file must be specified, not the name that appears on the icon or window. Program names have extensions of .EXE and .COM. For Windows applications, list the .EXE and .COM files in your windows directory to determine the exact filename.

Running Programs

A *running program* is one loaded in a window, not an icon, when Windows starts. The procedure for specifying a running program is exactly the same as that for specifying a loaded program, except the parameters are placed on the run= line of the WIN.INI file.

Locate the run= line under the [windows] heading in the WIN.INI file. Type the name of the program you want to appear in a window when Windows starts. Be sure to specify the program's exact name, which ends in .EXE or .COM. For example, to start the clock and display it in an open window when Windows starts, you would add the following to the run= line:

run= CLOCK.EXE

Specifying How Programs Are Listed

Recall from Chapter 7 that directory windows can be sorted in a number of ways. One method is to list only program files, which have the extension .EXE or .COM. If you select the Include option on the View menu and check only the Programs box, the File Manager will list only the files with extensions you have specified in the Programs= line of WIN.INI. The initial setting when Windows is first installed is

Programs= com exe bat pif

Files with these extensions are considered executable program files by Windows because you can click on them to start a program. Files with the .BAT extension are actually DOS batch files, and files with the .PIF extension are Windows Program Information

Files. You cannot add other files to this list, but you might want to remove .BAT and .PIF so only .COM and .EXE files are listed when you check the Programs box on the Include dialog box.

Specifying How Documents Are Listed

The Documents= line is similar to the Programs= line just discussed. You can specify the extensions of the document files you want to list in directory listings. Remember from Chapter 7 that document files are those associated with programs, so listing document files provides a way to view document files. To list only document files in a directory window, choose the Include option on the View menu and click on the Document checkbox.

Windows automatically includes the extensions used by its own accessories in document listings. For example, files with the .TXT extension are those associated with Notepad, and files with the .WRI extension are those associated with Write. If you create files that you associate with certain programs and you want those files to show up in document listings, you should add their special extension to the document line in the WIN.INI file. In the following example, .DAT (data) files and .DBF (database) files will be included in the document listing:

Documents= DAT DBF

Associating Filename Extensions

The [Extensions] section of the WIN.INI file specifies the types of file extensions automatically associated with applications. As you scan through the lines under [Extensions], you notice a common Windows filename extension associated with one of Windows' program files. For example, the following line associates the filename extension CAL with the Calendar accessory.

cal=calendar.exe ^.cal

Using the [Extensions] section of WIN.INI to associate files with applications is more convenient than using the Associate option on the File menu of the File Manager, which associates one file at a time. By including a line in the [Extensions] section, you can automatically associate a particular filename extension with a program. Then, by double-clicking on the file, you can automatically load the file and start its applications. For example, including the following line would associate files with the extension .MSG (message files) with the Notepad editor:

msg=notepad.exe ^.msg

The caret (^) is like a wildcard to specify all filenames. If you want to associate a specific file with an application, you must include its full filename, as shown here:

dat=cardfile.exe phone.dat

Saving and Rebooting

After you have made alterations to the WIN.INI file, you must save the file, quit Windows, and then start it up again. In this way the new settings will be made.

WORKING WITH YOUR SYSTEM'S STARTUP FILES

The system startup files, CONFIG.SYS and AUTOEXEC.BAT, contain command lines that set operating parameters, load memory resident software, and start various accessories and applications when your computer is first started. You may need to alter the commands in these files to run some software packages. You also may need to change or eliminate some of the commands if you have memory constraints. Some non-Windows applications may not run under Windows unless you make certain changes, as discussed in previous chapters.

> **Note** The Windows SMARTDrive and HIMEM commands are also discussed in this section for those who have reason to change their settings although the Windows SETUP program usually does an adequate job of installing these commands in your CONFIG.SYS file.

Editing the Startup Files

Most of the topics discussed here cover editing changes for the CONFIG.SYS file and the AUTOEXEC.BAT file using the Windows Notepad accessory. These startup files should always be located in the root directory of hard drive C or the drive used to boot your system. If the files are not in the root directory, the commands will not execute.

Most of the changes discussed here are intended to save memory or make your system more efficient.

LOADING THE FILES FOR EDITING Before you edit the startup files, make backup copies of them in case you want to revert back to the original versions. You also can create two versions of the file in case you need to switch from one to the other for different startup methods.

To edit either CONFIG.SYS or AUTOEXEC.BAT, start Notepad in the normal way. Choose Open from the File menu and type **\CONFIG.SYS** or **\AUTOEXEC.BAT** in the Filename field. Be sure to include the backslash to specify the root directory. Click on OK to load the file. The contents of the file appear on the screen, and you can make adjustments to each line.

Occasionally you may want to disable a line in a file rather than remove it. This gives you a chance to see how your system starts or to test a memory configuration without the line. If you decide you need the line, you can enable it again. To disable a line, type **REM** followed by a space in front of the line. REM is the batch file remark command used to place remarks in your files. When you reboot your system, you will get an error message for any remark statements in the CONFIG.SYS file, but you can ignore these until you remove the remark command or the complete line when your test is through.

When you have finished editing the file, choose the Save command from the File menu to save your changes. You must restart your system after making changes. This resets your system and starts it with the new commands.

The CONFIG.SYS File

The CONFIG.SYS file loads memory-resident software and device drivers into your system when it starts. These programs and drivers might specify an extended memory manager, network support, or other feature that is specific to your system. If you are trying to conserve memory because your non-Windows applications cannot run or are experiencing out-of-memory errors, you may need to temporarily disable these commands.

In the CONFIG.SYS file, Windows installs two commands of its own and may disable others during SETUP. The HIMEM.SYS and SMARTDRV.SYS commands should not be disabled. In later sections of this chapter you learn how to make alterations to the settings of these commands, although Windows setup usually does an adequate job of determining the best settings for your system.

Other commands that may be in your CONFIG.SYS file are DOS commands and are listed here. Not every command may be present nor are they required since DOS sets its own defaults for most of the commands. If you need more information, refer to your DOS manual.

- *FILES*. Specifies the maximum number of files each application can have open at one time. Microsoft recommends the following command for Windows:

  FILES = 30

- *BUFFERS*. Specifies the number of buffers (small blocks of memory) to use when accessing the disk drive. Buffers can improve disk access, but you need no more than ten if you are using the SMARTDrive cache utility supplied with Windows. Thus you can leave the command out altogether and let DOS specify its own default setting. If you do not use SMARTDrive, enter the following line in your file:

  BUFFERS = 20

  You can increase buffers at the expense of system memory.

- *LASTDRIVE*. Set this command to the total number of disk drives you may use at any one time, including RAM drives, rather than setting LASTDRIVE to Z. For example, if you have hard drives C through E and one RAM drive, set LASTDRIVE to F. See your DOS manual for more details.

- *SHELL*. Often used to increase the environment space on a system, which is the amount of memory space used for batch file variables and path statements. DOS sets a default environment space, but SHELL is sometimes used to increase it. If you are running low on memory, you may need to decrease the memory allocated to the environment space by SHELL. Refer to your DOS manual for more details.

HIMEM HIMEM is an extended memory manager that is used with systems running in Standard mode or 386 Enhanced mode.

The Windows SETUP program should have installed the command to load HIMEM in your CONFIG.SYS file.

> **Note** You rarely need to alter HIMEM settings, but they are described here for those who may have reason to do so.

The HIMEM command must come before the SMARTDrive command (discussed in the next section) because SMARTDrive uses the memory set up by HIMEM. The command takes the following form, assuming your Windows directory is C:\WINDOWS:

DEVICE=C:\WINDOWS\HIMEM.SYS /HMAMIN=m /NUMHANDLES=n

/HMAMIN=m specifies how much memory in kilobytes an application must use in the High Memory Area (HMA) for HIMEM to give that application use of the HMA. Only one application can use the HMA at a time, and HIMEM gives the HMA to the first one that meets the memory-use requirements set by m. The m parameter can be from 0 to 63. The switch is optional since HIMEM will give HMA to the first application that requires it, but you can specify a number equal to that requested by the application that uses the most HMA. This switch is not used in 386 Enhanced mode.

The /NUMHANDLES=n parameter specifies the maximum number of extended memory blocks that can be in use simultaneously. You can specify a value from 1 to 128, with the default being 32. Each additional handle requires 6 bytes of memory. NUMHANDLES is not used when running 386 Enhanced mode.

SMARTDRIVE SMARTDrive is a disk-caching program supplied with Windows. A command to load the program was most likely added to your CONFIG.SYS file when you ran the Windows SETUP program. This section further explains the SMARTDrive program and shows you how to change its options. If you have other disk-caching programs, you should remove them in favor of SMARTDrive. SMARTDrive is not only more efficient than most, but is designed to work with Windows to help your applications extend their memory reach.

SMARTDrive keeps information already loaded from disk in memory in case it is needed again. A good example is the Notepad accessory, which is a small program whose program code may stay in memory after loading, even if you completely close the window. This "ghost" code is reloaded if you call up Notepad at a later time. The data your programs use is also held in the same way as an attempt to decrease disk access and improve performance.

SMARTDrive has one important feature from which it gets its name. As you may know, information in memory is volatile and will be lost if your system is shut down. SMARTDrive knows when the information in memory needs to be written to disk and does so during idle microseconds, all in the background, so you don't have to worry about periodically saving the information to disk yourself.

As previously mentioned, a SMARTDrive command should already be in your CONFIG.SYS file with appropriate settings. Consider the following points if you need to change the settings:

- SMARTDrive requires 512K of extended memory when running in Standard or 386 Enhanced mode, or 256K of expanded memory when running in Real mode.

- Unfragmenting your hard drive often helps SMARTDrive run more efficiently. Refer to Appendix B.

- The SMARTDrive command must come after any commands that install expanded memory on systems running in Real mode, and should come after the HIMEM command on systems running in Standard or 386 Enhanced mode.

- Remove all other commands that perform disk caching.

Here is an example of a SMARTDrive command:

DEVICE = C:\WINDOWS\SMARTDRV.SYS 1024 256

The first part of the command, DEVICE =, is required for the CONFIG.SYS file. The drive and directory of the command is then specified. In this case, the command is located in the Windows directory. The last two numbers are the *normal cache size* and the *minimum cache size*. The normal cache size determines the size of the cache when SMARTDrive starts or when Windows is not running. In most cases you should set the normal cache size as high as possible. Windows often sets the parameter to the amount of extended memory available. The larger the cache, however, the more Windows has to work to manage it, so on some systems the best performance may be at the 1024K setting.

The minimum cache size limits how much Windows will reduce the cache size if memory must be recovered for its own use. When a cache is reduced, the information in it is moved to disk, so Windows may run slower.

The following additional parameters also may be required in the SMARTDrive command:

- /A. If you want SMARTDrive to use expanded memory, specify the /A parameter at the end of the command and make sure the command required to load the expanded memory manager is placed before the SMARTDrive command in the CONFIG.SYS file.

- /V. Allows SMARTDrive to run in conjunction with an extended memory manager other than HIMEM.SYS version 3.0. Do not use SMARTDrive version 3.0 with Windows/386 version 2.x or hard drive damage may occur.

- /b-. Prevents SMARTDrive from performing disk I/O double buffering. System speed may improve with this option if running in 386 Enhanced mode. Do not use this option with DMA hard drives.

- /b+. Ensures that SMARTDrive performs disk I/O double buffering. A slowdown in the system may occur. Use this option with DMA hard drives or if you use non-Microsoft virtual-memory programs like CEMM.

As mentioned previously, Windows SETUP sets these parameters to best match your system, so you may not need to make changes unless you have upgraded your hardware configuration.

The AUTOEXEC.BAT File

The AUTOEXEC.BAT batch file contains commands automatically executed by DOS when your system starts. Commands in AUTOEXEC.BAT can be used to start memory-resident pop-up utilities like Borland's Sidekick. You can even place a command in the batch file to start Windows.

One additional command you may want to include in the AUTOEXEC.BAT file for Windows is a SET command that specifies a special directory where Windows stores temporary files. Temporary files are often created by applications as a place to store data as they work with a document. This is especially true when memory is in short supply. It is best to specify a subdirectory where these temporary files can be stored, rather than letting the application store them where it wants. In this way, you can periodically clear the subdirectory of temporary files that are no longer essential. Microsoft recommends the following command be added to your AUTOEXEC.BAT file. Be sure to create the directory as well.

SET TEMP = C:\TEMP

19

OPERATING IN REAL MODE

Starting in Real Mode
Running Applications in Real Mode
Running Non-Windows Applications in Real Mode

The topics in this chapter are written specifically for those using the Windows Real mode. Remember that Real mode is used on systems with less than 1MB of memory or systems with Intel 8088/8086 microprocessors. In addition, if you normally run in Standard or 386 Enhanced mode, you may need to switch to Real mode to run some non-Windows or pre-Windows 3 applications.

One of the main differences between Real mode and Standard or 386 Enhanced mode is that Real mode uses expanded memory while the other modes use extended memory. Special startup procedures for using expanded memory are covered in the first section of this chapter.

The second section discusses how to use applications that run only in Real mode. If you normally run in Standard or 386 Enhanced mode, refer to the second section to run such applications.

STARTING IN REAL MODE

When running in Real mode, you should configure as much memory as possible as expanded memory. If you have additional memory boards installed in your system, make sure the boards are set to use expanded memory. You also must install an expanded memory manager for the board that conforms to the Lotus-Intel-Microsoft Expanded Memory Specification version 4.0.

Since the other operating modes do not use expanded memory, you may need to switch to Real mode when running applications that require expanded memory. Alternatively, you can configure just enough expanded memory for such applications, and then configure the rest as extended memory for use with Standard or 386 Enhanced mode. Refer to your expanded memory application to determine exactly how much expanded memory is needed and then refer to your expanded memory board documentation to determine how to set the board for both expanded and extended memory, assuming this can be done on your board.

Windows usually uses your system's expanded memory in the best way possible when running in Real mode. There may be times when you need to adjust how Windows uses expanded memory. The following information is supplied for those technically competent with expanded memory and how an application uses it.

Starting with Expanded Memory Switches

You can start Windows using one of the switches described here to control how it uses expanded memory which can be in either small-frame or large-frame EMS mode. Small-frame mode is more efficient if there is less conventional memory available and is best when running a single, large Windows application. Large-frame EMS mode is best for running multiple Windows applications simultaneously, but less memory is made available to each application.

- /E. Tells Windows how much conventional memory must be available in order to use large-frame EMS mode. If there is less conventional memory available than the amount you specify, Windows starts in small-frame EMS mode. Small-frame mode can be advantageous because it supplies more expanded memory to an application if that application is the only one running. Use this switch if you are running only one Windows application at a time to ensure that Windows is running in small-frame EMS mode. On the command line, you specify an amount of conventional memory normally unavailable to force Windows into the small-frame mode. For example, you could type **WIN /R /E 999** to start in Real mode and specify 999KB of conventional memory (an out-of-range amount).

- /L. Moves the EMS bank line up or down in 1KB increments. Applications running in large-frame EMS mode may display an error message that they have run out of either banked memory or global memory. Using a trial and error procedure, you can move the bank line down to make more banked memory available or move the bank line up to increase global memory. For example, to move up 8KB, you would type /**L+8**. To move down 8 KB, you would type /**L-8**. This switch is not used in small-frame EMS mode.

- /*N*. Prevents Windows from using any expanded memory.

RUNNING APPLICATIONS IN REAL MODE

Some older Windows applications and non-Windows applications cannot run in Standard or 386 Enhanced mode. Real mode offers an environment where these applications may run normally. The following sections provide information for getting those applications started.

When Applications Require Expanded Memory

If you run in Real mode because your system is based on an Intel 8088/8086 microprocessor or because you have 1MB or less of memory, you may not need to read this section. Your system probably is already set up with expanded memory and is running applications the way you want. This section is primarily for those who normally run in Standard or 386 Enhanced mode but need to run certain non-Windows or pre-Windows 3 applications in Real mode.

Sometimes an application requires expanded memory to run properly. This can pose a problem if the extra memory in your system is configured as extended memory, which is usually the case if you normally run in Standard or 386 Enhanced mode. To run an application in Real mode, you may need to reconfigure the memory on your system so that part is expanded memory and the remainder is extended memory. While this may take away from the extended memory used in Standard or 386 Enhanced mode, it will allow your non-Windows applications to run.

> **Note:** Your memory expansion board must be capable of being configured with both expanded and extended memory.

The procedure for configuring expanded and extended memory is to configure just enough expanded memory to run your Real mode application, and then configure the remaining memory as extended memory. This may require a trial-and-error process, or you can look through the application owner's manual to determine exactly how much expanded memory is required.

If all else fails, call the software publisher and request further information, or get an updated version of the program that runs under Windows 3.

RUNNING NON-WINDOWS APPLICATIONS IN REAL MODE

Program Information Files (PIFs) are special files that contain information about how Windows should run non-Windows applications—applications not specifically designed for Windows. Remember that Windows applications are designed to share memory cooperatively, while those not designed for Windows request memory on their own terms. Windows may have trouble running such applications, but you may be able to make them work in the Windows Real mode environment by creating PIFs.

Program Information Files may be included with many non-Windows applications. You should search through the files in the program's directory or search its original diskettes for PIFs. You also can look in the owner's manual for specific information about running the application with Windows. Remember, the application may run differently under Windows 3 than under older versions of Windows, so be aware of which version the program information applies to.

PIFs supplied with programs are usually ready to use, but you can still change their settings using the PIF editor accessory. The PIF editor comes with Windows and is used to create and edit Program Information Files. It is located in the Accessories group window of the Program Manager. Since the options and settings on the PIF editor window are the same for Real mode as they are for Standard mode, refer to Chapter 20 for information on how to use the PIF editor and how to set the options in a PIF file.

20

OPERATING IN STANDARD MODE

When Applications Require Expanded Memory
Running Non-Windows Applications

Windows runs in Standard mode on systems with Intel 80286 microprocessors that have 1MB or more of memory. You can also run 80386 and 80486 systems in Standard mode with some enhancement in speed, although the multitasking features are not available. Standard mode is accessed by using the /S option when starting Windows.

You need not know any special requirements or procedures when you run Windows applications in Standard mode. This chapter discusses running non-Windows applications and how to create or edit Program Information Files for use with those programs.

WHEN APPLICATIONS REQUIRE EXPANDED MEMORY

Some non-Windows applications require the use of expanded memory to run properly. This can pose a problem on systems configured to run in Standard or 386 Enhanced mode, because memory is configured as extended memory in most cases. To run an application that requires expanded memory, you must reconfigure the memory on your system so that part is expanded memory and the remainder is extended memory and then run the application in Real mode, as discussed in Chapter 19. While this may take away from the extended memory used in Standard or 386 Enhanced mode, it does allow your non-Windows applications to run.

> **Note** Your memory expansion board must be capable of configuring both expanded and extended memory.

For more information on configuring the memory in your system as both expanded and extended, refer to your memory board's instruction manual and Chapter 19. You may be unable to get such applications to work and keep your system configured for Windows at the same time, so it is recommended that you obtain an updated version of the software that runs under Windows 3 whenever possible.

RUNNING NON-WINDOWS APPLICATIONS

Program Information Files (PIFs) are special files that contain information about how Windows should run non-Windows applications. Remember that Windows applications are designed to share memory cooperatively while those not designed for Windows will request memory on their own terms. Windows may have trouble running such applications, but you may be able to make them work in the Windows environment by creating PIFs.

Although you can start and switch between multiple applications, non-Windows applications that run in the Real or Standard mode require the use of the entire screen. These applications suspend all other applications while they are active. The PIF file lets you set various screen options as well as memory options.

The features and functions of PIFs are as follows:

- PIFs are usually given the filename of their corresponding application and the .PIF extension. For example, a PIF to start Microsoft Word would be called WORD.PIF and would work with the WORD.EXE executable file.

- Information in a PIF is used to specify the path to the directory where a program is located and the path to use for retrieving and storing documents.

- PIFs can also specify any startup parameters for the application.

- You can start an application by double-clicking on its associated PIF.

- An application can have several PIFs, each with different settings. By starting from a particular PIF, the application is started with the settings specified in that PIF. One PIF could be created to use files from a business directory, and another PIF could be created to use files from a personal data directory. You might also want to change the memory settings of one PIF if you need to load documents or run programs that require the full system memory.

- A PIF can be created for a batch file. Commands in batch files are executed one after the other and can be used to run other commands before or after running a non-Windows application. For example, you could load a memory-resident package before starting an application.

Note: Many non-Windows applications come with PIFs for use with Windows. You should search the program directory or its original diskettes or look in the owner's manual for further information. PIFs supplied with programs are usually ready to use, but you can still change their settings using the PIF editor accessory.

Using the PIF Editor

The PIF editor accessory supplied with Windows creates and edits Program Information Files. It is located in the Accessories group window of the Program Manager. To load the PIF editor, double-click its icon, and the dialog box shown in Figure 20-1 appears. If you want to edit an existing PIF, choose the Open option on the File menu. All boxes and options on the PIF Editor dialog box are described in the sections that follow.

PROGRAM FILENAME The Program Filename text box is used to specify the path and filename of the program you want to run. The path is the directory where the file is located, and the

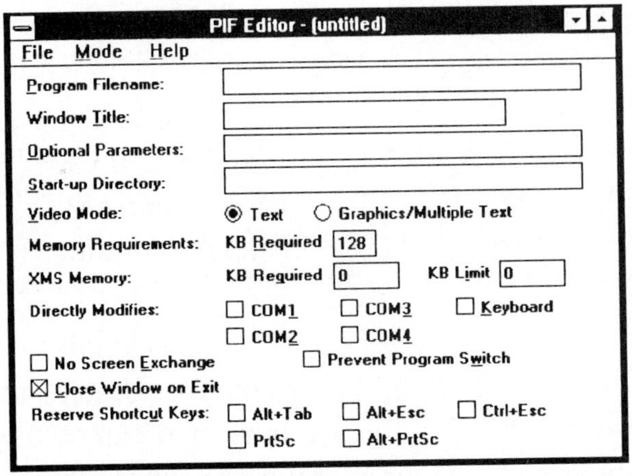

FIGURE 20-1. The PIF editor for Real and Standard modes

filename is its startup program file, which will have the extension .EXE or .COM. You also can specify batch files. For example, the following command line specifies the dBASE program in the DBASE directory on drive D:

D:\DBASE\DBASE.EXE

> **Note** To avoid problems, specify the paths of your program directories in the AUTOEXEC.BAT file using the PATH command. Refer to your DOS manual for more details.

WINDOW TITLE The Window Title is an optional text box in which you can type a descriptive name for the PIF. The name you type appears under the application's icon on the desktop. Keep the name short so it does not overlap other names on the desktop.

OPTIONAL PARAMETERS The Optional Parameters box is used to specify any additional startup parameters the application may require. For example, you can start Microsoft Word by typing **WORD /C**, so you would type /C in the Optional Parameters box. Some applications let you specify the name of a file you want to start with as a parameter, so you can type the filename, including its path, in the box.

If you want Windows to prompt you for a parameter whenever you start the application, type a question mark in the box. The question mark option is a good way to start an application that may require different startup parameters every time.

START-UP DIRECTORY You can use this field to specify the directory you want to use when the PIF is run. This field is especially useful if you want to work in different directories when you start an application. For example, when using Microsoft Word you might want to work in a directory of business files one time and in a directory of personal files another time. This requires that you create two PIFs, one to start from the business directory and one to start from the personal directory.

> **Note** You must set paths to your program directories if you plan to use them from other directories. Set the path in the AUTOEXEC.BAT file using the PATH command.

PIFs can be stored in the directory of the program, in your Windows directory, or in a directory of their own. No matter where you store PIFs, you need to make sure the options are set so the applications and files to be used can be found by the PIF.

VIDEO MODE The Video Mode option specifies whether the application uses a graphics display or a text display. It ensures that enough memory will be available when switching between applications. Select Graphics/Multiple Text if you are not sure, but using this mode requires additional memory that is wasted if your application is really a text-mode application. Always choose Text if you're sure your application is a text-mode application.

MEMORY REQUIREMENTS The Memory Requirements settings specify how much memory must be free before the application can be started. The setting of 128 is usually appropriate for most applications. This setting is not used to allocate a specific amount of memory to an application, since non-Windows applications running in Real or Standard mode are given all available conventional memory. The box is used merely to specify how much memory must be available before the application can be started.

XMS MEMORY Some applications use extended memory that conforms to the Lotus-Intel-Microsoft/AST Extended Memory

Specification (XMS). If you have Lotus 1-2-3 applications, for example, you can adjust the amount of XMS memory required by an application and the amount of XMS memory it should be limited to. Some applications use all available XMS memory, even that used by Windows. The two options are described here:

- *KB Required.* Specifies the amount of XMS memory that must be free and available before the application will start. In most cases, leave this option at 0. Other values slow the switching response time.

- *KB Limit.* Specifies the XMS limit. Set the option at 0 to prevent the application from gaining access to any extended memory. Set the option at −1 to let the application use all extended memory.

DIRECTLY MODIFIES Use the Directly Modifies option to prevent hardware conflicts, such as when two or more applications attempt to gain access to a communications port or keyboard shortcut keys. If the application uses any COM port, click on its box to prevent Windows from letting other applications use that port. Select the keyboard option if the application takes direct control of the keyboard and prevents you from using any of the Windows shortcut keys.

> Note: If any Directly Modifies option is selected, you may need to quit the application to return to Windows or other applications.

NO SCREEN EXCHANGE To conserve memory you can select the No Screen Exchange option. This prevents information from being copied onto the Clipboard using (ALT-PRTSC) or (PRTSC). Use this option only if you are running low on memory.

PREVENT PROGRAM SWITCH Select the Prevent Program Switch option to conserve memory. When you select it, you cannot switch from one application to another in Windows. Use this option only if you are running low on memory.

CLOSE WINDOW ON EXIT The Close Window on Exit option returns you directly to Windows when you exit an application. This prevents the information from being left on the screen.

RESERVE SHORTCUT KEYS The Windows shortcut keys, like ALT-ESC (to switch between windows) and ALT-PRTSC (to copy the screen to the Clipboard), are normally reserved for use with Windows when you are working in an application. The following describes how to resolve conflicts if the keys are also used by an application.

Alt+Tab	If left unchecked, Windows toggles between applications when this key combination is pressed. If checked, your application responds to the keystroke.
Alt+Esc	If left unchecked, Windows switches to the next application window. If checked, your application responds to the keystroke.
Ctrl+Esc	If left unchecked, Windows displays the Task List. If checked, your application responds to the keystroke.
PrtSc	If left unchecked, Windows copies a full screen to the Clipboard. If checked, your application responds to the keystroke.
Alt+PrtSc	If left unchecked, Windows copies the active window to the Clipboard. If checked, your application responds to the keystroke.

Changing the Default PIF Settings

Most non-Windows applications need no special PIF, because Windows has its own default settings for running applications that work in most cases. You can change these default settings if you wish to increase or decrease the settings for any reason. To do so, open the PIF editor, make any changes you want in the fields, and then save the settings to a file called DEFAULT.PIF.

21

OPERATING IN 386 ENHANCED MODE

Control Panel Settings for 386 Enhanced Mode
Running Non-Windows Applications in 386 Enhanced Mode
Control Menu Settings for Non-Windows Applications

The 386 Enhanced mode is Windows' most powerful mode. It allows you to do true multitasking and to run most non-Windows applications in windows of their own, making it easy to share information between applications and run other applications simultaneously. This chapter discusses configuration and program information you may need to refer to when operating in this mode.

CONTROL PANEL SETTINGS FOR 386 ENHANCED MODE

When you are running in 386 Enhanced mode, the Control Panel contains a 386 Enhanced icon. You can open the 386 Enhanced dialog box to set features such as time slicing and how your applications compete for peripherals. Recall from Chapter 1 that time slicing is a method of dividing the computer's time between each application it is running.

To view or set the options, open the Control Panel and double-click on the 386 Enhanced icon. The 386 Enhanced dialog box appears as shown in Figure 21-1. The dialog box is divided into two sections, which are discussed in the following sections.

Device Contention Options

The Device Contention box contains options for setting how applications simultaneously access devices like printers and mo-

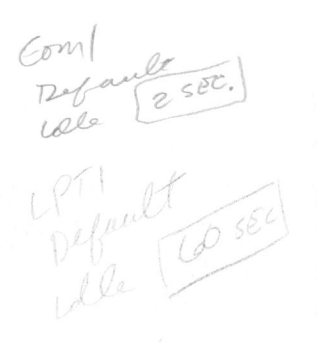

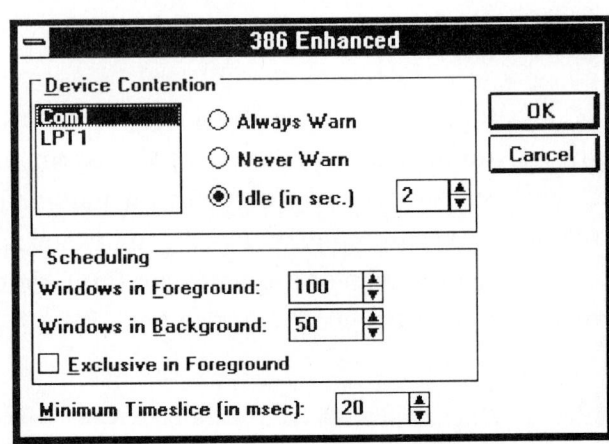

FIGURE 21-1.   The 386 Enhanced dialog box from the Control Panel

dems. If two applications compete for a device and one of them is a non-Windows application, you can use the following options to specify how Windows arbitrates the requests for the devices. Each option in the Device Contention text box is set separately; for example, in Figure 21-1 you would click on LPT1 to set its options.

- *Always Warn.* When this option is set, a warning message displays every time an application tries to use a device already in use. The warning message asks which application should be given access to the device. Select this option whenever possible.

- *Never Warn.* Lets any application get at a device at any time. It is not recommended because data collisions could occur, resulting in garbled data. This option is only set if you are sure other applications will not compete for the device.

- *Idle.* The idle time is the amount of time that elapses after an application stops using a device before it becomes available for use by another device. Set the number of seconds in the box to the right of the Idle button. The range is 1 to 999 seconds.

Scheduling Options

The Scheduling box on the 386 Enhanced dialog box has options for setting the multitasking features of Windows. The options are discussed here.

MINIMUM TIMESLICE Enter the number of milliseconds an application is allowed to run before Windows gives processor control to the next application. Increasing the time slice improves performance by minimizing how often Windows switches between applications to give each their allotted time slice. Decreasing the time slice makes Windows appear to run smoother, but the tradeoff in performance may not be worth it.

WINDOWS IN FOREGROUND Specifies the proportional amount of total time slices normally shared by all Windows applications. This number is used only when Windows-specific applications are being serviced in the foreground window. The number is relative to the time allocated to all non-Windows applications running in the background. The range is 1 to 10,000, but the important value is the ratio between this setting and the sum of this setting and the settings for the running non-Windows applications.

WINDOWS IN BACKGROUND Specifies the proportional amount of total time slices normally shared by all Windows applications when a non-Windows application is being serviced in the foreground window. The range is 1 to 10,000, but the important value is the ratio between this setting and the sum of the settings for the foreground application and all other non-Windows applications running in the background.

EXCLUSIVE IN FOREGROUND Specifies that all Windows-specific applications get the computer processing time when a Windows-specific application is being serviced in the foreground. All non-Windows applications are idle.

RUNNING NON-WINDOWS APPLICATIONS IN 386 ENHANCED MODE

Program Information Files (PIFs) contain information Windows uses when running non-Windows applications. Remember that non-Windows applications do not share memory cooperatively but request memory on their own terms. To overcome the trouble Windows may have running such applications, you can create PIFs.

Non-Windows applications that run in the 386 Enhanced mode may not require the use of a PIF, as they might when running in other modes. The 386 Enhanced mode is better able to handle the memory requirements of non-Windows applications and can even run them in their own windows. However, you can change the way these applications run by creating or editing PIFs for them.

The features and functions of PIFs are as follows:

- PIFs are usually given the filename of their corresponding application and the .PIF extension. For example, a PIF to start Microsoft Word would be called WORD.PIF and would work with the WORD.EXE executable file.

- Information in a PIF is used to specify the path to the directory where a program is located and the path to use for retrieving and storing documents.

- PIFs can also specify any startup parameters for the application.

- You can start an application by double-clicking on its associated PIF.

- An application can have several PIFs, each with different settings. By starting from a particular PIF, the application is started with the settings specified in that PIF. One PIF could be created to use files from a business directory, and another PIF could be created to use files from a personal data directory. You might also want to change the memory settings of one PIF if you need to load documents or run programs that require the full system memory.

- A PIF can be created for a batch file. Commands in batch files are executed one after the other and can be used to run other commands before or after running a non-Windows application. For example, you could load a memory-resident package before starting an application.

> **Note** Many non-Windows applications come with PIFs for use with Windows. You should search the program directory or its original diskettes or look in the owner's manual for further information. PIFs supplied with programs are usually ready to use, but you can still change their settings using the PIF editor accessory.

Using the PIF Editor

The PIF editor accessory creates and edits Program Information Files. Load the PIF editor by double-clicking on its icon in the Accessories group window of the Program Manager. The resulting dialog box, shown in Figure 21-2, offers the options described in the sections that follow. If you want to edit an existing PIF, choose the Open option on the File menu.

You access an additional dialog box by pressing the Advanced button on the PIF Editor dialog box for 386 Enhanced mode. The advanced options are used when you need to fine-tune the way the

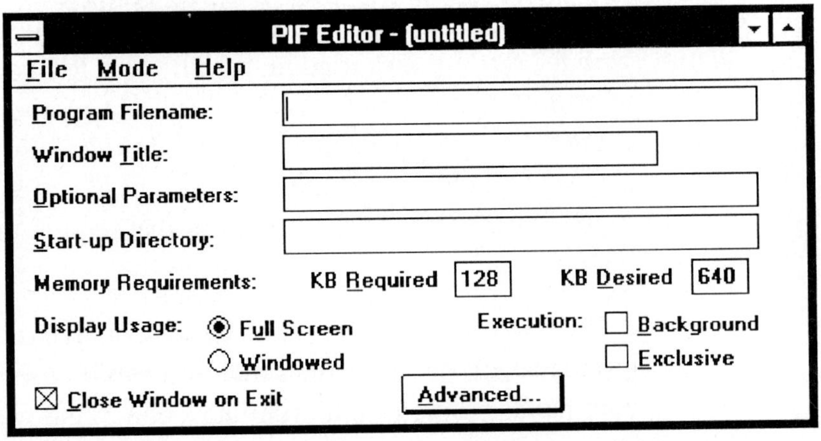

FIGURE 21-2. The 386 Enhanced mode PIF Editor dialog box

application will run. The Advanced options are covered later in this chapter.

PROGRAM FILENAME The Program Filename text box specifies the path and filename of the program you want to run. The path is the directory where the file is located, and the filename is its startup program file, which has the extension .EXE or .COM. You also can specify batch files. For example, the following command specifies the dBASE program in the DBASE directory on drive D:

D:\DBASE\DBASE.EXE

> **Note** You should specify the path to your program directories in your AUTOEXEC.BAT file using the PATH command.

WINDOW TITLE In the optional Window Title text box, you can type a descriptive name for the PIF. The name you type appears under the application icon on the desktop. Keep the name short so it does not overlap other names on the desktop.

OPTIONAL PARAMETERS The Optional Parameters box specifies any additional startup parameters the application may require. For example, you can start Microsoft Word by typing **WORD /C**, so you would type /C in the Optional Parameters box. Some applications let you specify the name of a file you want to start with as a parameter, so you type the filename, including its path, in the box.

If you want Windows to prompt you for a parameter whenever you start the application, type a question mark in the box. The question mark option is a good way to start an application that may require different startup parameters every time.

START-UP DIRECTORY You can specify in the Start-up Directory field the directory you want to use when the PIF is run.

This field is especially useful if you want to work in different directories when you start an application. For example, when using Microsoft Word you might want to work in a directory of business files one time and in a directory of personal files another time. This requires that you create two PIFs, one to start from the business directory and one to start from the personal directory.

> **Note** You must set paths to your program directories if you plan to use them from other directories. Set the path in the AUTOEXEC.BAT file using the PATH command.

PIFs can be stored in the directory of the program, in your Windows directory, or in a directory of their own. No matter where you store PIFs, you must make sure that the program you want to run is on the path, and the directory where they are stored is listed in the Start-up Directory field.

MEMORY REQUIREMENTS The Memory Requirements settings specify how much conventional memory (640K maximum) must be free before the application can be started and the maximum amount of memory Windows will give to the application. The options in the field are as follows:

- *KB Required.* In this field type the amount of memory Windows must have available before the application will start. This prevents error messages that might occur if you start an application without enough memory. Keep in mind that the number entered in this field is not a memory limit.

- *KB Desired.* In this field type the amount of memory you want Windows to allocate to the application. You can limit an application's use of memory to keep it available for other applications that run in a multitasking mode. If the option is set to −1,

Windows gives the application as much memory as possible, up to the maximum of 640K.

DISPLAY USAGE The Display Usage options specify whether an application is run on a full screen or in a window. Running an application in a window takes more memory but gives you all the advantages of a window, such as resizing, scrolling, and easier data transfer among other windows.

EXECUTION The Execution option controls how an application cooperates with other loaded or running applications. You can select one of the following options:

- *Background.* The application actively runs in a background window if you are using another application. If not selected, the application suspends during the period it is not the active window.

- *Exclusive.* Specifies that the application will be the only actively running application if its window is active. All other applications in background windows will suspend operation. If you intend to run an application in Exclusive mode, you should also select Full Screen in the Display Usage field to maximize the application's use of your system's resources.

CLOSE WINDOW ON EXIT If the Close Window on Exit option is checked, Windows closes its window automatically when you quit the application. You may want to clear the option to mark and copy information from an application that runs only in full-screen mode. If you select the Full Screen option and clear the Close Window on Exit option, Windows tries to display the application in a window when you quit so you can mark and copy information onto the Clipboard before closing the window.

Advanced PIF Options for 386 Enhanced Mode

You can access the Advanced options on the 386 Enhanced PIF dialog box by clicking on the Advanced button. These options let you fine-tune how the application will run in the 386 Enhanced mode and how it uses memory and the resources of your system. Those familiar with the technical aspects of the 80386, memory configurations, and multitasking may want to make changes to these fields, but the default settings are adequate for most applications. The Advanced Options dialog box, shown in Figure 21-3, is divided into four fields of options, which are discussed in the following sections.

MULTITASKING OPTIONS In the Multitasking Options field, you can use the following options to specify how an application will share the processing time of your system with other

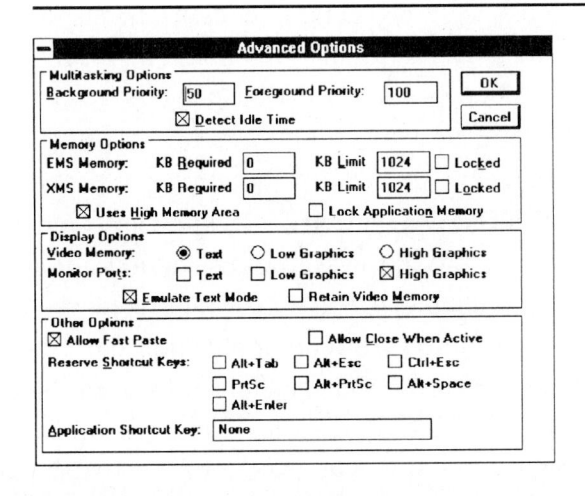

FIGURE 21-3. Advanced PIF options for 386 Enhanced mode

applications. The range of values you can specify in the Background and Foreground Priority fields is from 0 to 10,000.

- *Background Priority.* Specifies how much processor time an application should receive as it processes in the background. The value is only valid if the Background option on the PIF Editor dialog box has been set. Note that this option becomes meaningless if another active foreground application is processing with the Exclusive setting.

- *Foreground Priority.* Specifies how much processor time an application should use as it processes in the active foreground window. The actual percentage of time the application receives is dependent on how many applications are running in the background, if any.

- *Detect Idle Time.* Gives an active application's time to other applications if that application is waiting for your input. You should always leave the option selected to enhance performance. When an application is running abnormally slow, Windows may incorrectly see the application as idle, so you should clear the option to speed up the application.

Foreground and background processor times are added together to represent the total processor time. The final total does not matter since it varies depending on the number of running applications. The important value is the percentage of that total allocated to each application. It may be useful to come up with an arbitrary total value in advance (say 100 or 1000) as a point of reference, and then give each application a percentage of that total when you create the PIFs. Keep in mind, however, that the percentage varies, depending on the number of applications actually running with the application.

High Background Priority values can be given to applications you want to process in the background as you work with other applications in the active foreground window. If an application is highly processor-intensive, like an analysis package or chess game, you should boost its Background Priority value, especially if another application you plan to run in the foreground does not require a lot of processor time, such as a writing program. For example, assume two applications are running in the background, with Background Priority values of 50 and 25, respectively. In addition, a foreground application is running with a Foreground Priority value of 25. The total priority is then 100, which is a convenient number for determining the percentage relationship of each application's processor time. The background applications are given 50 percent and 25 percent of the processor's time, respectively, and the foreground application is given 25 percent.

MEMORY OPTIONS The Memory Options box controls how an application uses your computer's memory when running in 386 Enhanced mode. Each option is discussed here:

- *EMS Memory: KB Required*. Specifies how much expanded memory must be available before you can start an application. Set the option to 0 if the application does not require expanded memory.

- *EMS Memory: KB Limit*. Sets the limit on the amount of expanded memory Windows gives to an application. Set the option to 0 if the application should receive no expanded memory.

- *EMS Memory: Locked*. Prevents Windows from swapping the application's expanded memory to hard disk, thus increasing performance of the application at the expense of slowing the rest of the system.

- *XMS Memory: KB Required*. Specifies how much extended memory must be available before you can start an application.

Set the option to 0 if the application does not require extended memory.

- *XMS Memory: KB Limit.* Sets the limit on the amount of extended memory Windows gives to an application. Set the option to 0 if the application should receive no extended memory.

- *XMS Memory: Locked.* Prevents Windows from swapping the application's extended memory to hard disk, thus increasing performance of the application at the expense of slowing the rest of the system.

- *Uses High Memory Area.* Usually set on to allow the application to use the high memory area (HMA), which is the first 64K of extended memory.

- *Lock Application Memory.* Set this option to speed up some applications. It keeps the application in memory and prevents it from being swapped to disk. A slowdown in the rest of the system may occur.

DISPLAY OPTIONS The Display Options box contains options to set how an application appears on the screen and how Windows allocates memory to the application's display. Note that the Video Memory setting you choose is the initial memory setting made when an application first starts. Windows may adjust the setting as necessary. Each option is discussed here:

- *Video Memory: Text.* Set this field on if the application runs in text mode. A small amount of memory is set aside (usually 16K).

- *Video Memory: Low Graphics.* Set this field on if the application is to run in low-resolution graphics mode, which is usually the CGA mode that requires 32K of memory.

- *Video Memory: High Graphics.* Set this field on if the application is to run in a high-resolution graphics mode, such as EGA or VGA. This mode usually requires 128K of memory.

- *Monitor Ports: Text.* Set this option for text mode applications that interact directly with your system's hardware input and output ports to control display adapters. Few applications require this option.

- *Monitor Ports: Low Graphics.* Set this option for low- resolution graphics mode applications that interact directly with your system's hardware input and output ports to control display adapters. Few applications require this option.

- *Monitor Ports: High Graphics.* Set this option for high- resolution graphics mode applications that interact directly with your system's hardware input and output ports to control display adapters. Few applications require this option.

- *Emulate Text Mode.* Leave this option selected to increase the rate at which applications display text. If text is garbled or the cursor appears in the wrong place, try clearing the option.

- *Retain Video Memory.* Instructs Windows to not release the application's extra video memory to other applications. This may occur in applications that allow you to change to a different video mode that requires less memory. Setting the option ensures that the video memory is still available when you switch back to the other mode.

OTHER OPTIONS The Other Options box contains several unrelated options you can set to make your applications run properly in the 386 Enhanced mode.

- *Allow Fast Paste.* Leave this option set to allow an application to use the fastest method to paste from the Clipboard. If you are having problems pasting, try clearing the option.

- *Allow Close When Active.* Allows Windows to exit without requiring you also to exit from the application. This option is convenient because it lets you quit Windows without having to close each application separately. If the application does not use MS-DOS file handles in the standard way, clear the option.

- *Reserve Shortcut Keys.* The Windows shortcut keys listed here normally are reserved for use with Windows when you are working in an application. In some cases, you may need to use the same key combination for your application. If so, click on the key you want the application to respond to rather than Windows.

> **Note** If you check any of the following options, your application responds to the keystrokes in its own way.

Alt+Tab	If left unchecked, Windows toggles between applications when (ALT-TAB) is pressed.
Alt+Esc	If left unchecked, Windows switches to the next application window.
Ctrl+Esc	If left unchecked, Windows displays the Task List.
PrtSc	If left unchecked, Windows copies a full screen to the Clipboard.
Alt+PrtSc	If left unchecked, Windows copies the active window to the Clipboard.
Alt+Space	If left unchecked, Windows displays the Control menu for the application.
Alt+Enter	If left unchecked, Windows toggles the application in or out of a window.

- *Application Shortcut Key.* You can use the key sequence you specify in this field to quickly make an application the current active window. For example, you could specify (CTRL-F10) or (ALT-F1) as a shortcut key. The keys you select should not be in use by any other application. To make an entry in the field, press

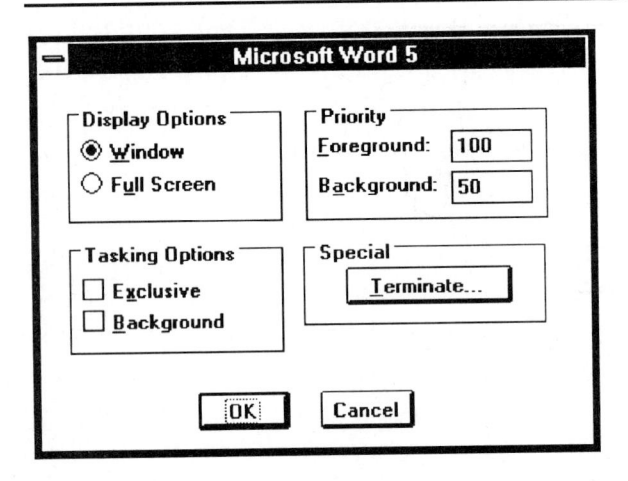

FIGURE 21-4. An example of the Settings dialog box accessible from the Control menu of a non-Windows application

the key combination you want. Windows interprets your keystrokes and displays them in the field.

CONTROL MENU SETTINGS FOR NON-WINDOWS APPLICATIONS

The PIF options discussed in the previous sections establish the initial startup options for a non-Windows application. Once the application is up and running, you can open its Control menu and choose the Settings option. Use the resulting dialog box, like that shown in Figure 21-4, to make changes to the current running mode of the application. These changes are not saved in the PIF; they stay active only during the current session. The following options appear on the dialog box.

- *Display Options*. Changes the way the application appears on the screen. You can select Window or Full Screen.

- *Tasking Options*. Sets how the applications share system resources with other applications. Either the Exclusive or Background application or both can be set. Select the Background option if the application should actively run in a background window. If not selected, the application suspends during the period it is not the active window. Select Exclusive to specify that the application be the only actively running application if its window is active. All other applications in background windows suspend operation. If you intend to run an application with the Exclusive setting, you should also select Full Screen in the Display Options field to maximize the application's use of your system's resources.

- *Priority*. Use Priority options to specify how much processor time the application should receive. For a discussion of these options, see "Multitasking Options" earlier in this chapter.

- *Special*. Click on the Terminate button in this field to quit a non-Windows application when the application is locked up. Use this option only as a last resort since data may be lost. Always save your other work and restart your computer after terminating an application in this way.

IV

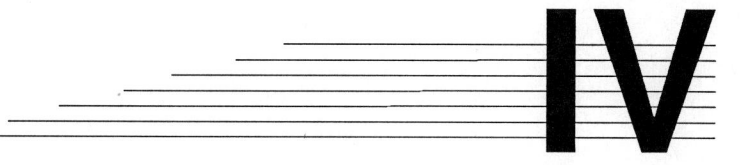

APPENDIXES

A

USING WINDOWS SETUP

Starting SETUP
Making Changes with SETUP

You can run the Windows SETUP program at any time to change the installation options. When you first installed Windows, the program ran automatically as part of the installation process. If you wish to add new or upgraded equipment to your system, you may need to run the stand-alone version of SETUP to tell Windows about your new equipment.

STARTING SETUP

To start the Windows SETUP program, double-click on its icon in the Main group window of the Program Manager. The Windows Setup dialog box appears with a list of the current settings.

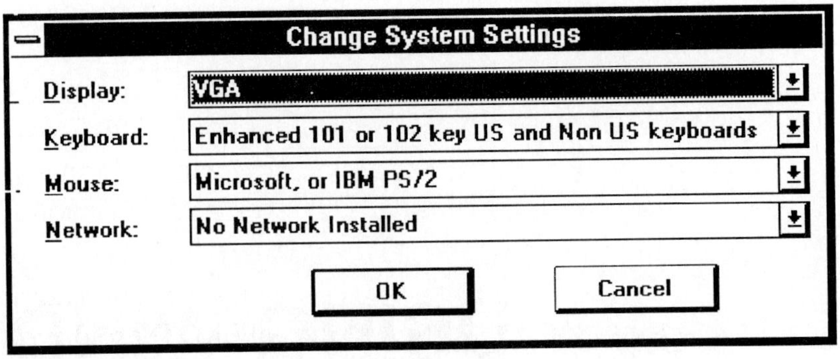

FIGURE A-1. The Change System Settings dialog box

MAKING CHANGES WITH SETUP

With the Windows Setup dialog box open on your screen, choose the Change System Settings option from the Options menu. From the Change System Settings dialog box, shown in Figure A-1, you can change the Display, Keyboard, Mouse, and Network options by clicking on the down-arrow buttons in their drop-down list boxes. These list boxes contain a complete list of available options. Simply use the down-arrow buttons or mouse methods to scroll through the list and highlight your choice.

To save the changes, click on the OK button. The SETUP program may request that you insert one or more of the original Windows diskettes in the floppy drive. These diskettes contain the software drivers required to operate the new hardware you have selected.

When the Windows Setup dialog box displays the new settings, choose Exit from the Options menu. The resulting dialog box offers you the option to restart Windows. The new changes take effect only after you exit and restart Windows.

Running SETUP from DOS

You may need to run the SETUP program from the DOS prompt in order to install device drivers not included with Windows, to install an updated version of a driver already on your hard disk, or to make a change to a device driver setting that you cannot do when running SETUP from Windows.

In general, you should follow the instructions supplied with new or updated drivers you are installing. These drivers are supplied by manufacturers to make their applications run under Microsoft Windows 3.

To start SETUP from DOS, exit Windows completely, and then type **SETUP** while logged into your Windows directory. Use the arrow keys to move to the appropriate Display, Mouse, Keyboard, or Network option, and press (ENTER) to display a list of options. Then click on the down-arrow buttons to scroll to the bottom of the list and select Other. This allows you to load a driver from a disk other than the Microsoft Windows disk set. Insert the disk in the floppy drive and follow the instructions on the screen to copy the driver to your hard drive.

As mentioned previously, hard drive performance degrades as files are deleted and new files are added. At first, files are stored one after the other on your hard drive, each occupying a new area of the drive. These files are stored contiguously from beginning to end. But DOS always fills the space left by an erased file with a new file. Usually the new file is not the same size as the erased file. If it is larger, DOS breaks the file up, storing part in the erased space and part elsewhere on the disk. This assumes that the erased space is somewhere among existing files, which is usually the case.

When a file is fragmented in this way, DOS has to work a little harder to retrieve the file when you need it. As more and more old files are erased and new files are stored, the fragmentation problem increases until the performance of your hard drive becomes noticeably slow. In addition, the drive itself has to work harder as it jumps from one place to the other to retrieve an entire file. The following sections discuss several ways you can correct disk fragmentation.

INCREASE THE DISK CACHE

One method of improving performance on a fragmented filing system is to increase the memory and in turn increase the size of the disk cache. While this method does not eliminate fragmented files, it does improve how your system accesses them to the point where fragmentation may not be a concern. If a disk cache is large enough, most of the data you need will be kept in memory. In this way, your system accesses memory instead of the hard drive, which improves performance.

USE A DISK OPTIMIZING UTILITY

Many disk optimizing utilities automatically unfragment files by moving them around on the disk until they are all in a contiguous form. This is the most preferred method because it can be done as often as required and is safe and easy to use.

Most optimizing programs work by unfragmenting one or two files at a time for safety reasons. If your system should lose power during the process, you will not lose any files because a copy of a file being moved is always kept on the disk. The process places each file in a temporary location while it reorganizes another part of the disk, so the file can be stored contiguously.

Popular disk optimizing programs are made by Peter Norton Computing, 5th Generation Systems (Mace Utilities), Softlogic Solutions, and others.

BACKUP-AND-RESTORE METHOD

The backup-and-restore method of optimizing a disk can be done with the DOS BACKUP and RESTORE commands. The process involves first backing up your entire hard drive to diskette or tape, formatting your hard drive, and then restoring the files. There are several essential things you need to include in this process to make it work properly. First, a file-by-file backup is important because it gathers each file that may be fragmented in a contiguous state on the backup set and allows you to restore files to the hard drive in this state. If you are using a tape backup, be sure to specify file-by-file backups instead of mirrored backup.

Formatting the hard drive is an important step because it clears the table DOS uses to keep track of files and their location on the disk. This information includes the location of the fragmented portions of a file. If you restore without clearing the drive, DOS uses the old table and puts the files back where they were. Formatting the drive causes a new file table to be built during the restore operation. Finally, you may want to remove all nonessential files from the drive before doing the backup. Removing these files in advance helps eliminate a lot of fragmenting that might occur in the near future when you erase the files. It also helps free up disk space on your hard drive.

ADVANCED BACKUP-AND-RESTORE METHOD

The advanced backup-and-restore method is the same as the method discussed in the previous section, with the addition of a few extra steps that can help cut down on the performance degradation caused by file fragmentation. Consider that your hard drive filing system has two types of files when it comes to fragmentation, *permanent files* and *transient files*. A permanent file has a fixed size and remains on your hard drive in a specific location for a long time. Program files and system files are good examples. A transient file shrinks and grows in size and eventually is moved elsewhere or deleted. Data files are transient.

Consider how the effects of file fragmentation can be decreased if all permanent files are kept in one area of your hard drive and all transient files are kept in another. Since transient files are no longer mixed with permanent files, fragmentation is confined to a physical area referred to as the *data area*. A data area is a physical area on a hard drive and should not be confused with data directories, which are used to organize files. Data directories however can help ensure files are placed in the physical data area of a hard drive, as you will see.

Initially you can control exactly which files occupy the permanent areas of your hard drive. After backing up and formatting your drive, you should restore all permanent program and system files first. In this way their position on the hard drive is contiguous and they are placed together where program access is fastest. After the permanent files have been placed, you can begin to restore your data files. The remainder of the drive is available for these files to shrink, grow, and fragment within their own area. When you want to optimize the disk again, all you have to do is back up only the data files. Since you probably have the original diskettes for the program files, you need not back them up every time.

Part of making this scheme work is to organize your files into distinct program and data groups at the drive and directory level. If you have two hard drives or a single hard drive partitioned into two, you can store all program files on one drive and all data files on the other drive. Optimizing then becomes a simple task of optimizing only the data drive, not the program drive. If you have only one drive, you can create distinct program and data directory trees. For example, you could create two directories at the root level, one called PROGRAMS and one called DATA. All your program files are then placed in subdirectories of the PROGRAM directory and all your data files are placed in subdirectories of the DATA directory. When it comes time to optimize, simply back up the entire DATA branch of the hard drive, delete the branch, and restore it. Remember that the PROGRAM branch does not need optimizing unless you have been removing program files from it.

C

USING WINDOWS WITH A NETWORK

Adding Network Support with SETUP
Using Network Drives
Printing on a Network

Microsoft Windows is compatible with a number of popular networks including Novell NetWare, Banyan VINES and Microsoft Networks. You can use the features discussed in this appendix when working in Windows with network drives or network printers.

You can install Windows programs themselves on the network file server, but you must install Windows on your own system from the network version using a special setup program. Contact your network administrator for more information. This appendix covers connecting to a network with a single-user version of Windows that is installed on a workstation hard drive.

ADDING NETWORK SUPPORT WITH SETUP

Before you can use the network features of Windows on your network, you must run the Windows SETUP program to change the system settings so Windows knows which network you are using. Double-click on the SETUP icon in the Windows Main group window. When the Change System Settings dialog box appears, click on the Network pull-down list box, and then click on the network you will be connecting to. If your network is not listed, choose one that is most similar to it.

Click on the OK button to accept your choice, and Windows may ask you to place one or more of its original diskettes in the floppy drive to copy the network driver. After the drivers have been copied, you will see the Exit Windows Setup dialog box. You should click on the Restart Windows option since the new drivers do not take effect until Windows has been restarted.

Network Features and Guidelines

When your network support is installed, you can connect your system to any network disk drive. Once connected to the drive, you can list its files or run the programs on the drive, depending on your access rights to the network. You may also be able to print to the network printers.

You should always make your network connection before starting Windows. If you attempt to start a network from inside Windows, your system may crash. The network drives and possibly its directories have special drive letters you use to switch among them. For example, when connecting to a Novell NetWare server, the first network drive is usually drive F. Your network manager may have assigned you a personal directory where you can store files on the network. You log into this directory using a drive letter such as G or H. Check with your network manager for more information.

Setting the Network Option in the Control Panel

When network support is installed and you have connected a network previous to starting Windows, a Network icon appears in the Control Panel window. Select this icon to open a dialog box that you use to view information about your network and to set special options specific to the network you are connected to.

The Network dialog box may include options to sign on and off the network, change your user ID and password, or send messages to other users. Check with your network administrator for more information.

USING NETWORK DRIVES

When you are logged into a network, certain network drives may be available for your use. On some networks an entire file server may be available, while on others the network administrator may limit your access to the file server. For example, you may be allowed to access only a personal directory and a directory that contains public files. Some networks allow you to access the hard drives on the systems of other users. These hard drives are available only if the user on that system has opened or "published" them for network use.

You can use the File Manager to work with network drives. Before attempting to do so, make sure you have already logged in to the network from the DOS level. This must be done before you start Windows. To connect to a drive, choose Connect Net Drive from the Disk menu of the File Manager. The Connect Network Drive dialog box appears with the next available drive letter at the top of the box. You can accept this drive letter or use another. Type the path of the directory on the network you intend to use. The File Manager makes this directory appear as a drive on your system. Also enter the password if one is required. If this is a new connection and you want to add it to a list of previous connections, click on the Add to Previous List box. When you are done, click on the Connect button.

> **Note** Use the Browse option to search for the network drive you want to connect to. This option may not be available on some networks.

When you need to disconnect from the network drive, choose the Disconnect Net Drive option from the Disk menu. A dialog box appears that lets you choose the drive to disconnect from.

PRINTING ON A NETWORK

Instead of printing your Windows documents on your local printer, you can use printers connected to a network, assuming you have connected to the network before starting Windows. This section covers the things you need to know for network printing.

Connecting to a Network Printer

To connect to a network printer, open the Control Panel and double-click on the Printers icon. When the Printers dialog box appears, choose Network. The resulting Printers-Network Connections dialog box displays a list of network printers currently available. Click on the Port pull-down list box and select the port you want to use for printing. If your local printer is connected to LPT1, you might want to choose LPT2 for the network printer. This lets you specify the LPT2 port from your application when you want to print to the network printer instead of the local printer. Windows redirects all output normally directed to the LPT2 port to the network printer.

You may need to type the network name for the printer in the Path text box or a password in the Password text box. This depends on the type of network you are connected to. Once again, check with your network administrator.

Click on the Connect button to connect the network printer and click on OK to return to the Printers dialog box. When you need to disconnect the network printer, click on the Network button on the Printers dialog box, select the printer to disconnect, and then click the Disconnect button.

Network Printing with Print Manager

If you are connected to a network and set up to print on a network printer, the Print Manager offers you a number of options. You can view the files in a network printer's queue instead of just the files you send to the printer. You can also view other network print queues, or bypass the Print Manager altogether to print directly to the network printer. The options discussed here are available from the Print Manager and are used to manage network print queues.

VIEWING THE ENTIRE NETWORK QUEUE When you send a file to be printed on a network printer, the Print Manager normally lists only the files you have sent. If you want to see all the files waiting to be printed on the network printer, highlight the line in the Print Manager window for the network printer queue. Choose Selected Net Queue from the View menu to display a window that shows the contents of the entire queue. Using this option, you can get an idea of where your print jobs are in the entire queue.

VIEWING OTHER NETWORK QUEUES You can view the contents of other queues if you want to see how many files are waiting to be printed before sending your own files. Use the method described earlier to connect to the other printer from the Control Panel, and then choose Other Net Queue from the View menu. A dialog box appears asking for the name and location of the network queue to view. Type the network pathname in the Network Queue box and choose View. The current contents of the queue are listed.

UPDATING THE NETWORK QUEUE STATUS   The queue listings just described may not be updated if you leave the windows open. To see the most current, updated listing, choose Update Net Queues from the View menu. If you reduce a queue list box to an icon, it is updated automatically every time you expand it back to a window. When high traffic on network lines slows the response of your system, you may not want an update to take place. To turn the update off, choose Network from the Options menu and clear the Update Network Display box that appears on the dialog box.

D

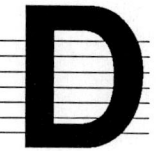

ADVANCED SCIENTIFIC CALCULATOR FUNCTIONS

Operators
Number Base Functions
Statistical Functions
Other Functions

The following tables explain the use of the advanced functions on the scientific Calculator. You can click on the Calculator button, or use the keystroke listed under the key column. For more information on the Calculator, refer to Chapter 12.

OPERATORS

Button	Key	Function
(	(	Starts a new level of parentheses. The current level appears below the display. The maximum number of levels is 25.
)	)	Closes the current level of parentheses.
And	&	Calculates bitwise AND.
Int	;	Displays the integer portion of a decimal value. Inv+Int displays the fractional portion of a decimal value.
Lsh	<	Shifts left. Inv+Lsh shifts right.
Mod	%	Displays the modulus, or remainder, of x/y.
Not	~	Calculates bitwise inverse.
Or	|	Calculates bitwise OR.
Xor	^	Calculates bitwise exclusive OR.

NUMBER BASE FUNCTIONS

Button	Key	Function
Bin	F8	Converts to the binary number system.
Byte	F4	Displays the lower 8 bits of the current number.
Dec	F6	Converts to the decimal number system.
Dword	F2	Displays the full 32-bit representation of the current number.
Hex	F5	Converts to the hexadecimal number system.
Oct	F7	Converts to the octal number system.
Word	F3	Displays the lower 16 bits of the current number.

STATISTICAL FUNCTIONS

Button	Key	Function
Ave	CTRL-A	Calculates the mean of the values displayed in the Statistics Box. Inv+Ave calculates the mean of the squares.
Dat	INS	Enters the displayed number in the Statistics Box.
s	CTRL-D	Calculates the standard deviation with the population parameter as $n-1$. Inv+s calculates the standard deviation with the population parameter as n.
Sta	CTRL-S	Activates the Statistics Box and the Ave, Sum, s, and Dat buttons.
Sum	CTRL-T	Calculates the sum of values in the Statistics Box. Inv+Sum calculates the sum of the squares.

OTHER FUNCTIONS

Button	Key	Function
cos	o	Calculates the cosine of the displayed number. Inv+cos calculates the arc cosine. Hyp+cos calculates the hyperbolic cosine. Inv+Hyp+cos calculates the hyperbolic arc cosine.
Deg	F2	Sets trigonometric input for degrees. This function is available in degrees only.
dms	m	Converts the displayed number to degree-minute-second format. Calculator assumes the displayed number is in decimal format.

		Inv+Dms converts the displayed number to decimal format. Calculator assumes the displayed number is in degree-minute-second format.
Exp	x	Allows entry of scientific notation numbers. The exponent has an upper limit of +307. You can continue to enter numbers as long as you do not use keys other than 0-9. Exp can only be used with the decimal number system.
F-E	v	Toggles scientific notation on and off. Numbers bigger than 10^15 are always displayed exponentially. F-E can only be used with the decimal number system.
Grad	F4	Sets trigonometric input for gradients when in decimal mode.
Hyp	h	Sets the hyperbolic function for sin, cos, and tan. The different functions automatically turn off the hyperbolic function after a calculation is completed.
Inv	i	Sets the inverse function for sin, cos, tan, PI, x^y, x^2, x^3, ln, log, Ave, Sum, and s. The different functions automatically turn off the inverse function after a calculation is completed.
ln	n	Calculates natural (base e) logarithm. Inv+ln calculates e raised to the xth power, where x is the current number.
log	l	Calculates common (base 10) logarithm. Inv+log calculates 10 raised to the xth power.
n!	!	Calculates factorial of the displayed number.
PI	p	Displays the value of PI (3.1415...). Inv+PI displays 2 * PI (6.28...).

Rad	F3	Sets trigonometric input for radians when in decimal mode. Input can be from 0-2*PI.
sin	s	Calculates the sine of the displayed number. Inv+sin calculates the arcsine. Hyp+sin calculates the hyperbolic cosine. Inv+Hyp+sin calculates the hyperbolic arcsine.
tan	t	Calculates the tangent of the displayed number. Inv+tan calculates the arctangent. Hyp+tan calculates the hyperbolic tangent. Inv+Hyp+tan calculates the hyperbolic arctangent.
x^y	y	Computes x raised to the yth power. Inv+x^y calculates the yth root of x.
x^2	@	Squares the displayed number. Inv+x^2 calculates the square root.
x^3	#	Cubes the displayed number. Inv+x^3 calculates the cube root.

TRADEMARKS

Aldus® PageMaker®	Aldus Corporation
Ashton-Tate® dBASE®	Ashton-Tate Corporation
AST® RAMpage!®	AST Research, Inc.
Banyan® VINES™	Banyan Systems Inc.
Hewlett-Packard® LaserJet Series II™	Hewlett-Packard Company
IBM® ProPrinter™	International Business Machines Coporation
Intel®	Intel Corporation
Intel® Above Board™	Intel Corporation
Micrografx® Designer®	Micrografx, Inc.
Microsoft® Excel	Microsoft Corporation
Microsoft® LAN Manager	Microsoft Corporation
Microsoft® Windows®	Microsoft Corporation
Novell® NetWare®	Novell Corporation
SideKick®	Borland International

Index

386 Enhanced mode 21, 50, 206, 234, 235, 386, 388, 389, 407
80286 Intel processor 397
80286 system options 43, 44
80386 Intel processor 397
80386/80486 system options 45, 397
8088/8086 391
8088/8086 system options 43

A

Accessories group window 12
Accessories, Windows 241
Active groups window 211
Active window 63
Airbrush Tool, Paintbrush 322
Alarms in Calendar 260
Anchor point 320
Application types 230-231
Application, starting 49
Applications
    installing 217
    non-Windows 235
    pre-Windows 3 233
    in Real mode 394
    running 208, 227, 398
    setup of 34, 41
    in 386 Enhanced mode 410

Applications, *continued*
    for Windows 232
Appointments in Calendar 258
Archive files 144, 373
Arranging windows 86
ASCII 120, 343, 347, 369
Associated document icon 139
Associating files 134, 162, 381
Attributes, viewing 143
Attributes of files 134, 160
AUTOEXEC.BAT 36, 55, 238, 382, 389

B

Background colors 320
Backup/Restore methods 433
Banyan VINES 437
Batch file startup 50
Baud rate 204, 343, 344
Beep 205
Binary files 347, 350, 351
Blink rate, cursor 198
Boilerplate letters 365
Boilerplates in Cardfile 366
Border width 199
Boss key 370
Box tool, Paintbrush 326
Brush techniques 322
Brush tip, Paintbrush 319
Buffer lines, in Terminal 343
BUFFERS 385

C

Cache, optimizing 432
Caching 386-388

Caching programs 24
Calculator 94, 248
    advanced functions 443
    Clipboard keys 250
    functions 250, 443
    number conversions 253
    paste commands 252
Calendar 95, 254
    alarms 260
    appointments 258
    date marking 261
    setup 257
    time increments 257
    everyday use 358
    personal use 358
Cancel printing 184
Capture of screen 108
Cardfile 95, 262
    creating boilerplates 366
    as scrapbook 371
    setup 265
Carrier Detect 345
Cascading windows 86
Catalog 372
CEMM 389
Change option, Write 287, 289
Character elements in Write 281
Character formatting 294
Check boxes 73
Chisel points, Paintbrush 323
CHKDSK DOS command 229
Circle tool, Paintbrush 326
Clear keys, Calculator 251
Clipboard 11, 92, 234, 237, 420
    options 107
    use with Calculator 250-251

Clipboard, *continued*
    use with Cardfile 268
       Window 109
Clock 96
Closing windows 77
Color eraser tool, Paintbrush 329
Color options 188
Color palette, Paintbrush 309
Color schemes 189
Colors, background 320
Colors, custom 191
Colors, foreground 320
Colors, new 193
Colors, Paintbrush 319, 332
Columns, in Terminal 343
COM ports 173, 203
Command buttons 72
Commands, DOS 166
Communications program 337
CONFIG.SYS 36, 54, 238, 382, 384
Connector 345
Contention options 408
Control menu 69
Control menu, 386 Enhanced mode 422
Control Panel 13, 91, 188, 439
Control Panel, 386 Enhanced mode 408
Coordinates, x and y 321
Copy 107
Copy disks 134, 167
Copying directories 157, 159
Copying files 134, 154
Country settings 200
Currency format 201
Cursor blink rate 198
Cursor in Paintbrush 314
Cursor position, Paintbrush 321

Cursor in Terminal 343
Curve tool, Paintbrush 325
Cut 107
Cut shortcut keys 113
Cutout in Paintbrush 331
Cutout tools, Paintbrush 327

D

Daily files 362
Data area on hard drive 434
Data bits 204, 344
Data files 120
Data transfer 6, 234
Date 194
Date format 201
Date marking, Calendar 261
Deleting cards, Cardfile 269
Deleting files and directories 134, 164
Desktop dialog box 194
Desktop granularity 198
Desktop organizing 359
Desktop patterns 196
Device contention options 408
Dialing in Terminal 345
Dialing in Cardfile 266
Dialog boxes 66
    elements of 70
DIF files 120
Directories 124, 125
    changing 136
    collapsing view 137
    copying/moving 157, 159
    creating 152
    deleting 164
    expanding view 137

Directories, *continued*
    organizing 128
    viewing of 136-138
Directory icons 133
Directory Management 361
Directory Tree window 91, 132, 135, 137
Directory, parent 138
Disk cache 24, 386-388, 432
Disk commands 134
Disk copying 167
Disk files 370
Disk formatting 166
Disk labeling 167
DMA hard drives 389
Document icons, adding 219
Document listings 381
Document windows 65
DOS commands 166
DOS Prompt 93, 228
Drawing area, Paintbrush 315
Drawing program 307
Drivers, printer 174
Drives, network 438, 439
Drop-down list box 73
Duplicating cards, Cardfile 268
Duplicating files 155
Dynamic Data Exchange (DDE) 15

E

Echo, in Terminal 342
Edit menu 107
Editing in Notepad 245
EMM386.SYS 45
Emulation, in Terminal 341
Enlarging in Paintbrush 331

Eraser tools, Paintbrush 328
Excluding files 147
Executable program icon 139
Exit option 107
Expanded memory 388, 391-394, 398, 418
Extended memory 23, 28, 387-388, 418

F

File
    archiving 144, 373
    ASCII 347, 369
    associations 134, 162, 381
    attributes 134, 160
    binary 347, 350, 351
    boilerplates 365
    catalog 372
    comparing 364
    concepts 118
    copying 134, 154
    copying between 364
    copying to disk 370
    creating 153
    daily 362
    deleting 134, 164
    directories 125
    duplicating of 155
    excluding in list 147
    fragmentation of 432
    hidden attribute 144
    including in list 147
    listing 124
    management tips 367, 368
    moving 134, 154, 361
    name extensions 122, 123
    naming 118, 120-122

File, *continued*
    new 102
    open 102
    permanent 434
    printing of 104, 134, 160
    pull-down menu 101
    read-only 144
    renaming 134, 159
    running a 134
    save 103
    save as 104
    searching for 165
    selecting for operation 149
    sending on disk 369
    sorting list 144, 145
    system 144
    templates 162, 208
    text 347, 348, 349
    transferring in Terminal 347
    transient 434
    types 119
    viewing 135, 142-143, 153
File Manager 17, 89, 90, 131, 220, 362, 368, 439
FILES command 385
Find and Change 287
Flipping in Paintbrush 332
Flow control 205, 345
Fonts 177, 199
    adding 181
    how printed 179
    raster 180
    sizing, in Write 295
    in Terminal 343
    vector or stroke 181
Footers 105, 336
Footers in Write 301

Foreground colors 320
Formatting disks 134, 166
Formatting paragraphs 297
Formatting, in Write 294
Fragmentation, file 432
Functions, Calculator 443

G

Games 353, 370
Granularity of desktop 198
Graphics
    files 120
    scrapbooks 371
    in Write 293
Group icons 62, 211
Group window 211
    creating 215
Groups,
    adding items 217
    deleting 216
    moving and copying 222
    renaming 216

H

Hard drives, DMA 389
Headers 105, 336
    in Write 301
Help menu 135
Help options 110
Hidden files 144
Highlighting/selecting 66
HIMEM.SYS 44-45, 383-386, 389
Hyphens 291

I

Icons,
    group 62, 211
    arranging 212, 213, 214
    directories and files 133, 138, 139
    document 219
    loaded 64, 211
    moving and copying 222
    program 6
    startup 362
    unloaded 62, 211
Inactive windows 63, 211
Indent slider 283
Indenting 298, 299
Index cards, Cardfile 265
Insertion point 111
Installation procedure 31
International settings 199
Inverting in Paintbrush 332
Invisible paragraph marker 282

K

Kermit 351
Keyboard,
    layout 200
    repeat rate 201
    techniques 79
Keystroke recording 270

L

Label disks 134, 167
Language settings 200
Large-frame EMS mode 393

LASTDRIVE 385
Layout in Write 299
Letterheads, creating 367
Line Size box, Paintbrush 311
Line tool, Paintbrush 325
Line width, Paintbrush 319
Line wrap, in Terminal 342
List boxes 72
List separator 201
Listing documents 381
Listing programs 380
Loaded icons 64, 211
Loading programs 379
LPT ports 173

M

Macro, Recorder
    playback 274
    recording 270
Make System Disks 134
Margins 106
Margins in Write 302
Maximize/Minimize buttons 69
Measurement settings 200
Memory keys, Calculator 251
Memory
    problems 236
    requirements 402
    usage 53
Memory, expanded 23-28, 388, 391, 392, 393, 394, 398
Memory, extended 23-24, 387, 388
Memory options, 386 Enhanced mode 414, 418
Memory-resident software 28, 53-55, 237, 238, 239
Menu bar 68
Menus, pull-down 68

Merging cards, Cardfile 269
Message boxes 74
Messages, warning 164
Microsoft Networks 437
Minimize/Maximize buttons 69
Modems 337
Mouse characteristics 202
Mouse techniques 74
Moving directories 157, 159
Moving files 134, 154
Moving windows 77, 81, 213
MS DOS Executive 131
Multiloading 10
Multitasking 5, 10, 21, 416

N

Network
    dialog box 439
    drives 439
    operation 437
    options 134
    printing 438, 440
    queue 441
    setup 438
Normal icon 139
Notepad 96, 242
    everyday use 359
    as scrapbook 371
    time-log feature 247
    tips 363
    use with calculator 251
Notes, consolidating 364
Novell Netware 437
Number base functions 444
Number conversions, Calculator 253

Number format 201

O

Opening a file 102
Operators, Calculator 444
Optimizing with Backup/Restore 433
Optimizing techniques 431
Optimizing utilities 432
Option buttons 73
Options menu, File Manager 147, 148
OS/2 6
Outdenting 299

P

Page breaks 291
Page layout in Write 282, 299
Page numbering in Write 302
Page setup 105
Pagination 291, 292
Paintbrush 96, 307
    color palette 309
    concepts 314
    drawing area 315
    Line Size box 311
    menus 312
    toolbox 309
    window 308
Paragraph
    alignment 298
    elements in Write 281
    end marker 281
    formatting 296, 297
    selection 283
    spacing 298

Parallel ports 173
Parent directory 138
Parity 205, 345
Passwords 439
Paste 107
Paste command, Calculator 252
Paste shortcut keys 113
Path 128
Patterns, desktop 196
Pause/resume printing 184
Phone number, Terminal 340
Picture, in Write 293
PIF (Program Information File) 34, 97, 231, 236, 239, 395, 398, 399, 410
PIF Editor 400
PIF Editor, 386 Enhanced mode 412
PIF options, advanced 416
Playing macros, Recorder 274
Polygon tool, Paintbrush 326
Pop-up programs 24
Port, printer 171, 172
Ports 173, 203
Presentation Manager 6
Previewing windows 84
Print Manager 92, 441
    queue 182
    window 181
Print priority 183
Print queue options 184
Print queue order 185
Printer
    active and default 176
    ports 172
    problems 186
    setup 34, 37, 106, 170
    topics 169
Printer drivers 170-174

Printer icon, Control Panel 205
Printing cards, Cardfile 269
Printing files 104, 134, 160
Printing in Notepad 246
Printing in Paintbrush 334, 335
Printing in Write 303, 304
Printing on networks 438, 440
Program files 119
Program icons 217
Program Information Files, advanced 416
Program listings 380
Program loading 379
Program Manager 16, 88, 207, 228, 362
Program Manager groups 209
Program running 380
Programs, adding 217
Programs, running 227, 231
Pull-down menus 68

Q

Queue 441
Queue, Print Manager 182
Queue order 185
Quitting Windows 51

R

Raster fonts 180
Read-only files 144
Real mode operation 20, 49, 235, 387, 391, 399, 400
    running applications in 234
    startup 392
Recorder 98
Recorder accessory 270
Recording a macro 272

Renaming files 134, 159
Repaginate 292
Repeat rate, keyboard 201
Restore methods 433
Restoring cards, Cardfile 269
Reversi 353, 370
Roller, Paintbrush 323
ROOT directory 126
Ruler in Write 280-283
Run option, File Manager 230
Running applications 227, 380
Running DOS commands 166

S

Saving a cutout, Paintbrush 334
Saving a file 103
Saving cards, Cardfile 269
Saving changes to Program Manager 214
Saving macros, Recorder 274
Saving in Notepad 246
Saving in Paintbrush 334
Saving in Write 285, 302, 303
Scheduling options, 386 mode 409
Scrapbooks 371
Screen capture 108
Scroll bars 69, 78
Searching for files 165
Searching for text 288
Searching in Notepad 245
Searching in Cardfile 266
Securing an Object 318
Select All 107
Selecting 66, 283
    files 149
    text 112, 289

Index 467

Serial ports 173, 203
SET command 389
Settings file, Terminal 339
Setup of printer 106, 170
Setup, page 105
SETUP program 27, 93, 378
    to add applications 221
    to install PIFs 240
    for networks 438
    starting 427
SHELL command 385
Shortcut keys 404, 421
Shrinking in Paintbrush 331
Sizing windows 75, 81, 213
Small-frame EMS mode 393
SMARTDrive 24, 44, 383, 386
SMARTDrive.SYS 384
SModem/CRC 351
Solitaire 353, 355, 370
Sorting files 145
Sound 205
Sound, in Terminal 342
Spray painting 322
Standard mode operation 21, 50, 234, 235, 388, 397, 400
Starting Windows 48
Startup 377
Startup files 36, 382
Startup icons 362
Startup, altering 377, 378
Statistical functions 253, 445
Stop bits 205, 344
Stroke fonts 181
Subdirectories 126
Subdirectory icon 139
Subordinate windows 65
Swap file 29

Sweeping in Paintbrush 330
Switching windows 84
SYLK files 120
System files 144

T

Tabs in Write 300
Task List 18
Template files 162, 208
Temporary files 389
Terminal 99, 337
    session, establishing 338
    settings 339
Text boxes 72
Text files 120, 347, 348, 349
Text scrapbooks 371
Text search 288
Text selection 111, 112, 283
Text tools, Paintbrush 324
Tiled windows 86
Tilting in Paintbrush 332
Time 194
Time format 201
Time increments, calendar 257
Time-slicing 11
Time-Log feature of Notepad 247
Timeout options 174
Timer, in Terminal 340
Timeslice 409
Title bar 67
Toolbox in Paintbrush 309
Translation, in Terminal 343
Tree options 135
Type Styles 295

U

Undo option 107
Undoing, effects in Paintbrush 319
Unloaded icons 211

V

Vector fonts 181
Video options 419
Viewing cards, Cardfile 266
Viewing directories 136
Viewing files 135, 142

W

Wallpaper 197
Warning beep 205
Warning boxes 74
Warning messages 164
Wildcard characters 124, 142, 146-147
WIN.INI 378, 379, 380
Window, active group 211
Window, description of 5
Window, group 211
Windows,
    active 63
    arranging 86, 148, 212-214
    cascading 86
    closing 77
    directory 137
    document 65
    elements of 66
    inactive 63, 211
    moving 77, 81, 213
    Paintbrush 307

Windows, *continued*
    previewing 84
    rearranging 135
    sizing 75, 81, 213
    startup 377
    subordinate 65
    switching 84
    Terminal 337
    386 caution 389
    tiled 86
    updating 148
    Write 277
WINWORD.BAT startup file 51
Word wrap in Notepad 244
Work area 67
Wrap, in Terminal 342
Write 99, 277
    character elements 281
    concepts 280
    creating boilerplates 365
    menus 279
    paragraph elements 281
    ruler 280
    as scrapbook 371
    starting 278

X-Y

Xon/Xoff 345, 346

Z

Zoom in Paintbrush 317, 321